THE POWER

OF

STRATEGY

INNOVATION

REVISED EDITION

A New Way of Linking Creativity and
Strategic Planning to Discover Great
Business Opportunities

Robert E. Johnston, Jr.
J. Douglas Bate

AMACOM

American Management Association
New York • Atlanta • Brussels • Chicago • Mexico City • San Francisco
Shanghai • Tokyo • Toronto • Washington, D.C.

Bulk discounts available. For details visit:
www.amacombooks.org/go/specialsales
Or contact special sales:
Phone: 800-250-5308
E-mail: specialsls@amanet.org
View all the AMACOM titles at: www.amacombooks.org
American Management Association: www.amanet.org

Library of Congress Cataloging-in-Publication Data

Johnston, Robert E.
The power of strategy innovation : a new way of linking creativity and strategic planning to discover great business opportunities/ Robert E. Johnston, Jr., J. Douglas Bate.
p.   cm.
Includes bibliographical references and index.
ISBN 978-08144-3365-2
1. Strategic planning.   I. Bate, J. Douglas.   II. Title.
HD30.28.J657   2013

658.4'012—dc23
2013008840

About AMA

American Management Association (www.amanet.org) is a world leader in talent development, advancing the skills of individuals to drive business success. Our mission is to support the goals of individuals and organizations through a complete range of products and services, including classroom and virtual seminars, webcasts, webinars, podcasts, conferences, corporate and government solutions, business books and research. AMA's approach to improving performance combines experiential learning—learning through doing—with opportunities for ongoing professional growth at every step of one's career journey.

Printing number
10 9 8 7 6 5 4 3 2 1

Contents

FOREWORD

The global competitive landscape has never been more challenging for a company wanting to achieve growth. Turbulence and uncertainty have become the new steady state. Companies that are accustomed to a predictable future are wandering and wondering. Many of these organizations view innovation as the key to success.

In the 2013 Insigniam Global Executive Survey, 87 percent of executives said innovation is the *most* important or a *very* important factor in their organizations' ability to succeed and strengthen competitive advantage in the next 12 to 36 months. Only 12 percent of the executives surveyed said they feel their organizations are very well prepared to generate the needed level of innovation.

The American Management Association, in concert with the Human Resources Institute, surveyed executives to assess the importance of innovation for longer-term success in a similar 2006 survey covering a longer time horizon. Eighty-five percent responded that by 2016, innovation would be "extremely important" or "highly important." This survey revealed that the top reason for innovation is customer demand, both now and moving forward.

Anyway you slice it, *innovation* is "hot!" Bob Johnston and Doug Bate, authors of this book, have been involved with corporate innovation since the days when innovation was not hot. In the 1980s, product innovation was accepted, but applying innovative principles to strategy in the C-Suite was just too risky. Over the years, Johnston and Bate drove future growth in many large organizations through strategy innovation. These two pioneers defined the landscape for strategy innovation—where an organization *invents* its future.

Simply put, strategy innovation is the creation of a compelling future state for the enterprise—a future that breaks the shackles of the past and of a predictable trajectory. Strategy innovation generates a remarkable future designed from the core values and inspired vision of the organization. Analyses and traditional strategic planning *cannot* accomplish the envisioning of this preferred future. An innovative and inspired future requires imagination and creativity. This book presents examples of how strategy innovation leads to extraordinary results. One of the most important books written on *innovation* in the last 10 years, *The Power of Strategy Innovation*, provides a methodology for any organization to define *and* create a preferred future.

Twenty-five years ago, Insigniam Performance also began a journey—that of catalyzing breakthrough results in the largest companies around the world. Our journey was born of one question: "Is it possible to take an already successful business, and elevate its performance to new, discontinuous levels?" Our ground-breaking methodology guided our clients to breakthrough performances, which arose from new, created futures. We guided them in seeing new perspectives and uncovering new possibilities. With this methodology, the leaders in these organizations catalyzed their people in thinking newly, acting differently, and ultimately delivering highly innovative, breakthrough results—over and over again.

So when Insigniam Performance met Bob and Doug (while facilitating a global leadership forum for the Product Development and Management Association), we found great synergies in our respective bodies of work. Results exploded when the two methodologies were combined.

The innovation process outlined in this book can be applied to *any* organization in *any* industry. However, success is often tied to the approach an organization takes to it. Adopting an "open" mindset is critical for strategy innovation. This is where Insigniam's methodology is powerfully employed.

Every organization contains invisible working assumptions and traditional ways of doing business that hinder the identification and pursuit of new growth opportunities. Johnston and Bate define these corporate constraints as "corporate gravity" and the "corporate immune system." These forces resist any attempt to change the current way of doing business. They are the "leash" that limits an organization from innovative growth. Once removed, the organization is poised for a dramatic leap in the perception of its future. The organization's default behavior is RE-SET to focus on innovative growth and breakthrough results.

Combine Insigniam's approach (*revealing* and *unhooking* the hidden constraints to innovation, then *inventing* and *implementing* a new and inspired future) with the methods in *The Power of Strategy Innovation*, and you have a formula for stunning, leading-edge innovation. With strategy innovation, there is no need to limit innovative thinking exclusively to R&D or marketing; innovation is embedded in each individual at each point in the enterprise. Now that's strategy innovation!

We at Insigniam are proud to provide you with the innovation tools you need to unleash the creativity of your organization, identify and execute the significant growth opportunities that can be found on your strategic frontier, and sustain continued dramatic growth by embedding innovation as a core competency in your corporate DNA.

Shideh Bina—Nathan Rosenberg—Michael Waldman
Insigniam Founding Partners

PREFACE

> The order is
> Rapidly fadin'
> And the first one now
> Will later be last
> For the times they are a-changin'.
>
> —*Bob Dylan*

If you didn't know that Bob Dylan recorded this song in the mid-1960s, you would think he was talking about 2013. We live in a dynamic world. The Internet puts newspaper publishers and travel agents out of business. Apple and Samsung steal the cellphone market from Nokia and Motorola. And China challenges the economic dominance of the United States.

What Has Changed

In these rapidly changing times, we decided to take a look at how the world of innovation has changed since we first published this book in 2003.

The past decade saw two of our highlighted corporate examples succumb to business challenges. Kodak, who recognized in the early 1990s the threat to their business of digital imaging, nevertheless refused to commit sufficient resources to this market shift soon enough, and suffered economic consequences that led to their recent Chapter 11 filing. Hewlett-Packard, an aggressive innovative force under CEO Lew Platt in the 1990s, lost its innovation luster as successor Carly Fiorina changed direction and pursued an acquisition growth strategy during her tumultuous tenure.

Another change in the past decade is our professional affiliation. The world of innovation has changed dramatically since we first entered this industry several decades ago—from a single-function activity to an enterprise imperative. Wanting to continue to have an impact on a larger scale, we decided we needed to be more than a two-person consulting firm (The Visterra Group). So we established for ourselves a strategic frontier of finding a global, high-quality partner where our capabilities would be a synergistic fit. Two years ago, we joined forces with Insigniam, a firm known as global leaders in breakthrough performance and cultural transformation in large corporations.

There is one thing that has not changed over the past ten years. We are delighted to report that the core concept of this book, the five-phased Discovery Process for strategy innovation, continues to be a relevant and valuable tool for the identification of new growth opportunities. Used by large and small organizations, it is a disciplined but creative approach for the exploration of strategic frontiers.

And, just as important, the use of these tools of creativity and innovation in corporations has grown dramatically over the past decade. Whereas Six Sigma programs and efficiency used to provide competitive advantage in many markets, it is now the ability to create ongoing innovative growth opportunities that give corporations the competitive edge they need.

Not only has innovation grown in importance, it has started changing form.

Era of Integration and the Corporate Innovation Journey

As we look back over the past decade, we see that the world of business innovation has entered an era of integration. Many corporations experimented with initiatives of strategy innovation that led to the successful identification of new growth opportunities. Believing that this capability must become an ongoing part of their corporate growth strategy, these corporations are now finding ways to integrate innovation as a permanent function. The recent emergence of the role of Chief Innovation Officer is a clear sign of this integration.

In Chapter 12, we predicted this integration, providing a blueprint for the creation of a *formalized* system of innovation. While the ad hoc teams used in the Discovery Process are a great way to experiment with strategy innovation, it is the creation of a dedicated, permanent function of innovation that will make innovation sustainable in a corporation. This move from ad hoc teams to a dedicated office for innovation defines the first stage of what we consider to be the "Corporate Innovation Journey."

Enterprise Innovation

In the Epilogue of this new edition, we introduce what we believe will be next in the world of corporate innovation. We predict that the current integration to a dedicated function will lead to a positive shift in focus for corporate innovation. Once inside the tent, the tools of creativity and innovation will be used by others in the corporation, not just those looking for new business opportunities. They will find innovative ways to provide new value for their customers, who may be internal corporate functions or external stakeholders other than customers.

We believe that all employees will eventually be trained in how to think creatively and find ways to add value in the work they do. After all, creating new value is the essence and definition of innovation. We call this next stage of innovation immersion "Enterprise Innovation," and believe that it is the next big thing.

There are many challenges associated with any attempt to integrate innovation to the traditional hierarchy and control-based policies of most corporations. However, we believe that the benefits outweigh the costs for those willing to make the journey. In the Epilogue, we share a case study of the successful first step on this journey to Enterprise Innovation.

ACKNOWLEDGMENTS

This book is possible only because of the contribution of numerous participants in strategy innovation initiatives across many different industries and dozens of companies reaching back to 1983. However, we wish to acknowledge here the special contribution and support of a few individuals who have helped us bring it to fruition.

We decided early on that the story was best told by some of the many pioneers who have championed strategy innovation on behalf of their companies. Individuals who contributed generously in terms of personal time and support include Bob Galvin, Motorola; Bill Coyne and Ron Baukol, 3M; Dieter Kurz and Marc Vogel, Carl Zeiss; Craig Wynett, P&G; Bob LaPerle, Eastman Kodak; Bruce Carbonari, Fortune Brands Home and Hardware; Maureen Wenmouth and Tim O' Brien, Moen; Dan Buchner, Design Continuum; Ken Cox, NASA; Gary Kaiser, Eli Lilly; Ray Siuta, Hewlett-Packard; Terry Tallis, Essential Possibilities, and Dana Seccombe, both formerly with Hewlett-Packard; and Garrett Bouton, Barclays Global Investors.

Although this book will highlight the stories of many companies, we would like to express a special thanks to two companies: Moen and McNeil Consumer and Specialty Pharmaceuticals. At Moen, CEO Dick Posey, the executive staff, and the Periscope II team have been extremely supportive of our efforts. At McNeil, we would like to express our appreciation to CEO Bill McComb; Bob Carpenter, vice president of marketing; Amy Weiseman, manager of innovation and new product processes; and the entire Edison team for their commitment to the exploration of a role for strategy innovation in their company.

We were warned that writing a book is one of life's challenges that will test our character, fortitude, and sense of humor. Thanks to the wisdom and disciplined freedom afforded us by AMACOM's staff, we found the process to be both enjoyable and fulfilling.

Published authors who provided seasoned support and encouragement include Chris Zook, Bain & Company; Sidney Parnes, Creative Education Foundation; Teresa Amabile, Harvard Business School; Stan Gryskiewicz, Center for Creative Leadership; Jonathan Low, Cap Gemini Ernst & Young; T. George Harris, University of California, San Diego; Lynne Lesvesque, Harvard Business School; and Brian Mattimore, consultant.

While the coauthors have collaborated for more than fifteen years, anyone who worked a day with IdeaScope Associates has made a contribution to this emerging field of strategy innovation. Former colleagues who have provided us with special support include Chris Von Pichl, Meg Dunn, Maxine Teller, Amy Weiseman, and Harvey Ehrlich. A special thanks to Stephen Cornell, who was an early conceptual catalyst in the mountains west of Banff and provided important polish later on.

Individuals not already mentioned who provided us with valuable feedback for ways to strengthen our strategy innovation story include Peter Carey, Worth and Louise Loomis, Dorie Shallcross, Ted Colson, Jeneanne Rae, K.T. Conner, Burt Woolf, Will Clarkson, David Arnold, Bella English, Maura Grogan-Cornell, and Melinda Merino. A special thanks also to Paul Wentzell and Terry Tallis, who provided us with timely graphics support.

Additionally, we would like to express our deep gratitude to Chris von Pichl, Peter Carey, Deborah Frieze, Bruce Landay, and Bruce Crocker for their helpful counsel in advancing the mission and impact of The Visterra Group.

Finally, our wives, Ty Johnston and Anne Bate, carried the special burden of living with authors, and we are genuinely grateful for their perseverance and care.

INTRODUCTION

We want you to use this book. Nothing would please us more than knowing that leading-edge companies around the world are developing their own Discovery processes for the pursuit of strategy innovation.

Strategy innovation is not a fad. It is not the latest management program of the month. It is a process of exploring your emerging future, understanding the changing needs of your customers, and using the insights gained in those explorations to identify new business opportunities for your company. That's it. Whereas many management programs help you shrink your costs to grow your bottom line, strategy innovation is aimed at growing your top line. New business opportunities help drive new company strategies, which drive future growth.

So, why aren't more companies doing strategy innovation? Because they don't have an internal structure or process to do it. Who in your company is responsible for the future? Who is feeding your strategic planning process with ideas that stretch your current strategy and get you into new markets? How are you going about identifying your next new business platform, the basis of your future growth and success?

What we describe in this book is a phase-by-phase approach to the process of strategy innovation, not step-by-step. We provide the blueprint and encourage you to customize it for the specific needs of your company and your industry. This blueprint has been evolving for more than a decade, based on our experiences in a wide range of companies and industries. We will share with you some of the stories that helped to create this process of strategy innovation. It is a process that works.

Creating a cross-functional process for strategy innovation in a corporate setting is not as simple as it sounds. This is especially true when the process ventures outside the current corporate strategy or business model. Escaping your "corporate gravity" and then avoiding your "corporate immune system" are two threats to the establishment of this process. We will point them out and help you address them.

We will also share what we have learned about selecting and preparing a "reconnaissance" team for this process. The alignment with senior management on which strategic frontier to explore is a critical consideration that will be explained in detail. We will show you where value-based insights can be found on your strategic frontier—with customers, with the emerging future, and with new business models. Taking the insights and turning them into new business opportunities is a crucial step, as is the creation of a strategic road map for the future. All of these elements form the basis of the five phases of the Discovery Process.

Through this book and the work of our consulting firm, The Visterra Group, we hope to advance the awareness and use of strategy innovation in corporations around the world. Whether you are a multimega global corporation or a cheese shop in Zurich, you can use this strategy innovation process to chart a future path of growth for your business. The fact that you are reading this book says that this is of interest to you. We hope to hear from you at www.the visterragroup.com

The Organization of This Book

Section One (Chapters 1 through 4) of this book outlines what strategy innovation is, what it is not, and how we propose that you integrate it to your organization. This section will be particularly important reading for senior management of a company or division.

Section Two provides specific guidance for implementing a strategy innovation initiative, which we call the Discovery Process. We begin in Chapter 5 with a real example of how the Discovery Process worked in a real company. Chapters 6 through 10 then provide details for the implementation of the five phases of the Discovery Process—Staging, Aligning, Exploring, Creating, and Mapping. Stories and examples are woven throughout these chapters to add a practical touch to the frameworks presented. Understand, however, that these stories focus primarily on the *process* of previous initiatives, as we consider the content generated in them to be proprietary information.

Section Three offers more in-depth discussion of the Discovery Process and strategy innovation in a corporate setting. In Chapter 11, we answer questions and share some additional insights related to the Discovery Process. Chapter 12 outlines the key considerations in formalizing a strategy innovation process in a company, moving the Discovery Process from an ad hoc initiative to an ongoing strategy innovation system. Finally, in the Epilogue, we challenge senior management in corporations everywhere as we share some of our thoughts about the future of strategy innovation.

Scattered throughout this book are boxes titled "Process Tip." They represent what we consider to be critical elements in the implementation of the Discovery Process. They come from more than a decade of experiences in the trenches and are things we would emphasize if we were talking to you. We put them in boxes so you wouldn't miss them.

If you are curious about the history of strategy innovation in corporations and its roots in the early work done in creativity and brainstorming, we encourage you to read the remainder of this introduction. It will provide a good context for understanding the evolution of innovation as it makes its way to the corporate boardroom.

The Migration of Creativity to Strategy in Corporations: Evolution to Revolution and Beyond

Many writers, researchers, innovators and strategists have recognized the value of an organization reaching beyond predictable, incremental growth to achieve greater profit in innovative ways. Gary Hamel, C.K. Prahalad, Constantinos Markides, Jim Collins, and Clayton Christensen all champion strategy innovation as a vehicle for creating "new value" and spawning new wealth. And, while most cite or imply the importance of a creative process in breaking the bonds of incrementalism, none prescribe an explicit process to do the job. As Hamel succinctly states, "No one seems to know much about how to create strategy."[1] To date, serendipity appears to be the secret solution to strategy innovation. In this sense, the relationship between strategy and creativity in the business literature is still somewhat remote. Few strategists have yet discovered or shared the decades of research in creativity and innovation that can be harvested for the purposes of creating new value and new profitability in their businesses.

Applying Imagination as a Skill

An emphasis on creativity first entered the corporate world in the 1940s and 1950s. The groundbreaking work on the creative process by Alex Osborn, cofounder of the advertising agency BBD& O, led to his fathering the process known as "brainstorming." His work also led to one of the first creativity guidebooks, the classic *Applied Imagination*.[2] While achieving legendary success with his creativity techniques in the advertising world, Osborn and his colleague, Sidney Parnes, recognized that every human being has the potential to be creative, if given the opportunity and the right environment. Their work was supported by the research efforts of J.P. Guilford, Paul Torrance, Don MacKinnon, Calvin Taylor, and others, which clearly proved that creativity is a developable skill inherent in everyone, not just a genius elite.

Parnes's research demonstrated, among other things, that creativity is a skill that can be strengthened with coaching and practice. Routinely, students in his courses were able to increase their idea-generating capacities by 100 percent or more. Of particular importance, Osborn and Parnes proved the value of a mental model for creativity, where "divergent thinking" is used to expand one's options, and "convergent thinking" enables the focus on a preferred, innovative choice. One believer, Robert Galvin, retired CEO and chairman of Motorola, used his imagination and inspired others to grow Motorola one-thousand-fold during his three decades of leadership. Galvin sagely observed, "Some think of this work of engaging the imagination to be the work of genius. Osborn demonstrated how it could be developed as a vocational skill." If creativity is a skill that can be developed, it becomes a tool that corporations can use for purposes of innovation.

Applying Imagination to Inventing

In the late 1950s, George Prince and William Gordon had the task of delivering proprietary new inventions to the clients of Arthur D. Little, Inc., in Cambridge, Massachusetts. As part of the R&D–focused Invention Design Group, they had the task of focusing on solving client problems in innovative, often patentable, ways. During many years of successful new product innovation, Prince and Gordon analyzed their process to determine the most effective thinking strategies for invention.

This research led to their founding in the 1960s of a new company they called Synectics, Inc. Synectics used the power of metaphor and analogy to spark creative thinking, leading to the identification of new products. They gave creativity a process that could be applied in corporations for the purpose of innovative inventions. In a span of a few decades, creativity had gone from an esoteric skill in an ad agency to the basis of a corporate process for generating innovative product ideas. Creativity was making progress but was still under the radar for most corporate managers.

Applying Imagination to Management . . .

In the 1960s Edward DeBono, a British neurologist, introduced the world to the concept of "lateral thinking," a fresh way to think about creativity. DeBono observed that in attempting to solve problems, most people think "vertically," in a straight line, probing deeper and deeper until the solution eventually presents itself. In problems involving a creative response, however, he noted that the solution is typically *not* at the end of a linear thought process, digging the same hole deeper and deeper. Instead, it involves "lateral thinking," digging a new hole somewhere else. Shifting the framework of the process often results in new and creative solutions.[3]

In thinking about thinking, DeBono believes that, between vertical and lateral approaches to creative thinking, lateral thinking is the more difficult to master but the more rewarding for innovation. DeBono has spent decades teaching corporate executives around the world the importance of "serious creativity" for inspiring innovative opportunities. During that time, the creativity message gained credibility with corporate managers as a tool for innovation.

In 1970, the Center for Creative Leadership in Greensboro, North Carolina, was founded to teach courses for individuals and teams to hone their creative talents. Stan Gryskiewicz—founding member, senior fellow, and vice president—organized and still leads a group called the Association for Managers of Innovation, which provides a forum for showcasing and networking of innovation practices across corporations. Corporate managers were beginning to recognize the potential for creativity in their organizations.

Applying Imagination to Strategy

According to Henry Mintzberg, former president of the Strategic Management Society, strategic planning is an oxymoron.[4] In most organizations it tends to neither provide a sufficient range of strategic options to consider nor present an engaging road map of a compelling future. This is not surprising since most strategic planning processes are numbers-oriented, lacking a creativity component. As a result, strategic planning in most companies is a process that merely extends the previous strategy into the future. Even when senior executives invite "out of the box" thinking, most managers do not know how to go about exploring beyond the existing strategic framework.

We had the opportunity, as a founding principal and associate at

IdeaScope, Inc., to work with senior executives of companies to discover and develop many new strategic opportunities. Initially, much of our work was product-centric. After working with many Fortune 100 companies on the creation of new product concepts, we had the privilege of assisting Procter & Gamble in the late 1980s with the development of an internal process called Concept Lab, for new product development across their many divisions.

Since we were known as leaders of a proven creative process in our product concept work, soon executives with *strategic* challenges began enlisting our services to provide the missing creativity ingredient from their analysis-based strategic planning approaches. Applying creativity to corporate strategy is more challenging than the identification of new products, and yet some of the process is similar. Through dozens of strategy innovation initiatives, we experimented with a variety of different processes and carefully analyzed the results. Then, following our departures from IdeaScope, we spent nearly two years researching and developing a new framework for strategy innovation—which represents a significant advance in the process. What you will see in this book is the result of more than a decade of work—a proven method for creating strategy innovation in corporations.

Early Pioneers of Applying Imagination to Strategy

From the mid-1980s on, companies like Eli Lilly, Procter & Gamble, 3M, Moen, BMW, Eastman Kodak, Hewlett-Packard, Fidelity Investments, General Mills, Dow Chemical, Motorola, Carl Zeiss, and Schott Glas have recognized the importance of infusing creativity into their development of new strategic opportunities. In a few of these companies, the quest for new strategic growth was vision-driven. Others were motivated by ambitious goals that extended beyond the reach of current capabilities. Still others were motivated by a severe competitive threat, which created an appetite for strategy innovation where none had existed before.

In every case, the organization was challenged by its situation to stretch beyond its self-limiting boundaries of how it viewed itself and the world. A shift to a new organizational self-image, a new industry perspective, or a new worldview was needed. The organization would then have to align on that new perspective, so it had to be a result of a credible, quality process.

Eli Lilly: An Early Strategy Innovator

In the mid-1980s, Eli Lilly and Company, a large and respected pharmaceutical manufacturer, speculated there could be a dramatic shift in drug discovery and development within infectious disease, home of its largest revenue stream. Most of Lilly's product portfolio for infectious disease was targeted to bacterial disease. Senior management wanted to explore the emerging trends in infectious diseases to determine if more attractive opportunities might exist in developing new products targeting viral and/or fungal diseases.

We were retained to act as "process architects" and "discovery guides" for the Infectious Disease Task Force, a half-dozen cross-functional teams assembled to create and develop new strategic options for Lilly in infectious disease. After much research of the available literature and the hosting of several panels of industry experts (called thought leader panels) sharing their views of the emerging future, the Lilly teams gained a new understanding of the opportunities for the future of pharmaceuticals. From this foresight, these scientists used creative techniques to generate a list of hundreds of new strategic options for Lilly, which they then refined to a few for presentation to management.

The advisory groups and senior management, up to and including the chairman of the board, committed to the new strategic opportunities developed by the teams. The organization was restructured around these new strategic options in infectious diseases, helping Lilly to remain a prominent player in that marketplace, as well as to anticipate and participate in the newly emerging field of biotechnology.

Impressed with the process of applying creative tools to strategy development, Eli Lilly later replicated the same strategy innovation process for both their cardiovascular business and for Elanco, their agricultural products business. Creativity had successfully entered the corporate boardroom.

Applying Imagination to the Economy

In his recent book, *The Rise of the Creative Class*, Richard Florida takes the importance of creativity and imagination to a new level, beyond that of corporate strategies to entire industries and our world economy. He writes:

> Many say we now live in an "information" economy or a "knowledge" economy. But what's more fundamentally true is that we now have an economy powered by human creativity. Creativity—"the ability to create meaningful new forms," as Webster's dictionary puts it—is now the decisive source of competitive advantage. In virtually every industry, from automobiles to fashion, food products and information technology itself, the winners in the long run are those who can create and keep creating.[5]

Creativity from the Mailroom to the Boardroom

Through this book we hope to extend this fifty-year migration of creativity in corporations. What started as a recognized, teachable skill in an advertising agency grew to become a tool for invention, and then a process for innovation throughout the company. This book will open the door for creativity in the boardroom, successfully marrying the processes of innovation and corporate strategic planning.

Although strategy and creativity may be strange bedfellows, the time is right for bringing them together in the corporate boardroom. It is not a matter of replacing your analytical, numbers-based strategic planning process with a less predictable, sometimes-serendipitous creative approach to strategy. The strategy innovation process outlined in this book will show how the two disciplines can be merged, with strategy innovation feeding the strategic planning process. The corporate need for innovation will demand this marriage, from a courtship that began long ago.

Endnotes

1. Gary Hamel, "Strategy Innovation and the Quest for Value," *Sloan Management Review*, Winter 1998.
2. Alex F. Osborn, *Applied Imagination*, 3rd edition (New York: Scribners, 1963).
3. Edward DeBono, *Lateral Thinking for Management* (New York: AMA-COM, 1972).
4. Henry Mintzberg, *The Rise and Fall of Strategic Planning* (New York: The Free Press, 1994).
5. Richard Florida, *The Rise of the Creative Class* (New York: Basic Books, 2002).

PART ONE

THE WHAT AND WHY OF STRATEGY INNOVATION

CHAPTER 1

STRATEGY MEETS INNOVATION

> If an organization is to meet the challenges of a changing world, it must be prepared to change everything about itself except its basic beliefs. The only sacred cow in an organization should be the basic philosophy of doing business.
>
> —*THOMAS J. WATSON*

No corporate strategy lasts forever. Companies that get all the components of their business models working together can often drive their success for many years. But at some point, they start to run out of gas. Many companies are shocked to hear the financial engine sputter, having never paid much attention to their fuel gauge. Others have an eye on the gauge but don't have a clue where the next service station is located, so they coast along, hoping to get lucky.

Then there are companies that have scouted out the road ahead and know their refueling options. With their eyes watching the road, the map, and the fuel gauge, they fill up the tank before it gets too low. Even older models, with the proper tune-up and constant refueling, can remain cruising at the speed limit for decades.

Your company needs strategy innovation initiatives to understand the road ahead and know your options for keeping the product tank full and the financial engine running smoothly.

What is strategy innovation?

Strategy innovation is shifting a corporation's business strategy in order to create new value for both the customer and the corporation.

In a dynamic marketplace, every business runs the risk that its current business model will become obsolete. As long as there is customer value to be delivered, there will be companies interested in delivering it. New companies will create innovative, more efficient business models in order to compete in profitable industries. Consider the case of Wal-Mart. Starting as a discount retailer to the underserved population of rural areas, it needed to develop a new, more efficient retailing business model in order to survive in that segment of the retailing market. Using sophisticated technology and a streamlined distribution system, Sam Walton created a new business strategy in the retail industry that created value for both his rural customers and for his company. The superiority of their innovative business model ultimately led to Wal-Mart's domination of that entire industry. The strongest survive.

In other dynamic industries of the twenty-first century, new technologies, new materials, and new distribution channels are continually changing the competitive landscape. Companies such as Nokia, Charles Schwab, and IBM recognized the potential of these changes, altered their business strategies, and have been able to take advantage of the emerging growth opportunities in wireless communications, financial services, and computer services. Companies such as K-Mart, USAirways, and Digital Equipment Corporation either did not see the trends in their industries or refused to alter their business strategies in times of change, and they have suffered the consequences. As Jack Welch, the highly successful former CEO of General Electric, once said about companies in dynamic markets, "When the rate of change outside exceeds the rate of change inside, the end is in sight."[1]

A Fight to the Photo-Finish

An example of the importance of strategy innovation in dynamic markets can be found in the photography industry. Back in the

1980s, Kodak and Polaroid were two prominent, global players in that industry. Kodak dominated the silver halide, 35-mm market while Polaroid, protected by its patents, owned the instant photography segment. At about that time, a new, disruptive technology was just beginning to emerge via the computer revolution, one that would threaten to make both conventional film processing technologies obsolete—digital imaging.

Kodak took the initiative in the late 1980s to understand the potential implications of this new technology. In two, large-scale strategy innovation initiatives, cross-functional teams of Kodak managers used panels of experts in this new technology to explore the emergence of digital photography and identify the potential new business opportunities of the future marketplace. From this work, Kodak understood the ramifications of digital photography on the industry and made important changes in their corporate strategy. R&D spending was immediately shifted from a focus on new silver halide projects to an interim, "hybrid" strategy, balancing the needs of the still-strong silver halide business with the growing potential of digital photography.

In the decade that followed, Kodak became a force in the world of digital photography, including the development of Picture CDs, Picture Maker kiosks, the purchase of their Japanese partner Chinon to manufacture digital cameras, the purchase of online photofinisher Ofoto, and a joint venture with America Online called You've Got Pictures. As this book is being written, Kodak is transitioning with the market to digital photography, rather than being left in its wake. It shifted its business strategy to create new value for both Kodak and its customers.

Polaroid, on the other hand, ignored the early signs of digital photography and decided to stick with and protect their existing corporate strategy in instant photography. They did not understand how to create value in this emerging marketplace, preferring to compete using their old strategy, crafted in a very different era. On October 12, 2001, Polaroid filed for bankruptcy protection.

Companies that are attuned to the changes taking place in the market and see them as potential business opportunities are practicing strategy innovation. Companies that are eager to create new value for customers are practicing strategy innovation. Companies that are willing to redefine themselves and how they operate in order to pursue new, more vibrant growth initiatives are practicing strategy innovation.

Strategy Innovation Goes Beyond Product Innovation

It is interesting to note how many companies in recent years have adopted "innovation" as a core value or as part of their mission statements. If we as a society have moved from the Information Age to the Knowledge Age, then this relatively new emphasis on innovation is quite logical. When information is ubiquitous and is no longer a source of competitive advantage, it is the innovative use of that information (via knowledge) that differentiates people, companies, and nations. Innovation may become the basis of all competition in the future. Innovation is the new competitive arena where present-day gladiators, equipped with similar information and access to similar resources, try to outsmart one another to victory.

As we work with and read about corporations today, we see the focus of innovation being placed primarily on the *products* that they are creating. Go to a company's Web site. If they talk about innovation or have an Office of Innovation, it is frequently related to the work done in their Research & Development labs. Innovation is usually thought of as invention. Innovation is usually new technology being turned into something unique and tangible that the company can sell. For those companies with strong R&D departments, this focus on the invention of innovative products is probably a key element of their corporate strategy.

There are, however, other elements of a corporate strategy beyond innovative products that can help companies compete in their markets. Besides having a product to sell, companies have to make that product and then get it into the hands of customers (and meet their customers' needs). To do this, companies create specific functions such as manufacturing, sales, distribution, and marketing. These functions and how they interrelate make up the company's business model. The effectiveness and efficiency of the business model is a critical element of a company's strategy. Michael Porter, the corporate strategy guru at Harvard Business School, highlighted the importance of "fit" of the functional activities that make up a company's strategy when he wrote, "Strategic fit among many activities is fundamental not only to competitive advantage but also to the sustainability of that advantage. . . . Positions built on systems of activities are far more sustainable than those built on individual activities."[2]

The implication here is that the most innovative *product* on the market may not be able to compete against a less advanced product that has a unique or superior *business model*. Dell Computer is a successful company because of its innovative business model (selling customized computers via the Internet and use of a very strong supply chain management), not because of its superior computers. Therefore, companies that do not have a world-class R&D capability may still be able to compete effectively in markets if they focus their efforts on building a superior business model.

Given the strategic importance of a company's business model in its ability to compete in the marketplace, it is logical that efforts put into improving the business model could provide real value to a company. If that is true, then companies should place at least as much "innovation" focus on the other elements of the business model (and how they interact) as they currently do on the product side.

Strategy innovation is a process of applying innovative thinking to the entire business model of a company, not just to its products or inventions.

Strategy Innovation as a Strategic Advantage

Although strategy innovation may be critical for success (or survival) in dynamic markets, it can also be a source of competitive advantage in more stable markets. The company that understands how to create value for both their customers and themselves can change the basis of competition in their industry. By creating efficient business systems aimed at delivering this new value in a market, companies not only redefine value but lock out competitors who are unable to replicate the efficient business model that delivers it. Like Wal-Mart, they play the same game with a different set of rules, rules that give them a decided advantage.

Strategy innovation has done for business what the forward pass did for the game of (American) football. Without a change in the rules, football would not have survived its early start-up years. Note in the following story the parallels between the early game of football and many businesses today:

The game of football first emerged on college campuses in the early 1800s. Styled after the game of rugby that was being played in England at that time, football consisted of a group of people moving a ball past another group of people, using whatever means they could. As the game evolved, teams adopted wild and dangerous tactics, such as the flying wedge, for moving the ball up the field. Defenses would respond to these new schemes with actions that bordered on assault. Games were won and lost in violent interchanges around the line of scrimmage, with both teams using brute force to maintain their positions. Plays were predictable, and the ball usually moved slowly, incrementally up the field. Some compared the game to warfare in the trenches of World War I. Injuries were common in those early days, and fatalities became a growing problem. When the number of deaths related to football rose to 33 in 1905, President Theodore Roosevelt stepped in with a mandate. He threatened to ban the sport unless changes were made to the style of play.

In 1906, the Rules Committee of the organization that would become the National Collegiate Athletic Association approved the use of the forward pass for football. This changed significantly the way the game was played. Soldiers in the trenches now had support from their airborne units. Teams now had more options for moving the ball. Rather than having to rely on the standard offense of running-the-ball-up-the-middle for a small gain in yardage, a team could throw a pass over the defense for a larger gain. The game became more complex. Predictability of offensive plays gave way to surprise attacks. Quarterbacks and coaches now had to make decisions on what play to use in any given situation, based on the strengths and weaknesses of the competition and the distance to the goal line. John Heisman and Knute Rockne were some of the first coaches who found effective ways to make the forward pass an integral part of the game. Football became a game of strategy.

The forward pass rule changed the basis of competition in collegiate football. Teams with big, tough players who could become human battering rams no longer had an advantage. Now teams with small, agile, quick pass receivers could compete with the big guys. More colleges fielded football teams, competition grew, and the game survived.

Strategy innovation is the process of finding a way to "change the rules of the game" so that your company's products, competencies, and assets provide you with a competitive advantage in the marketplace. If you are not the mammoth "battering ram" of a company that can compete in a market on the basis of size, strategy innovation allows you to define a new business where "small, agile, and quick" is the only way to provide customers with value. Starbucks could not have outmuscled and outspent Procter & Gamble and General Foods to gain advertising awareness for their new coffee and shelf space in supermarkets. So they set up small cafes where they not only sold their premium coffees but provided customers with the added value of a European café experience. Similarly, Minnetonka, Inc., was able to outmaneuver the giant soap companies in the early 1980s by introducing the first liquid soap product, later purchased by Colgate and renamed Softsoap.

In his book *The Innovator's Dilemma,* Clayton Christensen suggests that this small company advantage is an important force in the marketplace. He writes, "Large companies often surrender emerging growth markets because smaller, disruptive companies are actually more capable of pursuing them. Though start-ups lack resources, it doesn't matter. Their values can embrace small markets, and their cost structures can accommodate lower margins.

Their market research and resource allocation processes allow managers to proceed intuitively rather than having to be backed up by careful research and analysis, presented in PowerPoint. All of these advantages add up to enormous opportunity or looming disaster—depending on your perspective."[3]

This is the essence of strategy innovation: "changing the rules" of how customers receive value and having a business model that delivers that value better than anyone else. In that way, you make your weaknesses in an established market irrelevant, and your innovative business model becomes the new basis of competition in a market that you started.

Constantinos Markides, a professor at the London Business School and author of *All The Right Moves*, calls strategy innovation "a fundamental reconceptualization of what the business is about, which in turn leads to a dramatically different way of playing the game in the industry."[4]

In his book *Leading the Revolution*, Gary Hamel cites a number of companies that have dared to reinvent themselves by adopting innovative strategies and creative new business models. He believes that this capability will be required to compete in the markets of the future. "Unless you and your company become adept at business concept innovation, more imaginative minds will capture tomorrow's wealth."[5]

Strategy Innovation as a Source of Corporate Renewal

Strategy innovation is often considered the calling card of start-up companies looking to enter already-existing markets. However, established companies also use strategy innovation to their advantage, if they have the instinct for it. We recognize this instinct as a strong, internal emphasis on corporate "renewal." The instinct for renewal is something beyond a cultural norm; it seems to be embedded in the organization's DNA, what it sees when it looks in the mirror. These companies are never completely satisfied with who they are today, but are more interested in who they are becoming.

Companies such as Procter & Gamble, IBM, and Nokia have not experienced their sustained success by merely evolving. They have taken bold, strategically innovative steps at critical points in their histories to redefine who they were. How else does one explain the radical shift in the business of these companies from their origins? Procter & Gamble was once exclusively a soap manufacturer. At one point in their history, IBM made scales and cheese slicers. Before Nokia was in mobile phones, they were a paper products company. These companies are more concerned with their future than their past. They are proactive. They believe that corporate renewal is healthy, if not critical to their ongoing survival and success. All have confidence that they will still be in business in 2050 without believing it will be the same business they are in today.

Companies with an instinct for renewal as part of their corporate DNA are not on a treadmill. They are vigilant in the examination of their business peripheries, expecting the boundaries to change as the marketplace changes. And, when more radical opportunities present themselves, they are poised to respond. That is how a soap manufacturer becomes successful in the pet food business, how a producer of cheese slicers wins Nobel Prizes for physics, and how a paper products company becomes a world-beater in wireless communications. They expect to renew through strategy innovation and, in the process, be more vital tomorrow than they are today.

Summary

- Strategy innovation is shifting a corporation's business strategy in order to create new value for both the customer and the corporation.

- Strategy innovation is a process of applying innovative thinking to the entire business model of a company, not just to its products or inventions.

- Strategy innovation is the process of finding a way to "change the rules of the game" so that your company's products, competencies, and assets provide you with a competitive advantage in the marketplace.

◆ While strategy innovation may be critical for success (or survival) in dynamic markets, it can also be a source of competitive advantage in more stable markets.

◆ Established companies with an instinct for corporate renewal use strategy innovation to remain vital and relevant over time.

◆ Strategy innovation can provide new growth prospects for companies in any marketplace and should be a capability, if not a core competence, of every company hoping to survive in the dynamic business world of the twenty-first century.

Endnotes

1. Jack Welch, from GE's *2000 Annual Report*.
2. Michael Porter, "What Is Strategy?," *Harvard Business Review*, November/December 1996.
3. Clayton Christensen, *The Innovator's Dilemma* (Boston: Harvard Business School Press, 1997).
4. Constantinos Markides, *All the Right Moves* (Boston: Harvard Business School Press, 2000).
5. Gary Hamel, *Leading the Revolution* (Boston: Harvard Business School Press, 2000).

CHAPTER 2

STRATEGY INNOVATION IS
MANAGING THE FUTURE

> There are always two parties—the party of the Past
> and the party of the Future; the Establishment and the
> Movement.
>
> —*RALPH WALDO EMERSON*

When do you know that you need strategy innovation? In most
cases, it is when the projection of revenues for future products and
services does not add up to the company's growth targets. When
this happens, business leaders scramble around to find ways to address this "delta," the difference between the revenues they expect
to generate and the revenues they need to generate (see Figure 2-
1).

The Dreaded Delta and the Spiral of Incrementalism

The knee-jerk reaction to this revenue-target dichotomy is to pull
together a team of people to brainstorm some new product ideas
or acquisition targets to fill the dreaded revenue delta. Over the
years, creativity in the form of brainstorming events has earned its
reputation as a viable method of creating incremental new product

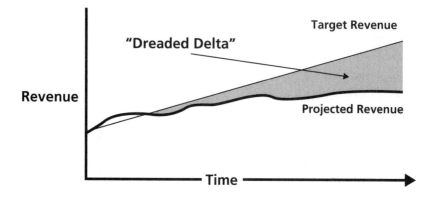

Figure 2-1. The dreaded delta.

and service ideas in corporations. However, the problem with many brainstorming efforts is that they are done within the context of the base brand or current business and tend to produce only line extension opportunities or incremental product improvements. They take current products and make them slightly more powerful, slightly more colorful, or slightly longer-lasting (at a slightly higher price). Often, these slightly better line-extension products can help fill the revenue delta, as long as the delta is not too big.

After years of creating line extensions to fill revenue gaps, corporations often evolve into "institutions of incrementalism." This is particularly true in companies that have had a successful product or brand on the market for many years. Whenever additional revenue is needed, a new line extension of the current product is introduced. With a strong brand, it is not too difficult to introduce a successful line-extension product. The line extension can usually use the same manufacturing facilities, the same distribution system, and the same sales force as the base brand, minimizing incremental costs. Because it leverages a known brand name, market acceptance is likely, and additional revenues (from the slightly higher price) are almost certain. Because it is similar to other products produced by this business system, the process for getting it to market is relatively easy, fast, and problem-free. A downside to leveraging the base brand through line extensions is the relatively low incremental revenue that results, as cannibalization of the base brand will account for some of the additional revenue.

Meanwhile, the business systems of the company adapt to this strategy of growth through incrementalism. We worked with a company once that had become a victim of its line-extension success. Its operations had become more efficient around dealing with line extensions, but less flexible in their abilities to accommodate new and unique products. Financial controls and hurdle rates for new products were set to the attractive level of line extensions, making it difficult for new products requiring additional costs or investment spending to be approved for development. The corporate culture, which rewarded people who quickly brought new line extensions to market, was less patient when nonincremental products had a longer time frame or required more attention or problem-solving to develop. When this happened, the company became caught in a spiral of incrementalism. It had become very efficient at developing low-volume, high-profit line extensions, and the internal systems prevented it from identifying, developing, or introducing significantly new products and services to the market. The company had lost its ability to significantly grow the business.

As long as the base brand remains vibrant with growth potential in the marketplace, the spiral of incrementalism can be an efficient and profitable way to run the business. If the brand saturates the market, the market undergoes some change, or the brand loses some of its previous vitality, growth slows, and the dreaded delta appears. Richard Foster and Sarah Kaplan, in their book *Creative Destruction*, write, "The reason IBM stumbled was that something was wrong with John Akers's view of the world—with his mental model. Akers believed in continuity in gradual, incremental change. But the world had become discontinuous."[1] When this happens, it is time to find a new growth platform for the company, a new "engine" to drive future revenues and profits. Akers's successor at IBM, Lou Gerstner, was successful in doing that and, as a result, was able to save the computing giant from break-up or collapse. By refocusing the company's expertise on computing services and its patents on technology licensing, Gerstner created significant new business platforms that will continue to drive growth in IBM's future.

The Corporate Dilemma of the Current Business vs. the Future Business

It is not easy for the senior management team of an existing company to navigate the whitewater conditions of a dynamic marketplace. Everything seems to be constantly changing—products, technologies, competitors, customer needs, distribution channels, and so on. How should the company respond? Is it better to take action or wait for the market to settle down? Should the company stick with their current strategy or move to a new one?

On the one hand, the company must manage its current business, which has been proven and time-tested in its ability to find a market and deliver a product or service to that market. This predictability represents a low-risk means for the company to meet its financial goals, ensuring its survival. It is the goose that laid the golden eggs. However, that current business is probably working off an older business model, created in the past when the market conditions were quite different. Being an older business model, it may have an infrastructure and overhead expenses that are inordinately high, keeping prices high and making the market an attractive target to new, leaner competitors. A start-up company with a Web site and access to cheap manufacturing capabilities overseas could replicate your products at lower prices and steal your market share. A global goliath could apply its considerable resources and technologies to offer your customers more than you can. All existing businesses are vulnerable, to some degree, to competitive pressures in a dynamic marketplace, making their futures uncertain.

On the other hand, there are countless ways for a company to create new business opportunities in a dynamic marketplace. Change in the status quo of any market component creates some degree of disequilibrium, which means that there are likely to be customers somewhere who are being underserved or business systems that are not working at full efficiency. This results in the potential to create value, which is the basis for new, future business opportunities. Revenue generated from these new ventures can help fuel the future growth necessary to keep the company financially vital and attractive to investors, suppliers, and employees. However, new business opportunities have a downside. They can introduce potential new risks to the company's financial equation, as the development and successful implementation of a new business opportunity is far from certain. Spending too much or taking too much time to pursue these new, untested opportunities may kill the goose, cutting off your golden egg supply.

This "tension" between focusing on the current, lower-risk (but vulnerable) businesses versus higher-risk new business opportunities is often a critical factor in the creation of a corporate strategy. It is the corporate strategy that identifies how the company will allocate and develop its resources to meet both current and future market needs, while keeping the company financially viable. Therefore, it is an important strategic imperative to consider how a company will balance the needs of today's business while pursuing the business needs of the future. Jim Collins and Jerry Porras, in their book *Built to Last: Successful Habits of Visionary Companies*, write, "Managers at visionary companies simply do not accept the proposition that they must choose between short-term performance *or* long-term performance. They build first and foremost for the long term while *simultaneously* holding themselves to highly demanding short-term standards."[2]

Although allocating time, attention, and resources to managing the future business will divert time, attention, and resources from managing the current business—and vice versa—this tension between the present and the future business is a healthy tension to foster in an organization. Linda S. Mayer, the senior vice president of marketing and product development at Moen, calls it the need for "bifocal vision." It requires everyone to always determine and strike a balance of the two, thus preventing the urgency of the present from overshadowing the importance of the future.

Business school professors Michael I. Tushman (Harvard) and Charles A. O'Reilly III (Stanford), in their book *Winning through*

Innovation: A Practical Guide to Leading Organizational Change and Renewal, address this difficult trade-off between the present and future businesses of corporations. "To succeed both today and tomorrow, managers must play two different games simultaneously." They go on to explain how the management of today's business requires a focus on efficiency and stability, aligning and improving the productivity of all facets of the business model. The business of the future, however, requires "streams of innovation," which can be a destabilizing force because they require corporate change. "Given these contrasting forces for change and stability, managers need to create ambidextrous organizations—organizations that celebrate stability and incremental change as well as experimentation and discontinuous change simultaneously."[3]

One way to foster this healthy tension is to create an internal corporate system focused on strategy innovation and the future. By formalizing such a system, senior management makes a corporate commitment to the importance of the company's future, while still running today's business. Chapter 12 outlines some important considerations in the formalization of a strategy innovation system.

Strategy Innovation Is Managing Your Business Toward the Future

Organizations that have found it difficult to focus on managing the future business provide a range of excuses, including:

- Corporate myopia
- Industry turbulence
- Future incompetence

Corporate Myopia

There are some companies that are so engrossed in managing today's business that they claim they cannot find the time or energy to think about tomorrow. We recently asked the senior management team of a billion-dollar corporation to speculate on the company's future, and on which direction it might take to identify new business opportunities. It was clear from our interviews that only two people on the team had spent any time thinking about the company's future beyond their current one-year planning period. This is probably not unusual. Especially in light of the downsizing and the relentless pressure to make the quarterly numbers in many organizations, the urgency of today's business supersedes the importance of tomorrow's business.

Industry Turbulence

Other companies, particularly those involved with fast-changing industries such as communications and technology, claim that attempts to understand the future are fruitless, given the chaos and unpredictability they see in their markets. With technologies, products, and pricing changing so rapidly, they maintain that it is impossible to speculate on where those markets might be in a three-to-five-year time frame. As a result, many of these companies take a reactive approach to the future, preferring to make decisions once market dynamics are clearer.

Future Incompetence

Finally, we have also run into companies that know it is important to understand the future and want to do it, but they do not know how to go about doing it. Their typical response is to try to find someone who "really understands the future," who can advise them on what to do about it. They want the answer delivered to them by an enlightened outsider. The search for this person is rarely "prophet-able." Futurists vary significantly in the assumptions they make and the factors they consider. None have the answer.

As a result of this lack of attention, the future is an unknown, mysterious place for many companies. The mystery even leads to some myths about the future, which can actually discourage its exploration. For example, many people see how sudden changes can have an impact on a market. Believing that these changes could not have been predicted, they assume that all "forecasts" of the future are too tenuous to be of value. Therefore, they do not bother to explore the possibilities of the future.

Assumptions About the Future

Strategy innovation can be a powerful means of managing your business toward the future. However, the effective pursuit of strategy innovation requires a few basic assumptions about the future.

1. *The future does not yet exist and can be created.*

   There are some people who feel that the future has already somehow been determined and will be revealed to us as it arrives. For them, the future is like an actor, with lines carefully rehearsed, waiting backstage for the right moment to enter the scene. Those who feel this way tend to be very *reactive* in their actions, for they fear that they cannot control the future. They will take no action until the future arrives. Then, they will "see what the future holds" and respond to it. Perhaps they feel the future is so powerful that it will nullify their actions, so why waste energy and resources now?

   By definition, the future does not exist and never will (once you experience tomorrow, it is no longer tomorrow, but today). Therefore, because the future is not a fait accompli, it can be influenced. Although maybe not a totally blank canvas, the future has considerable latitude for the artist to make an impact. Actions taken today by a company will result in some future effects in the marketplace. Therefore, *proactive* companies that take those actions today will have the greatest influence on the future. Reactive companies may survive into the future, but it is the proactive companies that will create that future. The proactive companies can, through their actions, "change the rules" in the marketplace, requiring the reactive companies to play the game a different way or perish.

2. *The future cannot be precisely predicted, but its forces can be identified.*

   If all trends were linear, constant, and noninteractive, it might be possible to predict the future. However, trends change, and so much of the future is shaped by events that cannot be predicted. We call these events discontinuities, things that shift the trend lines. They are inflection points that cause the future to be diverted from its previous path. The invention of the transistor, the evolution of the Vietnam War, and the development of the Internet were all discontinuities that had a significant impact on the future that we are now experiencing. The human genome project, the 9/11 terrorist attacks, and nanotechnology may have a similar impact on our children's future.

Although these elements cannot be predicted with any degree of certainty, the forces that led to them would have been quite easy to spot—by those who were searching for them. As we will discuss later in this book, we were involved in a strategy innovation initiative in the mid-1990s where an industry expert shared a concern that terrorist attacks could render city water supplies vulnerable. Back then, that seemed a very unrealistic possibility. But those who were in positions of responsibility recognized the potential because they were dealing with such issues every day. It is a valuable exercise to identify existing forces that could have an impact on the future. It is not the same as *predicting* the future, but it is gaining market foresight that can help understand and shape the future.

3. *The future is not one-size-fits-all, it is proprietary.*

When you see a cow standing in a field, what do you see? A farmer may see his chores. A toddler may see something scary. Ben & Jerry see a potential supplier. The point is that we all see things differently, based on our experiences and what is important to us (our values). The future is the same way. Companies perceive the future according to their past experiences, their core competencies, and their values and aspirations. Therefore, two companies from the same industry may see the same forces in the marketplace, but paint two totally different pictures of the future. The future you see is proprietary to you, based on your values. It cannot be delivered by a consultant, it must be discovered by you.

With these basic assumptions about the future, you are now in a position to explore the future for strategic opportunities that exist there.

Future Business Opportunities Will Drive a New Corporate Strategy

What does your company currently understand about its future? How might your markets change? What business opportunities will exist in these future markets? How will your company participate in these markets? Who in the company is focused on that question? These are important questions for all companies in all markets to consider as they create their business strategies.

In thinking about what your future business strategy might look like, there is often the question of which comes first—the new business opportunity or the new corporate strategy? Although not quite as perplexing as its chicken-egg cousin, this question might make for an interesting research project for an aspiring professor. Do corporations establish their strategies and then look for business opportunities to support those strategies or is it the other way around—first finding a business opportunity and then creating a new corporate strategy around it?

A case could be made for the strategy coming first. A quantitative analysis of markets done in the context of a strategic model (such as Michael Porter's Five Forces Model, or Bain & Company's Profit Pools Analysis) can identify "gaps" in the market, areas of profitability, or market segments where the company could have a sustained competitive advantage. In this case, a preferred company positioning in the marketplace can be identified first, leading to a search for new business opportunities to support that strategy.

However, we believe that new corporate strategies more often come from first identifying a new business opportunities. Many of the examples in this book reflect a new corporate strategy being created based on the identification of exciting new business opportunities. Having a portfolio of new business opportunities to choose from will provide senior management even greater flexibility in crafting a competitive strategy. Henry Mintzberg, a professor at McGill University and author of *The Rise and Fall of Strategic Planning*, observes that opportunities beget strategies. He wrote in the *Academy of Management Executives*, "Good strategies grow out of ideas that have been kicking around the company, and initiatives that have been taken by all sorts of people in the company. . . . That means that a lot of very effective, so-called strategists or chief executives don't come up with the brilliant new strategy."[4]

Robert Galvin, former CEO of electronics giant Motorola, claims that in his more than forty years at the helm, it was the new business options available to him that often drove his corporate strategies. He explained, "Strategy is determining the most worthy place to apply your resources. You allocate the resources to the ideas that have the most promising potential. Before allocating those resources, you should have surveyed all of your options and selected the best one."

Portfolio of New Business Opportunities: A Valuable, Intangible Strategic Asset

It stands to reason that if new business opportunities help drive the creation of new corporate strategies, then having a portfolio of many new business opportunities provides senior management with more options and more flexibility in their strategy-making. A portfolio of new business opportunities can provide the company with choices on how to grow the business. A diverse portfolio, consisting of shorter-term and longer-term opportunities as well as lower-volume and higher-volume options, can provide senior management with choices on how to meet the changing needs of the business.

The portfolio of business opportunities becomes, then, a strategic asset for the company. As an asset, it is worthy of investment by the company to develop, update, and maintain this portfolio. We believe that all companies should consider investing in a process of strategy innovation, either on an ad hoc basis or as an ongoing, core capability. Strategy innovation and the portfolio of new business opportunities created by a strategy innovation process is a valuable asset for competing in the future.

Much has been written recently about the growing importance of intangible assets on the ability of corporations to compete in today's economy. Tom Stewart, editor of *Fortune* magazine, wrote, "Intellectual capital—not natural resources, machinery, or even financial capital—has become the one indispensable asset of corporations."[5]

In their book *Invisible Advantage: How Intangibles Are Driving Business Performance*, Jonathan Low and coauthor Pam Cohen Kalafut write, "Threats and opportunities arise because intangibles have value. Value lies in the skill and knowledge of the people who manage a business and those who work for it. . . . It's built into how a company operates: the ideas that it pursues, the innovations it can bring to market, the information systems that tell managers what is going on in the world and in the organization."[6]

Low and Kalafut go on to say that intangible assets, including such things as products in the R&D pipeline, can have a significant effect on the company's valuation. In research they did for the Cap Gemini Ernst & Young Center for Business Innovation, Low and Kalafut found that "on average, 35 percent of professional investors' allocation decisions are driven by consideration of nonfinancial data or information about intangibles. In other words, more than one-third of the information used to justify these large-scale investment decisions is nonfinancial."[7]

We witnessed, in anecdotal form, the increase in corporate value that is possible based on the existence of intangible, strategic assets. Clinical Diagnostics was a division of Eastman Kodak when we first worked with them in the early 1990s to develop a ten-year strategic map for their business. Shortly after our initiative, Johnson & Johnson acquired Clinical Diagnostics to supplement their line of medical diagnostic equipment. According to José Coronas, the president of Clinical Diagnostics, Kodak received a premium price for their division because of the quality of their strategic map for the future.

Who Is Minding the Future?

Very few companies have a formalized process or infrastructure for creating new business opportunities for the future. Most are capable of generating new product ideas, which can often turn into new business opportunities. But few take the time to research the emerging marketplace and try to understand how it could differ from the markets of today and what opportunities might be available. Few take the time to understand customers and their unarticulated needs, which can lead to significant market opportunities of the future. Few examine the many ways that companies are rethinking and streamlining their business models in order to deliver customer value more efficiently and effectively.

Why is this the case? We believe it is because most companies do not have someone responsible for the future. In companies that phased out their corporate strategic planning departments in the mid-1980s (as Jack Welch did at GE), there is frequently nobody who is focused on the role that strategy can play in growing a business for the future. As a result, strategies are merely carried over from previous years and eventually become fixed as a way the company does business, something that is a "given" from year to year.

It does not have to be this way. Strategy innovation and its focus on the future can (and should) be senior management's responsibility and a core capability for any company. Finding innovative ways to deliver higher value to customers will create new markets and growth opportunities, giving the company first-mover advantage. It can also provide differentiation from competition, which keeps margins and profits strong. Companies with portfolios of new business opportunities will be more strategically agile in the nearer-term and better poised for corporate renewal in the longer-term.

Many companies invest heavily in R&D to identify innovative new *products* that can fuel future company growth. It only makes sense that companies should also invest resources to explore ways of creating innovative *strategies* for the future. Both are strategic assets that can be effective individually in a market but can be even more effective when they work together—an innovative product with an innovative business model.

To compete in tomorrow's markets, senior management needs a "road map" of the emerging future and a portfolio of new business opportunities aimed at creating value in that future. Being proactive and discovering new opportunities that fit the changing needs of a dynamic marketplace is the process of strategy innovation.

Summary

- ◆ At the point when companies experience the "dreaded delta," the gap between their projected revenue and the revenue required to maintain their businesses, they will need a capability for strategy innovation.

- ◆ If your business operates to annually introduce incremental product improvements (line extension products) to the marketplace, you may not have the business systems necessary to identify significant new business opportunities for strategy innovation.

- ◆ All companies must balance the needs of today's business with the needs of tomorrow's business. Strategy innovation can be a powerful means of managing your business toward the future.

- ◆ The effective pursuit of strategy innovation requires a few basic assumptions about the future:

  1. The future does not yet exist and can be created.

  2. The future cannot be precisely predicted, but its forces can be identified.

  3. The future is not one-size-fits-all, it is proprietary.

- ◆ The identification of new business opportunities in the future can drive new corporate strategies.

- ◆ Having a portfolio of future new business opportunities is an important corporate asset.

- ◆ To compete in tomorrow's markets, senior management needs a "road map" of the emerging future and a portfolio of new business opportunities aimed at creating value in that future.

Endnotes

1. Richard Foster and Sarah Kaplan, *Creative Destruction* (New York: Currency/Doubleday, 2001).
2. James Collins and Jerry Porras, *Built to Last: Successful Habits of Visionary Companies* (New York: HarperCollins, 1994).
3. Michael L. Tushman and Charles A. O'Reilly, *Winning Through Innovation: A Practical Guide to Leading Organizational Change and Renewal* (Boston: Harvard Business School Press, 2002).
4. Daniel J. McCarthy, "View from the Top: Henry Mintzberg on Strategy and Management," *Academy of Management Executives,* August 2000.
5. Tom Stewart (quote), www.vernaallee.com, January 2003.
6. Jonathan Low and Pam Cohen Kalafut, *Invisible Advantage: How Intangibles Are Driving Business Performance* (Cambridge: Perseus Publishing, 2002).
7. Ibid.

CHAPTER 3

STRATEGY INNOVATION IS NOT
STRATEGIC PLANNING

> Strategic positionings are often not obvious, and find-
> ing them requires creativity and insight.
>
> —*MICHAEL PORTER*

Although the concept of strategy innovation as a corporate capability is intriguing, it is an elusive goal for most organizations. The
reason for this is that most corporations have in place processes for
doing strategic "planning," but not strategic "innovation."

The Strategic Planning Process Will Not
Produce Strategy Innovation

In 1993, Bain & Company began a multiyear research project to
measure the management tools being used by senior executives to
improve the performance of their companies. In the results of the
2001 survey of 451 senior executives in companies around the
world, "strategic planning" was the most frequently mentioned tool
being used in corporations today, by 76 percent of executives.[1]

The Bain survey, however, does not specify what constitutes strategic planning in an organization. Our experience suggests that it
encompasses a wide range of different activities across companies

and even across different business units within the same corporation. On the one hand, some companies pull together their yearly budgets for the upcoming fiscal year and call that a strategic planning process. At the other end of the spectrum, there are companies that hire large consulting companies, such as Bain & Company, Boston Consulting Group, or McKinsey, and spend a significant amount of money analyzing the marketplace and competitors, and identifying any "gaps" in the marketplace that might suggest a new strategic opportunity. That is the deluxe version of strategic planning, done by larger corporations.

At the risk of overgeneralizing, we suspect that much of the strategic planning done in most business units of corporations is somewhere between these two extremes. It is likely that most strategic planning includes some review of the market and competition, such as updating market shares, revenue, and growth projections each year. It might also include a SWOT analysis (strengths, weaknesses, opportunities, and threats), reminding management where the company is strong relative to competition and where it is vulnerable.

However, the strategic planning in most companies is rarely an exercise in creating new and effective strategies for the future of the company. Instead, the strategic planning process is more often one that perpetuates, and at best revises, the current strategy every year. Richard Foster and Sarah Kaplan, in their book *Creative Destruction*, write, "Often today's strategic planning does not attempt to collect information that could challenge existing mental models. It focuses on reanalysis of the existing businesses and the analysis of similarly sized competitors, rather than attempting to understand what is happening at the periphery of the business and how it might change."[2]

Does your company have a standard "format" for the strategic planning presentation? Do you start this year's strategic planning process by referring back to tables and projections from last year's strategic plan? Are many of the tables already on spreadsheets that just need updating? If so, your strategic planning process is built around revising the strategy that is already in place. For a lot of companies, this is quite logical. If there are no dramatic changes in the market and the company is not hemorrhaging red ink, then continuing with last year's strategy is more efficient than starting from scratch. "If it ain't broke, don't fix it." Perpetuating the current strategy in your strategic planning process may be quite adequate for your market and your company's needs—but it won't lead to strategy innovation.

What financial targets are usually set for your business unit in the strategic plan? Do the targets encourage or require any risk-taking with the elements of the strategic plan? Is there any strategic "stretch" required? In many companies, there is an emphasis on steady, predictable financial growth from year to year. There are no surprises in the targets, which encourage no surprises in the strategic plan. Bets are placed on the tortoise, not the hare. These expectations send the business unit managers looking for incremental, predictable revenue growth each year. Introducing a lemon-flavored line extension of the current product does not raise corporate eyebrows the way an innovative, new-to-the-world product would. As a result of incremental financial targets, the strategic planning process in many companies encourages incremental growth within the existing strategy and business model.

Is number crunching an integral part of your strategic planning process? Do you spend a lot of time making all of the numbers in the plan "fit"? Numbers are frequently used in strategic planning to track sales, shares, and trends in a market. Those numbers are then used to make projections for the future of that market. When that is the case, the projections for the future are typically extrapolations of historical data. This process reinforces the notion that the future is expected to be an extension of the past. If it is believed that the future will look just like the past, then perpetuation of the current strategy is logical. However, strategic planning filled with statistics rarely leads to strategy innovation. Henry Mintzberg, in his book *The Rise and Fall of Strategic Planning*, wrote, ". . . nobody in the history of the world has ever created a strategy through an analytical process."[3] The analytical discipline of the strategic planning process with its year-to-year comparisons and extrapolations is one more reason why the strategic planning process is more of a perpetuation of the historical strategy and business model than the creation of the company's optimal strategy for the future.

Strategy Innovation vs. Strategic Planning

If you are intrigued by the potential of strategy innovation for your company, be aware that you will not get it from your current strategic planning process. You will have to create a separate process for strategy innovation, one that is:

+ Creative

+ Market-centric

+ Heuristic (discovery-driven)

Creative

Strategy innovation requires a creative process, not an analytical one. It requires people to listen to customers in new ways, design new types of products, and envision strategies for markets that do not currently exist. It is a process that is as disciplined and structured as strategic planning but uses creativity, rather than analysis, as the primary tool. The raw materials for strategy innovation are insights, which are new perceptions and new understandings of value. Insights can come from listening to or observing customers—their words, actions, emotions, and wishes. Insights can come from listening to industry experts or thought leaders as they explain their understanding of the present and future dynamics of a marketplace. Insights can also come from listening to people who are not entrenched in your industry, company, or culture, as they are in the best position of offering a fresh perspective.

The quality of the insights necessary for strategy innovation cannot come from statistics. People with a strong analytical orientation can participate in the strategy innovation process (everyone has the potential for creativity), but they must check their quantitative tools and mind-sets at the door. They can have them back when it comes time to evaluate and quantify the business opportunities developed by the strategy innovation process. However, the process for strategy innovation is a creative one, not an analytical one.

Market-Centric

Strategy innovation requires a market-centric process, not one that is company-centric. For many, this shift is as significant as the Copernican revolution. You will recall from high school science class that Copernicus identified the sun as the center of the universe (heliocentric model). Just like people used to believe that the sun and stars revolved around the earth, many of today's corporate executives believe that their companies are the center of their business universe, and that all other stakeholders (shareholders, suppliers, customers, and employees) revolve around them. Customers must shop at hours most efficient for the company. Suppliers must change their delivery schedules to meet the company's needs. Employees must move to a new location if the company wants them to. Strategy innovation proposes, instead, that customers and the dynamics of the marketplace are the center of the business universe (market-centric), and that wise companies will consider setting their orbits around them. If customers need call centers to receive the service they need, companies should consider changing their business models to create them. If Third World markets need household products at lower prices, companies should explore innovative ways of providing them.

To be clear on this point, we are not suggesting that companies meet all customer needs or sacrifice sound financial management to fulfill those needs. Successful strategy innovation requires that a new business opportunity add significant value for *both the customer and the company* to be worthwhile. However, the *starting point* for that consideration should be the needs of the customer/market, not the company's needs.

Heuristic

The strategy innovation process is not as predictable and linear as the strategic planning process in most companies. Revising plans and updating numbers have a predictability that allows you to schedule strategic planning sessions months in advance. Strategy innovation is a grassroots, discovery ("heuristic") process that is dependent on the quality of the insights gained along the way. Sometimes it happens quickly, sometimes it takes many iterations before a breakthrough is achieved. Customer interviews might not reveal new expressions of value in the first month of trying. An examination of future market dynamics may suggest several very different future scenarios that will take a while to sort out and evaluate. There will be starts and stops, dead ends, and a need to revisit previous work done. The iterative nature of the process means that the imposition of deadlines may affect the quality of the output. That is, a team may be forced to stop exploring because of a deadline, rather than because they have already discovered all the great insights they need. Flexible timing is more accommodating to the heuristic nature of the strategy innovation process.

Another difference between traditional strategic planning process and a strategy innovation process is the orientation toward time. There is a natural tendency in the strategic planning process to start the planning with "today" and then make projections, based on historical trends and today's statistics, out to "tomorrow." It is starting with the known and working toward the unknown. This near-term to long-term work flow reinforces the evolutionary nature of the strategic planning process.

The strategy innovation process, on the other hand, works best in the other direction: It starts with "tomorrow" and then plans backwards to "today." To be successful, the search for new business opportunities cannot be constrained by today's corporate conditions or today's market conditions. The search for opportunities cannot get bogged down in arguments over resource allocation. Strategy innovation is decidedly future-oriented. It must be able to transcend today's conditions and imagine what is possible in the future. After identifying potential new business opportunities in the future, the planning works *backwards* to identify the key strategic milestones to get there. In this way, the more tangible appeal of new growth opportunities acts as a "future-pull," which will help the company in its decisions on resource allocation (see Figure 3-1).

Strategic Planning Process	Strategy Innovation Process
Analytical	*Creative*
Numbers-driven	*Insights-driven*
Company-centric	*Market-centric*
Logical/linear	*Heuristic/iterative*
Today to tomorrow	*Tomorrow to today*
Extend current value	*Create new value*
Fit the business model	*Create a new business model*

Figure 3-1. The strategic planning process vs. the strategy innovation process.

Where traditional strategic planning focuses on building value in current markets, strategy innovation focuses on creating new value in new markets. In the 1960s, Xerox had a near monopoly on the sales and servicing of large copy machines to large businesses. Their business model consisted of a direct sales force that sold leased, high-end equipment, and an extensive service network (profit center) to keep the equipment operating. In their strategic planning processes at the time, much of Xerox's focus was no doubt on determining how to extend or improve the current value delivered to current customers, e.g., faster machines, new sorting methods, faster service response, or better leas-

Process Tip:

Strategy innovation is best achieved by leaping ahead and working backward.

You cannot discover distant lands if you remain tethered to your current one. Often we believe that some invisible constraints prevent us from seeking new and unique solutions to our problems. Make a conscious effort to break the bonds that hold you to your current operating system or business model and explore far-reaching possibilities. Dare to dream. When you find a dream out there that fits or helps solve your problem, figure out a way to take it back to your world. Leap ahead, work backwards.

ing plans. These means of value-enhancement can help grow revenues while leveraging the company's current strategy and business model.

However, there are also other ways of delivering value to customers. Canon discovered a different way to deliver value in the copier market. Using their skills in microelectronics and optics, they developed a copier with a replaceable cartridge, which they sold as the first personal copier. Aimed at small businesses and individuals, these copiers were inexpensive, required little or no maintenance, and could be purchased through existing retail channels. Canon used strategy innovation to redefine value in the marketplace for copying machines. As with Canon, the opportunity to create new value has tremendous revenue potential. At the same time, it will likely require a company to consider the development of a new business model in order to implement the new strategy. Xerox stayed with their old business model for a long time and suffered for it.

Strategy Innovation and THEN Strategic Planning

Developing an internal strategy innovation process to identify new ways of competing in the dynamic markets of the future does not mean that strategic planning is obsolete. In fact, we believe the strategic planning process and the strategy innovation process both need to exist and to work together. The way we propose that they work is for a strategy innovation process to be established that will "plug into" the strategic planning process. In other words, do strategy innovation and THEN do traditional strategic planning (see Figure 3-2).

In this case, strategy innovation becomes the "fuzzy front end" of the strategy creation process within a company. Its creative, market-centric view of the future will provide a portfolio of new business opportunities that exist, which the company can consider. These new opportunities can then feed into the company's current strategic planning process. There, the focus on numbers and fit with current corporate capabilities can help refine, evaluate, and ultimately integrate the opportunities identified. The creative process leads to the evaluative process. The ideas meet the implementation details. The strategy innovation process finds new ways to provide

Corporate Strategy Creation

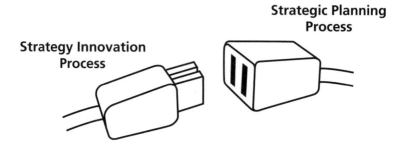

Figure 3-2. Integration of strategy innovation and strategic planning.

new value in the marketplace, and strategic planning determines if those opportunities provide new value for the company.

Corporations that choose to conduct strategy innovation on an ad hoc, initiative basis will want to consider planning a new initiative every few years to feed into the strategic planning process. They will find that the portfolio of new business opportunities they identify can remain robust for two to five years, depending on how quickly their markets are changing. At the end of that time, the market dynamics will have shifted, new technologies will be available, the strategic road map will have been played out, and it will be time to reexamine what the future might hold.

This was confirmed by Bob LaPerle, currently a corporate vice president at Eastman Kodak, who led two corporate-wide strategy innovation initiatives at Kodak in the 1990s. At that time, LaPerle noted, "I think it is valuable to do a study like this every two to three years, to look out five years. We need to challenge our paradigms every few years, especially if our business case is built on them or is sensitive to them. We should find out what the frontier looks like, challenge our thinking with outside experts, and see if our business case holds up."

For those companies that choose to conduct strategy innovation on an ongoing, formalized basis, they will want to find a way to integrate the strategy innovation process with their internal strategic planning process. It can be a formal "hand-off" of results from one group to the other, although that runs the risk of a not-invented-here reaction on the part of the receiving group. Preferably, there will be some inter-mingling of the strategy innovation and strategic planning groups, so that continuity is established and the opportunities flow seamlessly from their development stage to their evaluation stage. Since the 1990s, Eastman Kodak has moved from conducting strategy innova-tion initiatives to the development of a formalized strategy innovation process, which they call their Systems Concept Center. In it, they have created a separate venture board structure to help move new ideas from creation through to commercialization, providing the crucial link between strategy innovation and strategic planning. This center is beginning to play an important role in the identification and integra-tion of significant new business opportunities to Kodak.

Chapter Summary

♦ Strategic planning in most companies is rarely an exercise in cre-ating new and effective strategies for the future of the company, making it ineffective for strategy innovation.

♦ Strategic planning is typically a highly analytical, quantitative process that focuses on corporate issues of today and today's business model, extending out into the short-term future.

♦ For effective strategy innovation, companies must create a new process, one that is creative, market-centric, heuristic (discovery-driven), and focused on the future.

♦ A process of strategy innovation should be the "fuzzy front end" of an overall strategy creation process, leading seamlessly from opportunity identification and creation (strategy innovation) to opportunity evaluation and integration (strategic planning). Do strategy innovation and THEN do strategic planning.

Endnotes

1. Darrell K. Rigby, "Bain & Company Management Tools 2001 Global Results," Annual Survey of Senior Executives.
2. Richard Foster and Sarah Kaplan, *Creative Destruction* (New York: Cur-rency/Doubleday, 2001).
3. Henry Mintzberg, *The Rise and Fall of Strategic Planning* (New York: The Free Press, 1994).

CHAPTER 4

THE DISCOVERY PROCESS

> Our quest for discovery fuels our creativity in all fields,
> not just science. If we reached the end of the line, the
> human spirit would shrivel and die. But I don't think
> we will ever stand still: we shall increase in complexity,
> if not in depth, and shall always be the center of an
> expanding horizon of possibilities.
>
> —*STEPHEN HAWKING*

Do not outsource the strategy innovation process for your company! Regardless of how downsized, bogged-down, or downright busy your people are, they can find the time and energy to participate in a strategy innovation initiative. These initiatives are a welcome relief from employees' day-to-day responsibilities because they are opportunities to view the business from a much different perspective. Your people get to see the big picture, they get to see longer-term, and they get to embrace a companywide, cross-functional perspective that is often lacking in their functional silo-based daily activities. It is also a chance to explore, speculate, and imagine new possibilities for the future. A strategy innovation initiative is frequently the type of activity that pulls together organizations by aligning people and departments to a common goal, a shared purpose.

Try a strategy innovation initiative with an internal, ad hoc group before thinking about building a more formalized system for strategy innovation. Experiment with it. Try different approaches, with different teams of people—either sequentially or simultaneously. Every initiative will provide valuable insights and ideas to your company, which will turn into economic benefits. Some initiatives will yield short-term, business-building innovations, and some initiatives will produce the breakthrough, market-creating innovations of the future. After getting an idea of how strategy innovation can work in your company, then you can think about building a more permanent, in-house capability for it.

To launch a strategy innovation initiative in your company, you will need some resources (people and funding) and a process. If you supply the resources, this book will supply the process.

What Is the Discovery Process?

The strategy innovation process, which we have named the Discovery Process, is a method for creating a portfolio of innovative, new business opportunities that could become the basis for a new strategic direction for your corporation. Corporate teams that have taken these journeys liken themselves to reconnaissance teams, sent by their companies to explore the strategic frontiers of their industries. This imagery reminds us of Lewis and Clark, those brave explorers sent by U.S. President Thomas Jefferson in 1804 to learn what lay to the west of the Mississippi River, America's first frontier. The team gathered for that expedition was called the *Corps of Discovery*. Fast-forward several centuries to another frontier, outer space. Following the highly successful Apollo space program that placed Americans on the moon, NASA's space shuttle program launched the Hubble Space Telescope in 1990 to do reconnaissance work into inter-galactic space. The name of the space shuttle that delivered the Hubbell telescope was *Discovery*. It seemed appropriate to us that corporate reconnaissance teams would use the "Discovery" Process to explore and discover new business opportunities on their strategic frontiers, leading to innovative and competitive corporate strategies.

The Five Phases of the Discovery Process

The Discovery Process is a series of phases, not a linear series of steps (see Figure 4-1). By carrying out the phases, your company will avoid some of the process pitfalls that arise when doing cross-functional work at the strategic level. The specific steps to be taken within each phase must be determined by each company individually, as will be explained later in this chapter.

A summary of the five phases is as follows:

1. *Staging Phase.* In this phase, the Discovery team is selected, key roles are identified, the objectives of the initiative are established, and the team is prepared for the process.

2. *Aligning Phase.* The Discovery team and senior management align themselves on the focus and scope of the initiative, agreeing on the "strategic frontier(s)" to be explored.

3. *Exploring Phase.* The goal of this phase is the collection of new insights on the strategic frontier that can form the basis of new, value-producing business opportunities in the future. Depending on the strategic frontier and the scope of the initiative, teams will explore insights related to different exploration "vectors," including customer value, market dynamics, and/or business model innovation.

4. *Creating Phase.* Using the new insights gained, the Discovery team will create and refine a portfolio of new business opportunities for the future.

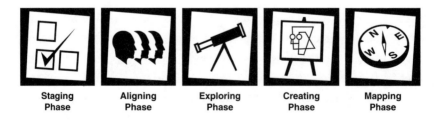

Staging Phase   Aligning Phase   Exploring Phase   Creating Phase   Mapping Phase

Figure 4-1. The five phases of the Discovery Process.

5. *Mapping Phase.* In this final phase, the team will create a strategic road map outlining key events, trends, market discontinuities, and milestones to move the company into its new strategic future.

Flexibility of the Discovery Process

All phases of the Discovery Process must be implemented for a successful strategy innovation initiative. However, just like fingerprints, no two Discovery Processes are alike. The activities that take place within each phase will vary significantly, based on the individual circumstances of the company and the goals for the initiative. Accordingly, the costs and timing of the process will vary also, depending on the activities undertaken. The scope of a strategy innovation initiative that is right for your company will typically depend on the following factors:

◆ Size of company

◆ Size of industry

◆ Type of industry

◆ Strategic frontier

◆ Degree of innovation desired

Size of Company

In general, larger companies have more resources available for strategy innovation than smaller companies. Yet the process of identifying new business opportunities is equally important, if not more important, for smaller companies to consider. The five-phase Discovery Process presented here is not dependent on a certain level of resources being available. We recommend that all companies carry out all five phases, regardless of how much time and money is spent on each phase. However, larger companies with their greater resources can afford to do more, on a larger scale, than the smaller companies can.

Larger companies, for example, can usually identify up to a

dozen people across all their functional areas that can be assigned to participate on the Discovery team. It is not unusual for each team member to be able to dedicate up to 20 to 25 percent of their time over a six-to-eight-months period for this initiative. In the Exploring Phase, larger-company budgets will allow for team travel across the country or across the world to participate in professionally organized meetings and customer visits. Depending on the scope, these global initiatives can last a year or more.

Smaller companies would experience this process very differently. With fewer people available, they might select three company executives and a college-age intern to participate in their Discovery Process. To take advantage of the availability of the intern, they may want to complete the entire initiative over the course of a summer, which is quite possible on a focused initiative. Instead of elaborate meetings at customer sites around the country or abroad, teams from smaller companies might concentrate their exploration efforts more on local visits with some customers, telephone interviews with others, and literature searches on marketplace trends via the Internet.

The implementation of the Discovery Process for strategy innovation is extremely flexible and can accommodate the different resources available in different size companies.

Size of Industry

Similar to company size, the size of the industry will also play a role in the scope of the Discovery Process. By size, we mean both the revenues generated and the number of industry "participants."

As you might imagine, being a strategic innovator in the multi-billion-dollar automobile industry will require a more significant Discovery Process than being an innovator in the unicycle market. The automobile industry is very complex, with many stakeholders (customers, suppliers, dealers, manufacturers, after-market suppliers, etc.) and market segments to explore. The Exploring Phase in the automobile industry would likely be quite extensive and take a great deal of time to implement. The unicycle market, on the other hand, probably consists of only a handful of manufacturers, a relatively limited number of distributors, and a small core of user/enthusiasts. Insight gathering in the Exploring Phase would be much simpler for the smaller, simpler unicycle market, requiring a Discovery Process that is much more limited in its scope and scale.

At the same time, making a significant impact on the automobile market through strategy innovation could result in significantly more revenue growth than making a significant impact on the unicycle market. The potentially higher return in automobiles would justify a greater investment in the Discovery Process in that industry than might be justified in unicycles.

Type of Industry

In addition to size of industry, the type of industry will also help dictate the scope of the Discovery Process. Industries undergoing a greater degree of change or transformation will usually require a more extensive Discovery Process than more stable markets. The reason is that it is more difficult to gain an understanding of a market's future if changes are taking place more rapidly. Very dynamic markets such as the telecommunications industry will have very complex forces at work—new products, new companies, new regulations, new technologies, and what some believe is an inevitable merging with the computer industry. Each market expert in the telecommunications industry may well describe a different emerging market scenario, making it difficult for your Discovery team to agree on what the future holds for the company. In these more dynamic markets, it may take multiple exploration efforts and a longer period of time before the future becomes visible and new business opportunities can be identified.

More stable markets are much simpler to explore because there are fewer future-changing forces to consider. A Discovery Process in the insurance industry, for example, would be a smaller scale effort than one in the telecommunications world.

Strategic Frontier

The selection of one or more strategic frontiers to be explored in the Discovery Process will have a critical impact on the size, scope, and timing of the initiative. A strategic frontier is a market, product, technology, or business process that lies beyond a company's current corporate strategy and business model. The identification of a single frontier allows the Discovery team to focus their efforts and activities in the Exploring Phase, interacting with one set of customers, projecting the future of one market, and seeking insights on a minimum number of business models. The selection of multiple frontiers will result in multiple explorations in these areas in order to best understand the opportunities available.

Besides the number of strategic frontiers being explored, the type of frontier will often dictate the activities necessary. As will be described in more detail in Chapter 8, insights on value in the frontier can be found along three different exploration vectors: customer value, market dynamics, and business model innovation. Some frontiers, such as repositioning the brand name or product to a different target audience, might require exploration in only one vector: the customer value vector. The insights from the new target audience would be most critical for the creation of a new business opportunity. On the other hand, leveraging an emerging technology may require exploration in all three vectors. Getting customer insights on the technology (customer value vector), a picture of how the future market might emerge (market dynamics vector), and an understanding of how to best organize for the new venture (business model innovation vector) will make that Discovery Process more complex.

Degree of Innovation Required

We saved the most important consideration for last. The scope and complexity of the Discovery Process is directly related to the degree of strategy innovation desired. Companies looking to identify new business opportunities that will create new-to-the-world markets and provide them with a unique, sustainable advantage over competition will need to plan on a robust, larger-scale Discovery Process commitment. These more visionary market opportunities will not emerge from merely holding a brainstorming session or two. It may require a longer-term effort for a team, or the company may decide to form two or three Discovery teams to pursue this level of strategy innovation simultaneously.

On the other hand, companies that have a new business opportunity already in mind and are searching only for a unique, strategic twist that will give it a proprietary advantage in the market will often find it after a brief, more concise Discovery Process.

The degree of innovation being sought is usually one of the first questions to be considered because it has a direct bearing on not only the scope of the Discovery Process, but the selection of the activities in that process.

Strategy Innovation by Degrees: Strategic Opportunity Spectrum

While Wal-Mart, Charles Schwab, and Dell are often among the poster-children of strategy innovation in business, they are not necessarily the norm. Strategy innovation does not have to be high-risk, market-creating new ventures that land their CEOs on the cover of *Fortune*. Strategy innovation just has to be something beyond today's strategy that provides new growth opportunities and/or a competitive advantage in the marketplace. When a company opens its first sales office outside its home country, it is strategy innovation. When Time Inc. introduced *People* magazine, it was strategy innovation. When Nike used its brand name to enter the new markets of clothing and equipment, they were practicing strategy innovation.

There is a wide range of the degree of innovation that companies can target. We define this range of strategy innovation as a Strategic Opportunity Spectrum, or SOS (see Figure 4-2). On one end of the spectrum are strategy innovations such as expanding sales offices, product offerings, and brand names into other markets. These are "visible" opportunities. They are not necessarily new-to-the-world markets or breakthrough products, but they do represent new value provided to customers and to your company, which makes them strategy innovations for you. Visible opportunities are likely to be

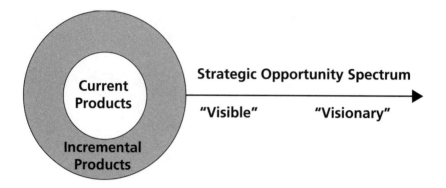

Figure 4-2. Strategic Opportunity Spectrum.

strategic options that management has been aware of for some time but which just need to be studied and defined before they can be introduced.

Parked at the other end of the Strategic Opportunity Spectrum are the classics of strategy innovation, such as Federal Express, amazon.com, and Starbucks, among many others. These are "visionary" opportunities because they required visionary thinking to create them. The markets that these companies dominate did not exist before they created them. They were created to provide value where customers did not realize they had needs. The moves were bold, considered risky by some, but resulted in the establishment of new-to-the-world products, services, and markets.

As with all spectra, the middle represents strategy innovations that fall somewhere between the visible and visionary ends. There are no hard-and-fast rules of how to categorize the level of innovation and where new innovative products or services belong on the spectrum. Think of this middle ground as consisting of products and services in already-existing markets, but ones that redefine those markets or represent a dramatic change over how that market has traditionally operated. Southwest Airlines is an example of a company that created an innovative strategy between the visible and visionary ends—a unique business model introduced to an existing marketplace. Digital cameras, wireless telephones, and electrostatic cloth sweepers might also be innovations that fall in the middle of the SOS.

Key Elements for Strategy Innovation

Strategy innovation can be done in a company on a one-time, ad hoc basis. Most of the examples contained in this book come from initiatives carried out by ad hoc teams. However, there is growing interest in the development of an internal capability for strategy innovation. Some of the elements necessary for developing a formalized, ongoing capability for strategy innovation can be found in Chapter 12.

Whether it is done on an ad hoc or ongoing basis, strategy innovation in any corporation must consist of the following four elements:

1. Management mandate
2. Corporate infrastructure
3. Innovation process
4. Corporate culture

Management Mandate

It is not until senior management in a company commits to strategy innovation that the company will respond. Employees will generally set their time commitments to be consistent with the perceived commitment of their management team. Therefore, the stronger the management mandate for strategy innovation, the sooner a higher-quality initiative will be accomplished. For a company looking to build strategy innovation as a core capability, this mandate must be built into its business systems.

Corporate infrastructure.

The infrastructure requirements for strategy innovation can be fairly simple, consisting of a team of people and some funding. Suggestions on finding the "right" people for the team will be examined in detail in Chapter 6, Staging Phase. For larger companies, the team should be a diverse, cross-functional team of eight to twelve people in upper-middle management who will have some responsibility for implementing new strategic initiatives in the company. Smaller companies will target teams of four to six people and include people who are directly involved with strategic decisions within the company. The team must have a captain to guide the process and a senior-level executive sponsor to fund it.

Funding requirements for a strategy innovation initiative will range significantly, depending on the size of the company, its industry, and how aggressive the team wants to be in exploring their strategic frontiers. Some companies have undertaken strategy innovation initiatives that cost in the $50,000 range, while others (usually large, global businesses) have had budgets well into the seven digits. It is the team that estimates the budget, based on the activities they identify as important to pursue.

Innovation Process

A good team needs a good process for how to go about creating new business opportunities that lead to strategy innovation. The Discovery Process is designated to meet that need. The five phases, described in detail in the next section, are designed to provide needed structure but allow for flexibility of activities within the phases to accommodate a wide range of industries and corporations.

Corporate Culture

If a strategy innovation initiative is being done on an ad hoc basis, the team can create for itself the type of creative, collaborative, and entrepreneurial environment or culture necessary for its success. However, if a company wants to develop a formalized strategy innovation capability, then there may need to be adjustments to the corporate culture to allow it to flourish. More cultural implications can be found in Chapter 12, Formalizing a Strategy Innovation System.

Output of the Discovery Process

The Discovery Process will yield a portfolio of new business opportunities that leverage the emerging trends in the marketplace and the needs of potential customers. In the Discovery Process, your team will seek out new insights on customer needs and their perception of value after talking to and observing potential customers in new ways. They will also learn of trends, market dynamics, and potential discontinuities in your industry as they work with experts to understand the emerging markets of the future. New business models being used successfully by companies in other industries will also offer insights on new ways of doing business.

Overall, there are three tangible outputs from this process:

1. The *insights* gained from the customer, market dynamics, and new business models are an important output of this process. Creating a database of these insights and sharing them with everyone in the organization will help stimulate new thinking and new ideas internally.

2. The insights will be used as the basis for the creation of a *portfolio of innovative new business concepts.* These concepts will range from short-term business opportunities to longer-term opportunities, providing your company with a valuable portfolio of strategic options for your future.

3. A third output of the Discovery Process is a *strategic road map* assembled by the team. On the basis of the new business opportunities that have strongest potential for the company, the team will create a strategic road map outlining a future plan based on implementation strategies and key marketplace factors.

The output from the Discovery Process will then advance to your in-house evaluation process for new business opportunities. There, the leading opportunities will undergo the quantitative scrutiny that is critical for determining market viability and financial attractiveness to your company. Business opportunities that receive the green light will then be ready for consideration in the company's strategic planning process (see Figure 4-3).

Although not every company is a Procter & Gamble, any company can be inspired by the success of their Corporate and Sector

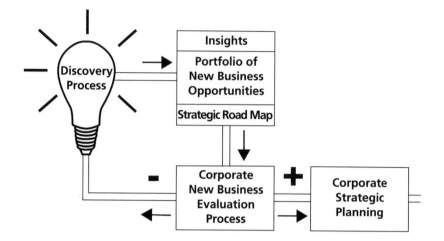

Figure 4-3. The Discovery Process integrated to strategic planning.

New Venture groups. These groups have infused new thinking, new growth, and new profits into this global consumer products giant. They have achieved this by identifying new insights to support the development of a portfolio of strategically innovative new business concepts, including the Swiffer mop, Crest White Strips, and ThermaCare self-heating pads. Over a four-year stretch, these groups conceived, developed, and helped launch "a third of all new U.S. packaged products with yearly sales above $100 million." While, by almost any measure, this level of success would be labeled a string of "home runs," each innovation was inspired by a new insight of a basic human need.

Risks Involved in the Discovery Process

There is very little at risk with a strategy innovation initiative, other than the time and money invested by the team. The internal team sets the overall budget so that costs (primarily in the Exploring Phase) can be controlled to whatever level represents a reasonable investment in the company's future.

We have never encountered an initiative where discussions with customers and industry experts did not lead to valuable insights for the company. The only question is whether the impact of those insights represents a significant business opportunity for the company (or only a minor business opportunity) and whether the company will choose to follow up with them.

Other things to watch for as critical success factors that can affect overall results include:

- ◆ The selection of the Discovery team, where lack of diversity in functions and skills can limit the quality of the output.

- ◆ The breadth and commitment of the management mandate to the team, as small mandates tend to produce small results.

- ◆ Alignment with senior management perspectives on the business, which greatly enhances the usefulness of the resulting portfolio of new business opportunities.

- ◆ The pursuit of *new* insights on customers and the marketplace, using techniques that are new to the company.

- ◆ The creativity of the team's working environment, where the identification of new business opportunities is not constrained by the company's current business model.

- ◆ The collaborative nature of the team's working environment, so that opportunities have cross-functional internal support.

Type of Company to Benefit from Strategy Innovation

A strategy innovation process may not be right for every company. However, it is difficult to cite what type of company would not benefit from understanding their customers better, gaining valuable foresight about their emerging marketplace, and considering how changes in their business model could provide a competitive advantage. If your company fulfills these requirements, you can benefit from a strategy innovation initiative or an ongoing strategy innovation process.

Listed below are those types of companies where strategy innovation would be most valuable:

- Companies that no longer want to compete on the basis of a similar, "commodity" product in the market
- Companies that seek a sustainable competitive advantage
- Companies looking to change their strategic direction
- Companies searching for the next growth platform for their business
- Companies that need new growth opportunities to meet long-term revenue goals
- Companies that are in declining markets
- Companies that have streamlined and downsized their businesses to improve the bottom line and now need to find profit improvements in growing the top line
- Companies facing a competitive threat and that need to respond with new ways to deliver customer value
- Companies looking to aggressively increase market share
- Companies that need to define a corporate mission or vision
- Companies that value management collaboration in the development of strategy

The following corporate environments are impractical for, or resistant to, a strategy innovation process and the new thinking it provides:

- Companies with a command-and-control management style
- Companies that have chosen to be a "fast-follower" or "low-cost provider" in their markets
- Companies where the collaborative culture is overshadowed by corporate politics

So, while it may not be right for every company, a strategy innovation process can be applied to many different types of companies and address many different corporate situations where new growth in new ways is the goal. What type of company is your company?

How might strategy innovation be incorporated to your strategic planning process?

In the next chapter, we provide an actual case study that will provide you with an understanding of how the strategy innovation process can work in a company. Following the case, we outline how to carry out the process through a detailed explanation of the five phases of the process.

Summary

- The Discovery Process is a market-tested approach for creating a portfolio of innovative new business opportunities for your corporation, leading to strategy innovation.

- The Discovery Process is a series of phases to guide a corporate team in doing cross-functional work at the strategic level. It is extremely flexible and can accommodate the different resources available in different size companies.

- The Discovery Process consists of the following phases:

  1. *Staging Phase.* In this phase, the Discovery team is selected, key roles are identified, the objectives of the initiative are established, and the team is prepared for the process.

  2. *Aligning Phase.* The Discovery team and senior management align themselves on the focus and scope of the initiative, agreeing on the "strategic frontier(s)" to be explored.

  3. *Exploring Phase.* The goal of this phase is the collection of new insights on the strategic frontier that can form the basis of new, value-producing business opportunities in the future. Depending on the strategic frontier and the scope of the initiative, teams will explore insights related to different exploration "vectors," including customer value, market dynamics, and/or business model innovation.

  4. *Creating Phase.* Using the new insights gained, the Discovery team will create and refine a portfolio of new business opportunities for the future.

5. *Mapping Phase.* In this final phase, the team will create a strategic road map outlining key events, trends, market discontinuities, and milestones to move the company into its new strategic future.

♦ The scope, timing, and costs for each Discovery Process will differ, based on size of company, size of industry, type of industry, the strategic frontier identified, and the degree of innovation desired.

♦ There is a wide range of the degree of innovation that companies can target, defined here as a Strategic Opportunity Spectrum. On one end of the spectrum are "visible" opportunities, representing nearer-term, lower-risk businesses that often extend the current business into new but established markets. On the other end of the spectrum are "visionary" opportunities, those longer-term, higher-risk businesses that introduce breakthrough products or establish new markets or industries.

♦ Companies can implement the Discovery Process on an ad hoc, initiative basis to meet a product line need or formalize it as an ongoing strategy innovation system. In either case, strategy innovation requires attention to four key elements—process, infrastructure (resources), mandate from management, and culture.

♦ Three tangible outputs from the Discovery Process include the insights gained from the Exploring Phase (into customers, market dynamics, and business model innovations), a portfolio of innovative new business opportunities based on those insights, and a strategic road map outlining a future plan based on implementation strategies and marketplace factors.

♦ There is very little at risk and much to be gained with a strategy innovation initiative, and nearly any company can benefit from one—learning more about their customers, the emerging marketplace, and new business model options.

PART TWO

A GUIDE FOR IMPLEMENTATION

THE DISCOVERY PROCESS

The Moen Story

> Transformation takes place when a new worldview re-
> places an old one.
>
> —*WILLIAM MILLER*

While Southwest Airlines, IKEA, Charles Schwab, and other high-
profile entrepreneurial companies tend to be associated with the
concept of strategy innovation, they are not the only examples that
exist. Strategy innovation does not always begin with a visionary
founder in a start-up mode—it can happen in fifty-plus-year-old
companies. It does not always germinate in technology-oriented
companies—it can happen in companies that bend metal for their
main business. It does not have to create a whole new industry—it
can happen in companies that just want to grow their businesses.

To illustrate how strategy innovation (specifically the Discovery
Process) can be implemented within a corporation, we selected an
example from a quality, existing company in a very common industry, plumbing products. The company is Moen, located in a suburb
of Cleveland, Ohio. Here is their story.

The internationally known Moen corporation has a long history
of "firsts" in the plumbing products industry. It created the first
single-handle faucet, the first washerless cartridge system, and a
"swing 'n spray" aerator, which can change a faucet's water flow
from a stream to a forceful spray. It was the first company to de-

velop a family of versatile faucets that could be lifted up to ten inches above a sink, and among the first to introduce pressure-balanced shower valves, as well as customer-friendly lifetime warranties and a toll-free help line.

Challenge for Growth

Yet in the early 1990s, this North Olmsted, Ohio–based company found itself in a challenging situation. Moen had just been purchased by American Brands (now Fortune Brands), and Bruce Carbonari had been installed as its new CEO. In assessing the company and its growth prospects, Carbonari quickly determined that he must transform the company in order for it to grow. The company was losing market share—it had become a distant number two brand in the market. It was also not positioned well for the changes that were beginning to take place in the market.

Moen's prior success had been achieved by focusing on faucet engineering and manufacturing. This was the approach to business that founder Al Moen established when he created that first single-handle faucet more than six decades earlier. The company's success as the number two brand in the plumbing products market was to make quality products and distribute them through plumbing wholesalers. Product styling, company marketing, and retail distribution were minor considerations in their business model.

But these old ways of competing would not sustain the new growth goals in the dynamic plumbing products market of the early 1990s. Female consumers were making more and more design decisions for kitchens and bathrooms, and they were looking for products that were as fashionable as they were practical. The number of shelter magazines and home shows was increasing to further fuel this interest in home renovation and design. At the same time, big-box retailers were changing how plumbing products were being merchandised and purchased, making them more accessible to the average homeowner. In a short time, Moen's strategic landscape had become dramatically more complex than simply selling a technically superior faucet to a plumbing wholesaler.

So CEO Bruce Carbonari started thinking about how to reposition the company for the future:

> These realities going on around us made it easier for us to start looking at change, because we knew we had no choice. We were the number two player, and dramatically smaller than the number one player. Roughly 90 percent of our sales were from products designed in the 1960s—and obviously not selling as well as we wanted. We needed to change, to evolve, and to get to a new and more sophisticated business model.
>
> But before we could change our product or how we do business, we had to change the way we viewed the business and, really, the entire culture of the company. Moen was a metal-bending company, not a consumer-driven one. We were a company with great faucet technology. But our faucets were of such great quality that most people only bought a new one every nine years. Our products were practical, but not designed with consumer input, and certainly not exciting. And exciting is what we needed.

The infrequent purchase rate of a Moen faucet, once every nine years on average, became a focus of Carbonari's new internal strategy for corporate transformation. Calling his new strategy *9-to-5*, he challenged his employees to create a company that produced such stylish and innovative products that consumers would be interested in purchasing new ones every five years, instead of nine years.

The company responded. New people and business processes were put in place to increase the flow of new, consumer-focused product lines. As new products were introduced to the market, sales increased, and Moen was back on a growth track. By 1994, however, Carbonari recognized that Moen needed even greater growth to achieve their corporate goals in the increasingly competitive marketplace.

Although Moen was doing a good job in developing new products, they did not have a reliable process for the identification of new products. Many different people within the company had many different ideas of what should be produced. They needed a way to determine a corporate strategy and accompanying product plan that would help them to meet the higher growth rate they desired.

Identifying Champions for Growth

The first thing he had to do was to get the organization aligned on the goal and get a group to lead the journey required to achieve it. To do this, Carbonari charged three members of his management team—Dan Buchner, director of new product concepts; Maureen Wenmoth, director of marketing services; and Tim O'Brien, director of technology innovation—to put together a diverse, cross-functional team from within Moen. Their challenge would be to lead the team in the creation of a "future product road map," outlining how Moen would achieve its growth goals over the next five-year period.

Carbonari and the Moen senior management team agreed that for the company to succeed, it needed the following from this internal team:

- ◆ A five-year strategic product road map
- ◆ A proactive competitive strategy
- ◆ Organization-wide commitment on the goal of being No. 1 in the industry
- ◆ Foresight on significant trends and events for the future
- ◆ An exploration of new technologies
- ◆ A shift from being "engineering driven" to being "consumer driven"

This last point—being consumer-driven—was very important to Carbonari. He believed that "you can be visionary, but if consumers aren't with you, and don't want your product, who cares?"

So with these considerations in mind, plus Carbonari's promise to provide the necessary support, Buchner, Wenmoth and O'Brien began wrestling with the identification of ingredients for success—engaging the right people, scheduling sufficient time, and allocating appropriate dollars. In other words, they had to figure out how to harness and organize Moen's talent and assets to move a plumbing fixtures company to a new level of excitement and innovation in the industry.

Organizing for Success

The tri-captains focused their initial efforts on forming the team that could meet this challenge. Buchner, Wenmoth, and O'Brien did not want employees who were comfortable with the status quo at Moen. They also did not want team members representing only senior management (senior vice presidents and above). Nor, for that matter, did they want team members whose contributions might be constrained by personal or political agendas for this project. They wanted to enlist individuals who were known to have "open minds," a track record for innovation, a collaborative style, and a passion about the future of Moen.

With these criteria and after a lot of back-and-forth, Buchner, Wenmoth, and O'Brien handpicked a team that represented a horizontal slice of directors, managers, and vice presidents from the marketing, research, product development, engineering, sales, operations, IT, finance, and advertising departments—a total of eleven team members. The group named itself the "Project Periscope Team," and appropriately so. Like a periscope, its mission was to examine Moen's future landscape from a position out of the direct line of sight. And like a submarine captain, Periscope team captain Buchner was at first unsure what the Moen Periscope team would see. According to Buchner:

> With a project this big, it's not initially possible to think too far ahead, or get a detailed implementation plan from the start. So the most important thing we needed to focus

> on here was the people. We needed people who were flexi-
> ble and available and committed. People who cared about
> the company, but weren't overly concerned about the im-
> pact change would have on their functional area. Several
> times, I had to go back to managers and say, "No, I want
> someone else from your department" because the person
> they recommended was not bringing the right level of tal-
> ent to the team or was not passionate enough.

The group committed to meeting weekly, or more often as the process and activities demanded. Buchner, Wenmoth, and O'Brien, as tri-captains, would invest more time, typically by arriving to work before others did or working later. In addition to this critical Periscope role and responsibility, the tri-captains also kept their "day jobs."

Additionally, an Extended Periscope team was formed, consisting of the key "doers" and "decision makers" from within Moen. Their involvement was designed to deepen the alignment among the decision makers and accelerate the implementation of the strategy once the process was complete. Involving CEO Carbonari, the senior vice presidents, and a carefully selected cadre of proven Moen innovators, this extended team would be engaged primarily for those events designed to yield customer insights or to identify and examine future marketplace trends. They would then have the opportunity to provide assistance to the Periscope team in its task of conceiving and developing new business concepts based on this new knowledge.

How often does the level of talent and experience represented on Moen's Periscope team and Extended Periscope team come together in any organization to focus on the future? In Moen's history, this was a first.

With the teams identified, Buchner, Wenmoth, and O'Brien worked to develop a common foundation of Moen knowledge so that everyone involved in the process would have a baseline of information on which to build throughout the process. This briefing document covered topics that would make up the Periscope "lens" through which each participant might more accurately view Moen's preferred future. The composition of this lens included current company competencies, resources, talents, and strengths. It also outlined areas for possible strategic growth and, perhaps most importantly, acknowledged the company's weaknesses. One weakness brought to light by the process was Moen's practice of using the "gaps" or "holes" in a competitor's line of products to dictate the type of new products Moen would develop. According to Tim O'Brien:

> In essence, we were letting the competition create our business strategies, and that, obviously, is not how things should be done. The central lesson from the brief was that to do things differently, we needed to see things differently.

Gaining a New Perspective

To see things differently, Moen enlisted the assistance of someone whose profession was seeing human behavior in a deeper, more insightful way—a cultural anthropologist. This anthropologist visited more than twenty homes and businesses across the country to observe how people use water and what role it played in their lives. He watched and photographed people doing the dinner dishes, washing their pet lizards, filling their pools, running through the sprinkler, hosing down the driveway, washing their cars, and bathing their children, among other things. He tracked people's moods, happiness levels, and feelings of satisfaction while carrying out each of these activities, plus how they felt when they were done. He wrote down how long each action took, and documented how people moved and adjusted their water faucet for the needs of that activity. He rated the importance people placed on water safety, flow, and efficiency, as well as the effectiveness and aesthetics of each fixture. The fun factor of each activity was rated too. He observed and noted the differences between the habits of men and women in their handling of fixtures. The final report from the cultural anthropologist did an excellent job of cataloging water use among consumers, providing the Periscope team with a much broader understanding of the uses and implications of their product line. As Maureen Wenmoth noted:

> The results of this insight safari was that people wanted more than just functioning faucets. We thought we knew all about water and faucet needs, and why not? Moen had been in the water business for many decades. But, by never before conducting observational research, we really were missing out on a lot. We were also limiting ourselves by working in self-created boundaries. We were working under the pretense that water is a commodity element—something people want and need. But the reality is that it's not so cut-and-dried. Water is many different things to different people. Yes, it's something people need. But it's also something they want to enjoy using and receiving. The information confirmed that we needed to be consumer-driven and think not just about faucets, but how they relate to a room, use, or surrounding space. Our future demanded it.

Enlightened by a new perspective on consumer behavior in and around water, the Periscope team wanted additional opinions or information on how this behavior might evolve or be influenced to change in the future. If this is our consumer today, who will be our consumer tomorrow? What will the world look like five years from now? What will be the key forces that could drive change in the marketplace? To create a "future view" to add to their newly found consumer worldview, the Periscope team decided to enlist the help and stimulation of a dozen globally recognized "thought leaders" from different areas of targeted expertise.

Bringing the Outside World Inside

Although the Periscope team was confident that an infusion of outside-the-company perspectives would be a positive stimulus, there was still some anxiety around picking the right topics and the right people to represent those topics. Observed Buchner, "The selection of the thought leaders and anticipating their interaction with our internal staff was an anxious time. Could we create a good outcome? We had lots of strong-willed people who had ideas that vertical integration was the way for us to go. What happens when you throw someone like a futurist into that discussion?"

The team decided that twelve thought leaders would be invited to two separate events. The first event, designed to provide Moen with a comprehensive "macro" view ten years out, would cover a series of broad topics. To identify these topics, Moen employees were asked if they could somehow, magically, achieve perfect knowledge, what would be the most urgent questions, the hottest issues, and the most enlightening topics to be addressed by a team of outside-the-company experts? The result of this exercise was a series of topics for the first thought leader panel, which included water quality, cost and availability, environmental regulation, trends in residential construction and building techniques, the relationship between people and water, the evolution and emergence of distribution channels, functionality and design in the homes of the future, trends in consumer purchasing options, and technologies and materials development of the future.

The First Panel

At this point, the recruiting of six thought leaders for this first panel began. Hundreds of people were contacted in order to identify the six that could best cover the topic areas. Thought leaders were selected based on both their knowledge of the topics and their style in communicating it. Thought leaders, to be effective in this role, needed to be confident of their expertise, open to being influenced by other thought leaders and the Moen team, and able to communicate their knowledge in an easy-to-comprehend way. These desired attributes in a thought leader made the search more daunting, but in the end successful. The selected thought leaders were then coached very carefully on how to play the role of "provocateur" in this panel, instead of an "expert with the answer." The goal was to stir up the thinking of the Periscope team and the Extended Periscope team, not to tell them what to do.

The first thought leader event was very successful. The thought leaders shared their perspectives, covered the topics well, and, most importantly, caused the Moen teams to think more broadly about their business. They learned that people outside the company had important perceptions and experiences that could help drive the move to a new growth strategy for Moen. "Short of clairvoyance, this was the best process for determining future wants and needs," says O'Brien. "It enabled us to look at, and be guided by, the present and the future, rather than the past."

The Second Panel

The second thought leader event was designed to deepen and advance the learnings of the first event. While the first panel had been intended to provide a wide-angle perspective on the industry's future landscape, this second gathering of thought leaders was focused on what it would take to have Moen's new business concepts and models successfully developed and launched into the marketplace. The thought leaders for this event were recruited for their expertise in kitchen and bath design, changing consumer values and lifestyles, water regulation and conservation, and trends in construction and building design.

The Probability of Terrorism

During the second event, a trend surfaced that had the potential to become an industry-wide discontinuity in the future—"environmental terrorism." In 1995—almost seven years before 9/11—multiple thought leaders had forecast the probability of terrorists purposely polluting or poisoning a public water supply with the intent to harm or kill many people. Following such a catastrophic event, it would be hard to imagine a parent drawing tap water from a faucet and then handing it to a child. The Periscope team heard from multiple experts that, regarding environmental terrorism, it was not a question of whether it would happen, but when. Consequently, it was not difficult for the team to see the need at some point in the future for a product that would filter pollutants and poisons from a home faucet and signal when it was safe to drink. Maureen Wenmoth observed:

> These were people who saw, and knew firsthand, how people want to use water, from many different perspectives and areas of expertise. They gave us a deeper understanding of the topic. How people want water faucets that are as safe as they are attractive. How they want fixtures that don't actually look like fixtures. And so on. Water safety, in fact, was a recurring theme that really got us thinking and focusing on the potential importance of water filtration.

With new perspectives and knowledge from the cultural anthropologist and the thought leader events, the Periscope team was ready to start creating a robust portfolio of new business opportunities. In a series of sessions, they created a wide range of opportunities, spanning the short-, middle-, and longer-term time horizon for their five-year plan. To combat the probable trend of environmental terrorism and assure water safety, the Periscope team conceived a new product/business concept they called "PureTouch." It would be the world's first faucet with a built-in filter and electronic signal to indicate when the water is safe to drink. Moen partnered with Culligan, a leading water filtration company, to provide the replaceable filter in PureTouch. The innovative business design for PureTouch provided new growth potential for Moen via follow-up filter purchases by those who bought the product.

Since Carbonari, his executive staff, and American Brands management had all been members of the Extended Team and involved throughout the process, there was no need for the Periscope team to do the traditional "selling" of their new business concepts up the corporate ladder. Instead, the time and energy typically invested in selling senior management at the back end of a process was freed up to do more and better future planning. So the Periscope team, using tailored market research, did additional fine-tuning of their new business concepts and the five-year road map. The Moen Future Road Map described a preferred future for Moen as it looked to compete in the plumbing products market for the next five years. It outlined the major events, milestones, and potential conditions of the world and marketplace over that time, including such things as:

- Target launch dates for new products, with key milestones
- Anticipated trends and significant events at retail, with consumers, and in government regulations
- Probable competitive tactics and responses

As Dan Buchner explained:

> We took the output from the thought leader panels and built a detailed Future Map that captured our new learnings regarding the industry, the economy, and our competition, anticipating what might happen over the next five years. We updated the Future Map as part of our annual planning. It helped us focus and showed us the difficult decisions that we would have to make. Before, we had been trying to do everything in the marketplace, so the map helped us focus our attention and our efforts. The events on our Future Map played out faster than we expected. Three-quarters of the things happened, but in half the time that we expected.

It took several years of intense development and problem-solving for Moen to actually produce PureTouch. In the process, the company brought in new people with new skill sets to broaden its ability to create innovative products. They also set up systems to efficiently develop new products and take them to market. The Moen tradition of engineering excellence would remain essential to product development. But also added to their development strategies was a closer examination of water containment, water forming, the water-user interface, valving, product intelligence, installation/retrofit, treatment, temperature, and style.

It was the development and launch of PureTouch, along with other similarly innovative products, that significantly changed Moen. No longer did Moen view itself as merely a faucet company. With their new internal slogan H2O-4-U ("water for you"), team members were set to position Moen as a full-service water supply company, offering "Water the way you want it." In the market-place, this new product line and new company attitude signaled to consumers and the plumbing products trade that Moen was serious about their new, long-term strategy of "leadership through innova-tion."

Award-Winning Innovation Spurs Growth

The PureTouch Filtering Faucet System won *Popular Science's* pres-tigious "Product of the Year" award for 1999 (along with the new Volkswagen Beetle and Viagra!). Awards are nice, but for some on the team, it was almost as satisfying when the CEO of a leading competitor was discovered, by an after-hours security camera at a major trade show, fondling an early PureTouch model. And, within six months of PureTouch hitting the shelves, Moen became the number one brand in North American residential faucets.

Fast forward to the end of 2002. Moen has tripled in size and is pushing $1 billion in sales. Its market share is up 72 percent since the early 1990s, and the brand is now number one in consumer awareness in all of Moen's product categories. Bruce Carbonari is now the CEO of Fortune Brands Home and Hardware. Maureen Wenmoth and Tim O'Brien have been promoted to vice presidents at Moen, and Dan Buchner has taken a position leading the Indus-trial Design group for Design Continuum, an international design firm.

In assessing the success of the Periscope project, many believe that this strategy innovation initiative was the catalyst for creating organizational alignment around a number of new growth platforms for the company. The resulting development of internal systems and capabilities for those platforms allowed the company to launch a series of new products that fueled company growth for the next five years, keeping Moen the industry leader and allowing them to meet their financial targets.

As this book is being written, Moen has recommitted to its strategy of "leadership through innovation" by launching a new five-year strategy innovation initiative, called Periscope II.

Strategy innovation can have a dramatic impact on a company's growth and its future. Identifying the business opportunities for strategy innovation is a process that can be carried out in any company willing to make the commitment to it. In the next five chapters, we describe the process used by Moen in their successful transformation. Use it in your company to eliminate the dreaded delta, navigate the whitewater of your changing marketplace, or revitalize your business. You too can do it.

CHAPTER 6

THE DISCOVERY PROCESS

Staging Phase

> Producing major change in an organization is not just
> about signing up one charismatic leader. You need a
> group—a team—to be able to drive the change. One
> person, even a terrific charismatic leader, is never
> strong enough to make all this happen.
>
> —*JOHN KOTTER*

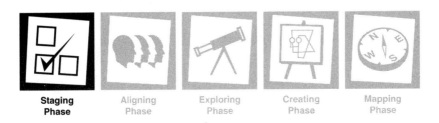

| **Staging** | Aligning | Exploring | Creating | Mapping |
| **Phase** | Phase | Phase | Phase | Phase |

The Staging Phase is the creation and preparation of an internal team for a strategy innovation initiative. The Staging Phase consists of three important activities:

1. Creating the right team and support structure

2. Creating the right working environment

3. Implementing the staging meeting

These three activities are driven by the internal sponsor of the Discovery Process and coordinated by the Discovery team captain. Their efforts culminate in the launching of the strategy innovation initiative.

Initiating the Discovery Process: The Importance of a Management Mandate

It is senior management that is responsible for the creation of the corporate strategy. They have the corporate perspective necessary to understand the strengths and weaknesses of the current business model and its implications for the future. They can foresee when the current business model may be incapable of meeting the needs of all of its stakeholders. They know when the current corporate strategy may not be sufficient to remain viable in a dynamic marketplace. Therefore, it is essential that senior management initiate the call for new strategic options and commit to the pursuit of a stronger, more innovative corporate strategy.

Regardless of who first identifies the need for strategy innovation, it is critical that the senior management level makes a commitment to the effort. A successful initiative requires this commitment because it signals to the Discovery team and the rest of the organization that their efforts are important and are making a meaningful contribution to the long-term success of the organization. When the team sees that commitment, they, too, will be committed to the effort.

This mandate from senior management for strategy innovation may be the single most critical element in the ultimate success of the initiative. Teams that believe that their work will likely result in a positive impact on the organization will be much more engaged and productive than those who believe that their work is just another corporate program. At the very least, we encourage corporate CEOs to communicate the importance of this effort directly to the team. To the extent that this mandate for strategy innovation can be expressed even more forcefully—such as the commitment to enter one new market every two years or to have a certain percentage of revenue from products less than five years old—it will significantly boost the team's commitment and energy level.

A number of companies have benefited significantly from a senior management commitment to strategy innovation. At 3M, the most recent CEOs, Desi DeSimone and now James McNerney, carry the banner for breakthrough strategy innovation by inspiring the business units and labs to innovate beyond, for example, the next Post-it Note line extension. During his tenure as CEO of IBM, it was Lou Gerstner who, to drive innovation, would routinely visit IBM Research to communicate customer "needs" he had observed during his travels. At Procter & Gamble, it was CEO John Pepper and COO Durk Jager who sponsored and maintained a direct link with Corporate New Ventures, helping steer and support the discovery of "white space" opportunities for that consumer packaged-goods giant. At Moen, the CEO Bruce Carbonari championed the importance of strategy innovation to both dramatically grow his business and, importantly, remold his organization's culture from a commodity producer of faucets to a leading edge innovator of new kitchen and bath products. At Barclays Global Investors, it was the CEO for Global Individual Investor Business, Garrett Bouton, who sponsored and shepherded the creation of iShares, a breakthrough in publicly traded index funds. Indeed, the larger surprise for us would be the identification of a company with the capacity for strategy innovation where senior management is *not* directly engaged as champion and primary supporter of those efforts.

When senior management commits to a strategy innovation initiative, they are agreeing that there is value in each of the following:

- ◆ Involving an internal team of managers in the development and implementation of corporate strategy

- ◆ Using the emerging marketplace and the needs of customers in the formulation of a corporate strategy

- ◆ Considering new business opportunities that may require some change to the current business model (infrastructure, processes, or resource allocation)

Of these three, it is senior management's unwillingness to consider changes in the current business model that most often derails successful strategy innovation initiatives. Discovery teams *will* identify exciting new business opportunities for the future. However, the pursuit of those opportunities often requires, for example, the creation of a new distribution channel, the licensing of a new technology, the outsourcing of a critical skill, or the establishment of a new partnership in order to meet these new customer needs. When management will not consider any changes to its current business model as part of the future strategy, they are wasting the potential of strategy innovation. It is better to observe and follow the lead of companies like 3M, IBM, P&G, Moen, and Barclays, among many others that we will present in these chapters, to consider new corporate structures when necessary to harness the full potential of strategy innovation.

Creating the Right Team and Support Structure

Why an internal team for strategy innovation? The history of strategy innovation in the corporate world is filled with examples of brilliant strategies identified by insightful and talented individuals. Sam Walton of Wal-Mart, Steve Jobs of Apple, Fred Smith of Federal Express, and Howard Shultz of Starbucks are frequently cited for their abilities to perceive a need in the marketplace and conceive of a unique business model to meet that need. Because of their success as individuals, wouldn't it seem better to assign one or two of your best people to do strategy innovation rather than create an internal team to do it?

A Corporate Team, Not a Lone Pioneer

We believe that a corporate team is the most successful approach for identifying and developing innovative business opportunities. A team of dedicated people can outperform an individual in identifying new business opportunities because of the following factors:

1. New ideas require different perspectives

2. Complexity requires support

3. Successful implementation requires alignment

Different Perspectives

Identifying innovative business opportunities requires a new way of looking at customers and the marketplace. Taking on a new perspective can be difficult for people who have developed or supported the current view of customers and the marketplace. A team of people with diverse perspectives is more likely than a lone pioneer to be able to see the world differently. In addition, the process of discovering new business opportunities requires both right-brain creative skills to identify a new customer need and left-brain rational skills to create the appropriate business model to meet that need. Unless the designated strategist is mentally gifted, a team of people with a mix of different perspectives and thinking skills is much more effective in this process of strategy innovation.

Complexity

The process of creating an innovative strategy for a corporation is not a simple one. There are many issues and questions to address, many options to consider, and much uncertainty in the decision-making process due to an inability to accurately quantify the future. In this complex and often ambiguous journey, a team of people can offer support and problem-solving ideas to each other where an individual would have to shoulder the entire burden alone.

Alignment

The most important reason for using a team is the need for gaining internal agreement or "alignment" with the strategy being developed. Many of the famous strategy innovators of the past started their own companies and did not have to deal with the often shark-infested waters of a complex bureaucratic organization. If you ever had an idea where you needed support from a variety of other functional areas in your company in order to implement it, you know that "convincing" others of a need to change is a daunting task. Aligning others, who often have a different set of needs and priorities, can take a long time. It often requires persistence, diplomacy, good luck, and maybe some political horse-trading to align all parties to bring a new idea to fruition. How many market-changing innovations have not seen the light of day because their inventors could not get the necessary cooperation or could not convince other functional groups of their viability?

Internal, cross-functional teams greatly enhance the internal alignment process. When the team members from different functional areas together hear customers complain about the call center or the redesigned packaging, they do not need to spend time understanding, questioning, or verifying the problem. Rather than trying to decide who is to blame and who must solve the problem, they brainstorm potential solutions together. When faced with reporting their findings back to management, they unite around their preferred solution together. The process of internal alignment for strategic action is made significantly easier when a cross-functional team is involved rather than a lone strategy creator.

Bob LaPerle was a director of business planning in the photographic products group at Kodak in the early 1990s when he helped organize a critical strategy innovation initiative for that photographic giant. He recalls:

> **Process Tip:**
>
> *People support what they help create.*
>
> If you have played a role in the creation or development of something, you are much more likely to be committed to it than if you were not involved. You know the thinking that went into it, the trade-offs that were made, the problems and issues that were addressed, the time invested. Your fingerprints are on it. You are proud of your group's output and want to see it implemented. You will help defend it, if necessary. People support what they help create.

> I had no staff and no budget, so how was I going to make
> a difference? Pulling together the folks from the business
> units and R&D in a cross-functional team was key. It made
> a huge difference when we went to the first thought leader
> panel. There we found out together what industries were
> likely to interface with photography in the future. As a re-
> sult, we gained agreement on a dramatic change in the
> R&D spending. It was a significant shift in spending away
> from silver halide projects towards projects aimed at digi-
> tal photography and hybrid approaches.

Think about the impact on your company if there were a team of people across all functional areas that was aligned around the company strategy and committed to its implementation. The strategy would have momentum from its wide-ranging support and would probably help speed the time to market. What if that small team were supplemented by a much larger group of managers that had also been involved in the process at critical points and felt a similar sense of "ownership" and commitment to it? The impact on the efficient and coordinated implementation of your corporate strategy would be significant. That is the power of a team approach to strategy innovation.

Key Roles in the Discovery Process

Participation in the Discovery Process will vary for each corporation based primarily on its size and reporting structure. For a small company with fewer layers of management, members of the senior management team would be directly involved in the process. Because these team members are also the strategy decision makers in the company, the Discovery team would, by definition, always be aligned with the interests and perspectives of senior management. In the case of smaller companies, the Discovery team needs only to select a cross-functional team and appoint a team captain.

In larger corporations with much more complex organization charts, the selection of the team and identification of roles requires more careful consideration. The primary reason for this is that Discovery team members who search for and create the new business opportunities will be different from the company's strategy decision makers. This requires the identification of a role (such as sponsor) that will act as a liaison between these two groups to help keep them aligned. Secondly, a larger corporation usually has a greater breadth and depth of functional areas that play important roles in the implementation of any corporate strategy. With more people who can have an important influence on the strategy, there needs to be a way to involve a larger group without making the team unwieldy (Extended Discovery team).

When planning a strategy innovation initiative, there are some roles that are crucial for success and others that are valuable but should be considered optional (see Figure 6-1).

Key Roles

- *Sponsor*
- *Team Captain*
- *Discovery Team*
- *Extended Discovery Team*

Optional Roles

- *Facilitator*
- *Advisory Team*
- *Support Team*

Figure 6-1. Staffing the Discovery Process.

Sponsor

Working closely with 3M CEO Desi DeSimone on bringing strategy innovation to the top of the innovation agenda was William Coyne, senior vice president for research. It was Coyne's active sponsorship of strategy innovation, with vocal and visible support from DeSimone, that led to the formalization of 3M's highly successful strategy innovation capability called Pacing Plus. As in this example with 3M, the sponsor is typically a higher-level management executive who has responsibility for the strategic growth of the corporation or of a division. Good sponsors understand that their personal futures, as well as the futures of their organizations, are at stake, and they are committed to the challenge. It is important that they have a vested interest in the outcome of the work.

In addition, the sponsor of the Discovery Process must believe that corporate growth should be achieved through strategy innovation, not just incremental improvements to the current corporate strategy. There will be pressures throughout the organization to look for short-term, incremental growth opportunities because they are the lowest-risk programs and easiest for the company to implement. The Discovery team will turn to their sponsor to defend their pursuit of innovative growth opportunities that meet the needs of customers and the emerging marketplace, not primarily the short-term, risk-reduction needs of the corporation. For Bruce Carbonari, CEO at Moen, there were numerous hurdles in the development of PureTouch, their innovative, prize-winning filtration faucet. Still, for him, as sponsor, it was never a question of whether this breakthrough opportunity would be launched as a new business, it was only a question of, "How breakthrough could it be?" It was his insistence on innovation and persistence through the hurdles that ultimately led to its introduction.

There are three primary roles of the sponsor in this Discovery Process:

1. Liaison

2. Mentor

3. Spokesperson

Liaison

As liaison, the sponsor is the primary point of contact between the Discovery team and both senior management and the Extended Discovery team.

Mentor

As mentor, the sponsor provides the guidance the Discovery team needs in the design of the initiative, the securing of resources, and their presentations to management. Additionally, in this mentoring role, if the organization or senior management has a vision for the company, the sponsor is the primary cheerleader of that vision to the Discovery team on behalf of the rest of senior management. If the organization lacks a vision, then it is incumbent on the sponsor to personally be visionary enough to not constrain the Discovery team. Typically, this means being open-minded and willing to be stretched by the team in the way he or she views the future of the enterprise.

At the Hewlett-Packard Inkjet Business Unit (HPIJBU), it was Dana Seccombe, as general manager and sponsor of a strategy innovation initiative, who provided the compelling future vision for computer printing—that some day printers will be given away for free, and, therefore, future revenue and profit must be generated by ink and paper. Understanding this fundamental trend before anyone else put HPIJBU in a strong position to strategically out-innovate the competition. Seccombe's vision, combined with his foresight to sponsor key strategy innovation initiatives, is part of the reason HP's Inkjet Business Unit was able to average 45 percent growth over ten years through 2000.

Spokesperson

As a spokesperson for the Discovery team, the sponsor plays a key role in the communication of the purpose, impact, and results of the Discovery Process to the rest of the organization, as appropriate.

However, sponsors are not considered members of the Discovery team and generally do not attend its regular meetings, unless invited for advisory purposes. The team must feel that they are driving the process and are not just there to carry out the directions and wishes of the sponsor. Sponsors stay in touch with the efforts of the team through the team captains.

As sponsors become engaged in the Discovery Process, it is critical that they adopt the innovative work style that the team has adopted. Be they CEOs, EVPs, or general managers, it is important when participating in Discovery Process activities that they not require the decorum that typically accompanies their title and office. Although this hierarchical demeanor might have value in the day-to-day running of the business, it has a countereffect on individuals and teams who are conceiving and developing new business concepts.

Consider the example of the CEO of a consumer products company that had assembled and charged a strategy innovation team with identifying new business opportunities. The CEO had requested to "observe" the team's meetings without any direct involvement. Think for a moment about how this type of participation would affect you, as a Discovery team member. Your sponsoring CEO walks into your meeting and sits at the back of the room without saying a word. Would that change the dynamics of the meeting? Would you feel more relaxed about offering the next speculative new business possibility on which the future of the organization will be based?

In this case, the CEO was advised to go ahead and attend the meeting *and* participate in the same manner as other participants at the meeting. In that particular meeting where the purpose was to generate a wide range of new business possibilities, this would specifically mean:

- Listening to others with an open mind for new learnings, surprises, and insights
- Offering ideas with the same frequency as other members of the team
- Being a model for risk-taking by offering speculative ideas along with others

The CEO took the advice and made valuable contributions to a highly productive session. The dynamics of the meeting greatly improved with his involvement. The team was even more fluent and targeted than it had been in prior sessions. The experience of their CEO listening, learning, offering ideas, and speculating on new, out-of-the-box possibilities seemed to energize and encourage the team. They were seeing the management mandate in action.

To optimize the contributions of a sponsor, sometimes even sub-tle changes in attitudes or behavior can have a positive impact on the output of the Discovery Process. There is a German manufac-turing company that had, over its hundred-plus-year history, re-fined bureaucratic hierarchy to a new level. Higher ranks within the organization brought with them a deference bordering on rever-ence. However, the current CEO/chairman was determined that the future would be different in both strategic substance and style. He chartered a Discovery team and challenged them to create a process that would result in a new strategic portfolio for the company. One of the first signals to this team that the CEO was serious about creating a new future was a simple one: He agreed that in all the meetings where he and other sponsors (other executive officers and a general manager) were involved, titles would be dropped, and everyone would be on a first-name basis. This was a dramatic de-parture from traditional meetings in this company and indicated to the team that this was, indeed, a bold new initiative. The CEO rea-soned that they were all in this project together and shared a com-mon goal—the creation of an innovative portfolio of proprietary business opportunities that would fuel the growth of the enterprise for the next decade.

Team Captain

A crucial role in the success of a Discovery Process initiative is that of team captain. Dan Buchner, one of the team captains on the Moen Periscope project, had this to say about the role of team cap-tain:

> The role of team captain was pretty exciting. We were at a point where we had to do something different, think in a different way, and we had a lot of support to do that. I was curious on how it would play out, in both the process and the results. I had organized and directed efforts like this before, so I was not scared or concerned. I value naiveté.

> If you take on big challenges, it is better to not know exactly what you are taking on.

Typically, the team captain is personally recruited by the sponsor, as the two of them will work closely in the coordination of the initiative. Team captains need to be leaders who can command respect from team members and are enthusiastic about the initiative. They need to be able to think strategically while simultaneously managing the details of an organization-wide strategic effort. Because of the cross-functional and highly collaborative nature of the team and its work, the team captain must be more of a "first among equals" leader than a "command-and-control" leader.

Good team captains can come from any department or function in the company, although in many companies it is the R&D section leader or the senior marketing manager who fulfills this role. Even though most of the team members continue to hold their "day jobs" while participating in the Discovery Process, team captains who are relieved of most of their other responsibilities during the initiative are much more effective.

The team captain needs to be an enthusiastic supporter of the initiative, a good communicator and listener, and someone able to deal with both the "big picture" (corporate strategic options) as well as the "little picture" (reserving conference rooms). Personal characteristics of good team leaders include knowing how to get things accomplished in the organization, being flexible in planning, being willing to experiment and take risks, and being respectful of the needs and different perspectives of others.

The sponsor should clarify to a prospective team captain what the value of the initiative is to the organization and what the "risks and rewards" are for him/her personally. This will begin to lay the foundation for the trust and openness in their relationship, which may be the most important one in the initiative. When this is done, it greatly increases the probability of success for both the relationship and the initiative. We have seen team captains, after showcasing their talent in leading successful strategy innovation initiatives, propelled to greater responsibility and positions at some of the largest and most respected global companies.

The Discovery Team

Recruiting the right mix of people to form the Discovery team is a critical element of the success of the initiative. On the topic of his Periscope team, Dan Buchner of Moen said, "I was quite concerned about who would be on the team. I was concerned about the right balance of perspectives in both functional areas represented as well as individual perspectives. It was also very important to me that team members be open-minded and have the ability to change. But there weren't a lot of people like that in our organization at the time. We had lots of debates internally on who should be on the team."

As for how he went about recruiting the team, Buchner explained:

> I would go to the head of a functional area and ask for their best person but often they would offer the person most loyal to the thinking and direction of that area. Sometimes I had to go back and say, "No, I want someone else." Another approach I took was to get the people I wanted on the team excited about the program, and then they would request to be on it. It's more about the people you put on the team than having a detailed implementation plan before you start the process—it's not possible to think that far ahead. If I were to form a team again, I wouldn't do anything differently. A key issue was the availability of people. We got the right group of people at the right levels in the organization. It would not have worked with the VPs. The manager and director levels are much better because there are no politics there and no one is overly concerned about the output of the program having an impact on their particular functional area. In addition, these are people who can get stuff done in the organization.

> At the higher levels in an organization, people have less time to be involved—plus people sometimes start questioning their motives.

Think of the Discovery team as a reconnaissance group that is charged with exploring the future and reporting back the business opportunities they find there. Who from your company would you send on a reconnaissance mission? Because reconnaissance work is done in unknown, uncharted territories, you would probably want people who are comfortable with, and capable of, making observations and decisions in new environments and contexts. You would also probably want to include people who are excited about the opportunity to be involved in this type of work and would be committed to the responsibilities that it entails. Beyond that, team members should be selected based on both internal corporate considerations and the attributes the team needs to work effectively.

The following are key considerations when recruiting a highly effective Discovery team:

1. Cross-functional implementers
2. Diversity of its members
3. Team players

Cross-Functional Implementers

Cross-functional teams used in the Discovery Process will help facilitate the process of corporate alignment and implementation of a new strategy. When the Discovery team is made up of individuals from all major functional areas of the company, it will create business opportunities and a strategic future that reflects the interests, needs, and capabilities of the entire company, not just those of R&D or marketing. This pays significant dividends when it comes time to aligning the organization around a strategy for the purposes of implementing it. People support what they help create. When all functions have helped create the new strategy, they will be more easily convinced to support it in its implementation phase.

A key implementer for Discovery teams that is often overlooked is the public relations or corporate communications function. Having been part of the initiative and the creation of the new strategic direction, a team member from this function will speak with even greater knowledge and conviction when communicating the new strategy to both internal employees and external stakeholders.

Diversity of Its Members

The single most important attribute of the Discovery team is its diversity. This diversity, however, has nothing to do with being "politically correct" or sensitive to a broad representation of employees. Do not create team diversity in order to avoid age or gender discrimination lawsuits.

Diversity has a very tangible benefit for a Discovery team. Strategy innovation is a creative process, with a goal to identify markets, products, and business models that may not yet exist. Success will depend on the team's ability to ask new questions, perceive new insights, and imagine new solutions. It is very difficult for a group of individuals who all share the same backgrounds, thinking styles, and experiences to think new thoughts when they are together. They share the same assumptions and mental models of how things work. On the other hand, an "outsider" added to this group will likely introduce a new way of looking at something, which will help the group break out of their old patterns and consider new ideas. When the entire group is made up of "outsiders," the possibilities for new thinking increase exponentially. Having diverse perspectives, thinking skills, and expertise on the team will significantly enhance the group's creative potential.

An example of the importance of diverse thinking and new perspectives comes from Wilson Greatbach, the inventor of the cardiac pacemaker. He was an engineering student at Cornell when he would, on occasion, lunch with the students from the Cornell Medical School. Listening to the medical students discuss the dissection of cadavers where death was caused by cardiac arrest, Wilson heard the discussion, of course, not in medical terms but in his terms— engineering principles. His insight of an engineering solution to this medical problem led to the development of the first cardiac pacemaker. This invention became the core of a billion-dollar business and was the first of 240 patents granted Wilson Greatbach, an individual with a different perspective who was able to listen and make new connections between seemingly unrelated disciplines.

Having cross-functional representation on the team will automatically add an important element of diversity. However, also consider including people for reasons other than functional diversity. For example, perhaps the team could benefit from some company veterans and some newcomers, some big-picture people and some detail people, some older people and some younger ones, some from different cultures or backgrounds, some extroverted people and some more reflective ones, some conservatives and some liberals, or some right-brain thinkers and some left-brain thinkers. Often teams will use standardized aptitude tests or personality tests, such as Myers-Briggs, to help them define these dimensions. The more variety on the team, the greater your chance of finding innovative opportunities that can become practical new businesses.

Also consider going outside the company for recruiting Discovery team members. People from your advertising agency, design firm, or other suppliers can bring a valuable "outside" perspective to this effort. A Kodak team included a science fiction writer on the team to help them in imagining future marketplace scenarios. A P&G team included a major foods wholesaler who had been developing a "grocery store of the future." Blue Cross and Blue Shield of Virginia involved a maverick hotel entrepreneur to help them stretch their concept of "service."

Team Players

The third important consideration for a Discovery team is recruiting people who are team players. Effective teams interact well, respect each other, listen to each other, and create new things together. People who feel they have "the answer" or in some way try to control the output of the group will end up destroying the creative dynamic of the team. Focus on finding team members who look forward to discovering and creating the future together with others.

It is important to point out that Discovery team members do not have to have experience in, or even an understanding of, corporate strategy. The team will focus on identifying business opportunities that are stimulated by hearing about customer needs and emerging marketplace dynamics. Those opportunities will eventually be handed over to individuals or organizations with strategy experience for further refinement and evaluation for the company.

Size matters somewhat when it comes to a Discovery team. We have found that the ideal team for larger corporations or business units usually consists of eight to twelve members. Larger companies with many different departments find it difficult to provide good cross-functional representation with fewer than eight members. With more than twelve members, meetings can become unwieldy and team decisions more difficult.

In smaller companies, it may not be possible to identify eight available people to make up a Discovery team. It is difficult to say what the "minimum" number of members should be for a team, as it will depend on the people who participate. With fewer than five or six members, the team will not benefit

Process Tip:

Ask for a small portion of each team member's "mind-share" to be dedicated to this initiative on a 24/7 basis.

It is better to have 20 percent of someone's mind thinking about this initiative *all* the time than it is to have 100 percent of someone's mind for a meeting once every few weeks. Between meetings, team members should be scanning their world for new data, trends, insights, and connections that could affect the company's future. This turns initiative "downtime" into fruitful "incubation" time, when the brain subconsciously works on a problem and often finds solutions while we are doing something else.

from the diversity of perspectives and thinking styles that will foster innovative thinking. However, we can imagine that even four committed, curious, and open-minded individuals could be a dynamic and effective team. An alternative approach for a smaller company is to add outside expertise to the internal team, perhaps tapping talented people from advertising agencies, vendors/suppliers, or other affiliated companies.

Because most companies do not have the luxury of a dedicated staff to do this discovery work, they must find people who already have "day jobs," who can dedicate part of their calendar, energy, and passion to this effort. The part-time nature of the team working over an extended period of months can introduce issues of continuity and momentum. If the team only meets once every week or two, the pressures of the day jobs can steal valuable attention from the Discovery Process. To address this, we recommend asking team members to always keep the initiative on their mental radar screens.

The Extended Discovery Team

In most companies, there are people in management who will play a role in helping to decide on or implement the corporate strategy, but who cannot be included as a member of the Discovery team. Those people can still play an important role in the Discovery Process by being part of the Extended Discovery team. Typically a group of ten to fifty people from middle management up to senior management ranks, they participate in the process at the key review or alignment meetings, as well as in any high-profile exploration activities that might involve industry experts.

The Extended Discovery team consists of individuals who assist the Discovery Process in one of three ways:

- ◆ Their deep, sometimes specialized, experience enriches the quality of the Discovery team's work for generating insights and developing opportunities.

- ◆ They increase the Discovery team's sensitivity to implementation considerations.

◆   As stakeholders in the organization's strategic decision-making process, they will play a vital role in the future alignment
of the organization on the preferred opportunities.

The Extended Discovery team provides a vehicle to involve a
greater breadth of expertise from the organization in the strategy
innovation initiative. Regardless of the size of the Discovery team,
there will always be a need for a valuable perspective outside the
team at various points along the way. The Extended Discovery team
is the way to efficiently enlist broader organizational expertise at the
appropriate time. Some strategy innovation initiatives are highly
technical in nature and might require a greater involvement of the
R&D community in the exploration phase. In others, a greater skew
toward the marketing side could be most appropriate when it
comes time to creating the business opportunities. Establishing an
Extended Discovery team will allow you to involve the types and
depth of organizational expertise that is necessary in the Discovery
Process.

In any successful Discovery Process, there is always "one eye" on
the implementation of new business opportunities throughout the
process. The Extended Discovery team is the way to involve individuals, sometimes deep in the organization, who are known to
play pivotal roles in the successful implementation of a strategy
innovation by the organization. Because members of the Extended
Discovery team will be involved in the implementation of the new
strategy, they should be part of its evolution. Their insights and
advice typically prove to be valuable to the Discovery team as it
helps them understand possible implications of the new business
model they are creating. Get them involved early.

Since the sponsor is often a single member of a much larger
senior executive staff, forming an Extended Discovery team will add
other key decision makers to the Discovery Process. This will enable
these decision makers to better understand the future forces that
will influence the new opportunities that they help create. In his
Kodak initiative, Bob LaPerle felt that having some involvement of
senior executives on the Extended Discovery team was particularly

valuable. "It was good to have senior managers at the thought leader panel, as it opened their eyes significantly that imaging as an industry was going to transform. It aligned them around that idea. Forcing them to participate in the process was a big step forward."

Optional Roles in the Discovery Process

Because every company is different, every strategy innovation initiative will be configured differently. Team members bring a mix of skills and talents that might or might not be sufficient for the needs of the Discovery Process. For that reason, other skills and talents must be recruited to provide the necessary help. The optional roles of facilitator, advisory team, and support team can play valuable roles.

Facilitator

The team captain is often the logical choice to facilitate the meetings of the Discovery team. In some companies, however, the team captain is not one who has the necessary experience to facilitate meetings with a team of managers through a lengthy process. If that is the case, then consider identifying a skilled facilitator to lead the team meetings.

The Discovery Process requires someone who can focus a team's energy, encourage unconventional thinking, and help a team reach consensus. Larger companies often have in-house meeting facilitators who can play that role. If you use an in-house facilitator, make sure the facilitator is experienced in leading dynamic processes and has a good sense of the overall business of the company.

If your company does not have anyone in-house who is "process-savvy," consider finding an independent facilitator who has these skills. That will free up the team captain to focus on the "content" of the meeting and be able to provide direction to the team without jeopardizing the preferred "neutrality" of the facilitator role. According to Dan Buchner of Moen, "We could not have carried out our project without an independent group leading the process."

Advisory Team

Some strategy initiatives are so crucial to the viability of the organization that senior-level management prefers to play a more hands-on role during the Discovery Process. In those cases, consider the creation of an advisory team. The advisory team could consist of the team sponsor plus a couple of senior managers who provide guidance, advice, and counsel to the Discovery team on an ongoing basis, perhaps through update meetings with the team or the team captain.

For the German manufacturer mentioned earlier, an advisory team consisted of the CEO/chairman, the COO, a third board member, and the general manager of a highly entrepreneurial and successful business unit in the United States. They would meet periodically with the Discovery team to hear progress reports and provide seasoned advice. Additionally, this advisory team participated in key Discovery events and provided valuable insights and feedback to the Discovery team in the debriefing sessions at the close of each event. The CEO/chairman served as the leader of the advisory team and made himself available for frequent meetings with the team captain.

Although these meetings greatly facilitate the alignment of the Discovery team with management, it is important that the advisory team does not dictate all of the team's activities. The Discovery team must feel some autonomy in their work and be allowed to explore and discover new opportunities on the strategic frontier. If they are only carrying out the wishes of the advisory team, they will feel less ownership of the output, which will negate the alignment advantage of using a team approach.

Support Team

Some initiatives require frequent meetings, travel, and arrangements with external individuals or organizations. The administrative details involved may require the identification of a person or team to help coordinate these efforts. The support team can relieve the team captain of these administrative responsibilities and provide the Discovery team with a central point of control over production of meeting notes, communications, coordination, and budget tracking.

Figure 6-2 shows the various roles and how they interact in the Discovery Process.

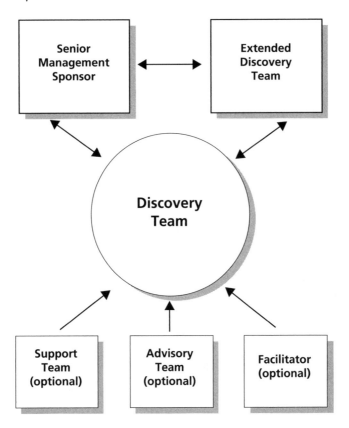

Figure 6-2. The Discovery team and support structure.

Funding the Initiative

The team's sponsor typically arranges for funding for the Discovery Process. Sometimes the funding is built into the annual budget, but other times the sponsor needs to go door-to-door seeking small change from management colleagues.

The "positioning" of the strategy innovation initiative will usually have an impact on its ability to be funded. Strategy innovation initiatives that are considered an investment in the future of the company tend to be funded more quickly than initiatives perceived merely as an expense item in this year's budget. Initiatives that fit the strategic agenda of senior management will be more compelling and of higher visibility than initiatives positioned as an experimental pursuit of a new internal process. When all functional groups in a company are committed to involvement in the process, it will attract funds faster than if it is primarily a project in one functional area, such as a marketing or product development activity. Perhaps because of the exploratory nature of strategy innovation initiatives, some corporations consider them to be similar to an R&D effort, and often look to the R&D budget for funding.

There is no "standard" cost for a Discovery Process. Focused initiatives at smaller companies or business units may generate exciting new business opportunities for less than $100,000, while large, global companies may spend over $1 million on exploration activities all around the world. It is the number and scope of the exploration activities undertaken by the team that will determine the overall cost of the initiative.

Creating the Right Work Environment

When Discovery team members are first asked to be part of a strategy initiative, it probably conjures up images of enough computer printouts to deforest Montana, spreadsheets endlessly calculating the impact of different sales estimates, and notebooks filled with presentation charts and tables. After all, strategic planning in the minds of most people is all about gathering and projecting numbers. Those numbers are related to today's corporate strategy and help identify how today's strategy must be adjusted to meet the projected needs of tomorrow.

However, as we emphasized previously, strategy innovation is not about incremental adjustment to today's strategy, and it is not about numbers. It comes about as a result of a process of exploring the future, discovering new business opportunities on your strategic frontier, and creating a strategic road map to move the company toward its preferred future. Therefore, the strategy innovation process (the Discovery Process) will differ significantly from a traditional strategic planning process, as outlined in Figure 6-3.

	Strategic Planning	Strategy Innovation
Process:	*Analytic/quantitative*	*Creative*
Based on:	*Current business model*	*New business model*
Goal:	*Extend current value*	*Create new value*
Focus:	*Company-centric*	*Customer-centric*
Assumes:	*Future similar to the present*	*Dynamic future*
Principles:	*Abide by rules/traditions*	*Break the rules*

Figure 6-3. Strategic planning vs. strategy innovation.

As a result, the Discovery team's working environment will be much different from a traditional strategic planning process. It will be:

1. Creative
2. Opportunistic
3. Dynamic
4. Collaborative

Creative

Because the team will be imagining new products, markets, and business models that do not currently exist, they will need to be creative together. All people are born with the potential to be creative, and it is the environment that will determine whether their creative abilities are realized. Environments that are highly judgmental or critical, risk-averse, or dominated by one set of beliefs will suppress creative potential. Therefore, it is important that the Discovery team create a working environment that welcomes all new thoughts and ideas, that is willing to experiment, and that is egalitarian in its operations.

There is one other aspect of a creative working environment that reflects the creative heritage of this Discovery Process. As with early "brainstorming" work done in corporations, a two-step, creative process consists of a "divergent phase" followed by a "convergent phase" (see Figure 6-4).

Divergent Phase

In the divergent phase, a team gathers together ALL ideas they can think of that will help solve the issue or problem they were dealing with.

"Rule of 100"

When Bob Galvin was CEO of Motorola, he once requested that his managers enter a meeting with at least a hundred ideas on how to solve a particular problem they would be addressing. This exercise forced people to "stretch" their thinking and be willing to entertain a wide range of options before committing to a decision. Said Galvin, "On that one, I tested things to the extreme, and it worked." This is the essence of divergent thinking, the critical first phase of the creative process.

Without regard to feasibility, practicality, efficiency, or effectiveness, the team creates a great quantity of new ideas, ranging from the ridiculous to the sublime. By ignoring the evaluation of each

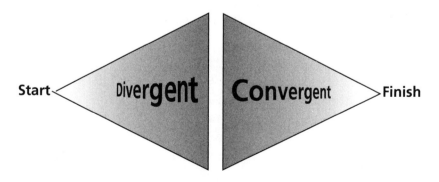

Figure 6-4. The creative process.

idea as it is presented, the divergent phase allows for a much greater quantity of ideas to be considered. Perhaps more importantly, however, deferring judgment on each idea allows the team to explore together and mentally wander into new and innovative ways of solving the problem. It is often the more absurd ideas offered in the divergent phase that will cause people to look at the problem differently, resulting in creative solutions. The divergent phase has a daydreaming quality to it that some people find exhilarating but more practical or action-oriented people find more frivolous. However, it is the crucial step that any group must take when they are interested in identifying innovative ways of solving problems.

Convergent Phase

As all business creativity must ultimately be feasible, practical, efficient, and/or effective to have value, the creative process must then move to a second phase—the "convergent phase." In the convergent phase, team members review the hundreds or more ideas generated in the divergent phase and apply some evaluation criteria to the list. It is the *quantity* of options created in the divergent phase that increases significantly the odds of finding an appropriate solution. This convergent phase is the work that most managers do well because their jobs typically require them to evaluate new options for appropriateness to the current business.

Divergent-convergent thinking should permeate all activities of the Discovery team. It is built into all the activities in the five phases of the Discovery Process outlined in this book. Try using it on your own activities. For example, if your team is considering where to go out for dinner some evening, first make a list of all possible restaurants that you could consider (even those that you normally would not consider) and then apply your team's decision criteria to that list. Innovation is a two-step process: Create, then evaluate.

Opportunistic

The Discovery team, acting in an entrepreneurial fashion, will be freed from any corporate constraints when exploring for new business opportunities. Without the pressure of having to find marketplace needs that fit nicely into today's corporate business model, the team will be able to pursue any customer need, emerging marketplace opportunity, or business model innovation that would create value at some point in the future.

Once team members can successfully disengage from corporate constraints, they are then able to disengage from marketplace or business model constraints also. After identifying a customer need, they look for the best way to meet that need, regardless of whether it uses traditional business practices or not. At this point, they are no longer "following the rules" or traditions in an industry but daring to "change the rules" in a way that creates customer and corporate value. This freedom from constraints creates a working environment that is highly opportunistic and filled with an anything-is-possible attitude among the team members. It is this attitude that is most conducive to the identification of innovative strategies.

Dynamic

Throughout the Discovery Process, new insights and information gathered will create an extremely dynamic working environment. The customer need that the team identified in Week One of the exploring process may appear worthless compared to what you found in Week Ten. Perhaps the new business opportunity you created with great enthusiasm fell apart when an industry expert said that the technology necessary would not be ready for ten years. In such a dynamic environment, Discovery team members must consider all ideas to be emerging and evolving, not fixed and unchangeable. We use the terminology of "building" ideas and opportunities to reflect the fact that each new insight and fact can help improve an already-existing idea or start a new one. Thus, the working environment for the Discovery team is one of constant change and improvement rather than "we created it already, it's done."

Collaborative

The results of the Discovery Process are created by the entire Discovery team, not any individual. The collaborative working environment encourages everyone to "build on" or help improve any idea or concept that has been created. By the time the concepts are fully developed, many of the Discovery Process participants have their fingerprints on them and feel part of their development. This is not an environment where anyone tries to push a personal agenda or pet project. It is not one of internal coalitions or behind-the-scenes maneuvering for support for different positions. Ideas are created from new information and insights that the team discovers together. At the inception of the initiative, the canvas is blank. Through collaboration, the Discovery team creates the mosaic of the future together.

Collaboration is a critical element of the Discovery Process. It is offered here in contrast to more common corporate behavior of one group identifying or developing an idea or proposal and then "selling" or "handing off" that idea to another group. The process of having to sell ideas to other people or departments is frequently a challenging, politically charged, time-intensive process. Handing off ideas to a different department invites not-invented-here passivity and significant time delays until all of the development issues and questions are discussed and agreed upon. We have found that having all relevant parties present at key information-sharing and idea-creating events results in significantly greater alignment of those parties for decision making and enhanced implementation.

Implementing the Staging Meeting

At this point, the Discovery team has been recruited and understands the working environment for the Discovery Process. The final preparation step is the staging meeting, where team members:

1. Understand the scope of the initiative
2. Share the Discovery brief
3. Create the team

Understand the Scope of the Initiative

Senior management and the sponsor will "launch" the Discovery team at the staging meeting by outlining the reason for the initiative and the impact that it will have on the company. They will also share their expectations for the results of the Discovery Process. These expectations should be significant enough to challenge the team but not so significant that they feel overwhelmed by the task before them.

It is reasonable to expect that the Discovery team can identify three to five short to mid-term new business opportunities that would have an important impact on a company's revenues plus one to three longer-term opportunities that could have a dramatic impact on future business.

Share the Discovery Brief

The Discovery brief is a document containing information that would be helpful to the Discovery team as it begins the initiative. The document is prepared by the team members prior to the staging meeting and then presented at that meeting. Because the team is cross-functional, each function prepares information from their field or expertise that will educate their teammates on that area. The presentation of this information will provide a "working knowledge" of each area and give the Discovery team a common vocabulary for their discussions.

The Discovery brief has two distinct sections:

- The field of today
- The seeds of tomorrow

The Field of Today

In this first section of the Discovery brief, each department or functional area will prepare a short overview of the current conditions in that field. Marketing might share current market data, a short competitive review, and customer usage information. The R&D section of the Discovery brief might review how current products work, the materials/ingredients used, and consumer benefits. The sales department might outline how the various distribution channels have evolved over time.

The important focus of all areas should be to remove any "mystery" about how things work in that area and to introduce a working vocabulary for the Discovery team to use throughout the initiative. It is our experience that about one-third of the focus of the Discovery brief should be on the field of today.

The Seeds of Tomorrow

The remaining two-thirds of the Discovery brief should be future-oriented. Each functional area should share with the rest of their Discovery teammates what they see as possible influences on the business of tomorrow. Perhaps the operations group is aware of a new automated manufacturing process overseas that will allow for customized production. Product development may be working on a new product design that could provide customers with added benefits. Or finance has discovered a leasing company that is willing to finance some new equipment purchases.

The seeds of tomorrow are everywhere, once you start looking for them.

- What intangible assets do you have that could be leveraged in the marketplace?
- What trends are you seeing that could affect the future of the business (either positively or negatively)?
- What is taking place at the periphery of the market or within a small market niche that, if it were to grow, might have an impact on the future?
- What group of customers is changing their behavior for some reason?
- What are your suppliers or vendors doing that might affect you in the future?
- What new technologies or materials did you recently read about in a periodical?

- ◆ What is missing that your company could provide to the
    world?

The purpose of this part of the Discovery brief is to inventory
what the team already knows or has contemplated about the future.
It is not important at this point that these future seeds be certain
to or likely to affect the future—only that it is "possible." Waiting
for trends to become probable influences on the future is waiting
too long, putting your company in a reactive mode to the market
and competitors. It is the collection of these seeds before they have
germinated that gives a company a strong, proactive future-orienta-
tion.

When Eastman Kodak launched a strategy innovation initiative
in the early 1990s, called the Future Imaging Strategies Team
(FIST), it was the first broad-scale effort by management to assess
and develop a strategy for the impact of digital imaging technology
on their chemically based silver halide business. For over a century
Kodak had been expanding and protecting primarily a single technology in silver halide that had historically delivered over a 70 percent global imaging market share. The emerging Pacific Rim
technology for producing electronic images was soon to provide a
textbook technological disruption, which the FIST effort was
formed to address. The team captain, Robert LaPerle, noted that
the development of a briefing document had special value to the
team, given the scale of the threat to Kodak's traditional business.
"The planning brief got our mind-sets around 'digital' and the role
that it would have. We started to see it more as a long-term opportunity than a threat. It helped us to get senior managers exposed to
it and thinking about it. The brief took on a life of its own and was
distributed to individuals at the company who otherwise were not
involved in the FIST project."

By providing an inventory of the present and future elements
they have to work with, the Discovery team will begin to look at
their business differently. Dan Buchner of Moen claimed that the
writing of the Discovery brief for the Periscope project was one of
the "ah-ha" moments for the team. "We divided up the areas and

started digging in and came to realize how complex the issues were. We spent a huge amount of time pulling the planning brief together, and that helped a lot. We identified a lot of myths, things that were no longer true. We were running a company based on some ideas that were not true anymore."

In our experience of working with Kodak and Moen, as well as many other companies, in the development of a successful planning brief we have observed the following common threads:

- The quality of the Discovery brief is often "predictive" of the Discovery team's final output. A high-quality, thoughtful brief presented in the staging meeting dramatically increases the ultimate value of the initiative to the organization.

- The more candid the Discovery brief, the better. With the identification of corporate strengths, capabilities, competitive threats, knowledge gaps, and assumptions regarding the future, the brief becomes a metaphorical "mirror" that the Discovery team reflects on during the course of the process. Accuracy and honesty in this exercise sets the stage for greater strategic insights later on.

- The Discovery brief should not be a lengthy document. Attempts to fully educate teammates in the workings of a functional area can lead to confusion. Hit the highlights, keep it simple, and provide some sense of priority of information presented.

Create the Team

With the staging meeting being the first time the entire Discovery team has met as a group, time should be spent on issues related to the team and its working relationship. Team members need to establish how they will communicate with each other, the logistics of subsequent meetings, any ground rules for working together, and a first attempt at a time line and key milestones for the initiative.

Because the smooth interactions of the team members are so crucial for the success of the Discovery team, the staging meeting is a good time to begin to define the team. Just as Moen named their team "the Periscope team," your team might want to give itself a unique identity that bonds the members in its quest and captures the spirit of the initiative. We have been involved in some initiatives where the Discovery team, in an attempt to create more entrepreneurial thinking and be less tied to the constraints of their company, adopted a new company name for their team.

A final word regarding Discovery team chemistry. It is not uncommon for Discovery teams to experience a "bump" or two in their formation. Often, a functional area needs to be added, a team member needs to be replaced early in the process, or there are mild disagreements on the team's charter. These things generally work themselves out when team members become committed to the process and begin to work as members of a team. Occasionally, however, there are situations where it is obvious to the team captain and to the team that an individual is working contrary to the goals of the team or, put another way, not able to carry his or her weight in fulfilling the strategy innovation mission of the team. The sooner these individuals are replaced on the team, the better. One individual, consciously or unconsciously working to sabotage the Discovery Process, can derail the entire initiative. The team captain must act swiftly to either coach the individual toward being a contributing member of the team or replace that person.

Summary

- ◆ A mandate for strategy innovation from senior management is a critical first step to any strategy innovation initiative.

- ◆ A corporate team is the most successful approach for identifying and developing innovative business opportunities that lead to strategy innovation.

- ◆ The key roles in the Discovery Process consist of a sponsor, a team captain, the Discovery team, and the Extended Discovery team. Optional roles include a facilitator, an advisory team, and a support team.

- ◆ Key considerations in the creation of a Discovery team include the identification of cross-functional implementers, the diversity of the team, and the willingness of the members to be team players.

- Although there is no "average" cost for conducting a strategy innovation initiative, it is important that the team determines its needs and that management fund it adequately.

- Because the Discovery Process is a creative process, the team must establish a working environment that is conducive to teamwork and creativity. Specifically, the working environment needs to be creative, opportunistic, dynamic, and collaborative.

- The preparation of the team for the Discovery Process culminates in a staging meeting, where team members gain an understanding of the scope of the initiative, share the findings of a Discovery brief, and begin the formation of the team.

Chapter 7

THE DISCOVERY PROCESS

Aligning Phase

> The principal mark of genius is not perfection but originality, the opening of new frontiers.
>
> —ARTHUR KOESTLER

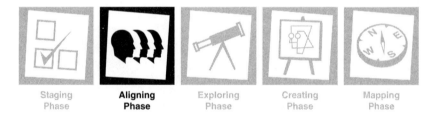

| Staging Phase | **Aligning Phase** | Exploring Phase | Creating Phase | Mapping Phase |

While the staging phase involved team preparation and primarily process-related issues, the aligning phase focuses the Discovery team on the *content* of the initiative. Where should the team begin to explore for the best new business opportunities? What new areas are most consistent with the mission, strategy, or capabilities of the organization? What are the company's "strategic frontiers"?

The Aligning Phase consists of two important activities:

1. Identifying the company's strategic frontiers.

2. Aligning with senior management on the proposed strategic frontiers to be explored.

Current Corporate Strategy vs. New Corporate Strategy

One of the primary benefits of having a clearly defined corporate strategy is its ability to provide focus for the organization. It is the corporate strategy that aligns the behavior of all functional groups in the organization, coordinating how they spend their time and budgets. This focused and coordinated use of corporate resources will increase the likelihood of reaching corporate goals and help maximize the overall efficiency of the organization. A corporate strategy is a valuable tool for senior management to help control the activities and direction of the company.

Strategy innovation initiatives similar to the process presented in this book are intended to explore business opportunities that are *beyond* the current corporate strategy. They are initiated when the incremental execution of the current strategy will not provide the growth necessary for the company's future. Therefore, strategy innovation processes will venture outside the current corporate strategy, outside of the current purview of senior management, and sometimes outside the comfort zone of the organization.

This exploration beyond the current corporate strategy, beyond the current business model, beyond management control is an important consideration for the Discovery Process. Some companies encourage their people and teams to explore into new areas and welcome the discovery of new opportunities wherever they can be found. Other companies prefer to keep their exploring teams on a shorter tether, believing that exploring into areas that the company cannot (because of current resources) enter would be a waste of corporate resources. If your senior management team wants to maintain tight control over the strategic options it considers, then this is an important issue that needs to be discussed in the launching of a strategy innovation initiative.

This potential conflict between the exploratory work of a Discovery team and the narrow boundaries of acceptable results by senior management is a critical issue in strategy innovation initiatives. By its very nature and definition, strategy innovation involves searching for ways to "change the rules" of a current marketplace, in an attempt to increase value or market share for a company. Although strategy innovation can have a substantial positive impact on a company's growth, it may also require changes to the company's infrastructure or business processes to achieve that growth. While senior management desires the growth, they are also responsible for the current business model and are often wary of changes to it. This trade-off provides a "creative tension" that is present in all strategy innovation initiatives. The Discovery team needs the freedom to explore new business opportunities wherever they exist, *and* senior management needs to maintain some control over the process to protect against changes too risky to the business model.

Rather than try to resolve this "creative tension," we would argue that it is a necessary component for the success of the initiative. The Discovery team should know that senior management will not embrace every new business opportunity they identify, especially if the opportunities represent too radical a departure from today's core business. At the same time, senior management must understand that the Discovery team will need to recommend some changes in the current business model in order to create new value in the marketplace. These two forces should be held in a dynamic tension that keeps both groups from wandering too far away from their mutual goal, which is the identification of business opportunities that the company can implement to provide significant new value.

"Discovery Drift" and the Importance of Alignment

In some instances senior management has granted the Discovery team carte blanche at the beginning of the process to explore business opportunities wherever they can be found. This results in a very empowering and productive process for the team. Each new insight gained in the process uncovers value potential for customers, perhaps with only a slight change required to the current business strategy. After many months of exploring, all those *slight* strategic changes begin to add up so that by the end of the initiative, the Discovery team has identified some very exciting and significant business opportunities, but they are *very* different from today's corporate strategy and the company's current business model.

When the team presents its findings, senior management, not having been as involved in the process, notices the big shift in business strategy suggested by these opportunities and fears that the corporation cannot afford such dramatic changes. As a result, they may hesitate to endorse these new business opportunities, in spite of their significant revenue potential. Because senior management did not experience the gradual drifting from the current business strategy as the team did, they are not ready to make the big strategic leap to a whole new way of doing business. We call this movement away from the current business strategy "discovery drift," and we see it as one of the primary reasons why the output of such initiatives may not always be embraced by the company (see Figure 7-1).

To prevent this "discovery drift" and increase the possibility that the outputs of the Discovery Process will be embraced by senior management, phase two of the process establishes "alignment" between the Discovery team and senior management. By understanding the expectations of senior management for this initiative and the degree of stretch, change, and risk they are willing to consider,

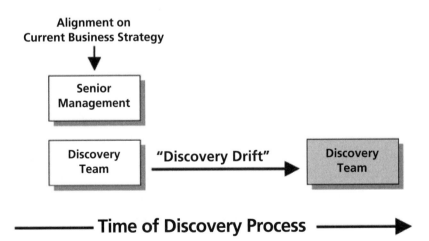

Figure 7-1. Discovery drift and the need for alignment in the Discovery Process.

the team can appropriately focus their exploration and creation outside the current business strategy.

Senior management doesn't always play the role of curmudgeon in this process. We have seen cases where they had higher expectations for the team than what was delivered. We once worked with a team from a major consumer package goods company that had recently received FDA approval for a proprietary food technology. This technology, if leveraged properly into new products and businesses, promised to have a powerful impact on the company's profitability and shareholder value. However, senior management's charge and objectives to the team stopped short of suggesting, or even influencing, the new business areas that could be explored by the team. Without the encouragement to explore beyond the current business model, the team limited their explorations and their speculations to opportunities that fit the current business model. The result was that senior management was underwhelmed and unaligned with the new business opportunities developed by the team, feeling they were too close to existing businesses. The lesson from this experience is to engage and align senior management early on in determining the territory to be explored in the discovery work.

Alignment on the Flexibility of the Business Model

One way for the Discovery team to align with senior management around this question of how much change can be tolerated is to clarify what elements of the current business model they perceive as fixed and which they consider flexible. Either through a discussion with the Discovery team sponsor or a meeting with senior management, go through the elements of the current business model and ask how much change they would tolerate in that area. Will they consider serving a different customer base? Does a new business opportunity have to use current technology? Is senior management flexible in considering new business arrangements, such as joint ventures? Are they fixed in their insistence on using the company's current sales force or distribution channels for any new venture? Do the new products have to be manufactured in current facilities?

In this discussion, senior management will likely prefer to leverage all of the current elements of the business model because that represents the least change and will likely provide the greatest efficiency. However, if all of the elements of the current business model are to remain more fixed than flexible, the Discovery team has very little room to identify growth opportunities. The most important output of such a discussion is the sensitization by both senior management and the Discovery team that some changes will likely be necessary for the identification of new business opportunities. A second output is a prioritized list of business model elements that should remain fixed (or flexible). While the Discovery team will not necessarily use this list to limit their exploration of new business opportunities, they will use it as evaluation criteria to help screen and prioritize the opportunities they create in the Creating Phase.

Alignment on Business Assumptions

Another way for the Discovery team to align with senior management is to examine business assumptions together. Since no one can know the future, as previously noted, we all make assumptions about it. If not based on new knowledge, our assumptions about the future are typically based on our past experience. We assume that the competitive landscape of tomorrow will be similar to today's landscape. We assume that the channels of distribution today will be the ones we use to grow the business. We assume we will adapt our current manufacturing capabilities to meet the needs of future markets.

However, all markets are dynamic. Sometimes the changes will obsolete a business assumption that is crucial to the company's strategy. Moen ran into this situation in the plumbing fixtures market. Their previous strategy was based on the assumption that plumbers would continue to be a primary means of selling/influencing the purchase of plumbing fixtures to consumers. By offering the highest-quality faucet to the plumbers who appreciated this quality, the company believed that their business would continue to grow. Then along came Home Depot, offering consumers the opportunity to select the fixtures they wanted. Seeing products side-by-side on the shelf, consumers made decisions based more on style (what they could see) than on quality (what they could not see). What helped Moen turn around their business was their willingness to surface key business assumptions, question the viability of those assumptions for the future, and then make a strategic shift based on marketplace changes. As a result, their faucets became more stylish.

How many companies based their futures on the business assumption that the dot-com revolution would continue at its torrid pace?

Following some thought leader panels in the mid-1990s, 3M recognized that they had many processes in place to identify customer insights but nothing in place to collect market foresight. As a result, the business assumptions for the future were inconsistent and sometimes contradictory across their many different divisions. In response, 3M formalized a corporate capability for generating proprietary foresight. A group was established to identify and track emerging trends and possible discontinuities, providing a clearer and more consistent basis for the establishment of future business assumptions across divisions.

The Discovery team should spend time with senior management discussing the assumptions on which the current and near-term business strategy is based. Then ask how confident they are that the assumptions will remain valid in the future. Gaining alignment with senior management on which business assumptions will likely remain valid, which will probably change, and which are questionable is a potent alignment exercise.

Strategic Frontiers

"What's next for your company?" Can you answer that question? Is your answer, "More of the same"? If so, you are stuck in an *incremental* way of doing business, trying to eke out a little more revenue from the same marketplace using your same business model. Roll out the next line extension, charge a little more for it, and hope that competition is asleep at the wheel. Incrementalism is a safe strategy designed for modest growth. In some markets (those that are more static than dynamic), this can still be a viable strategy. If it still works for your company, you are probably not getting much from this book. When your company's financials or growth prospects need a boost that your incremental strategy cannot provide, it is time to rethink your strategy and consider "what's next."

Beyond Incrementalism

Process Tip:

A strategic frontier is that unexplored area of potential growth that lies between today's business and tomorrow's opportunities.

We call this area a frontier because it is considered to have potential for growth but has not yet been fully explored. When we talk to people in companies, many have opinions on what are (or should be) their strategic frontiers. However, because there is no process in place to do it, they rarely discuss these frontier options with others. A discussion of the future should begin with a discussion of a company's strategic frontiers.

We have run into a few companies, such as 3M, that usually know "what's next." In their yearly planning process, the 3M business units are required to account for their progress in developing their *next* strategic business platform for growth. That platform is identified and developed so it is ready to be introduced when revenue from the current platform begins to wane. The next platform becomes the basis of their corporate growth in subsequent years. If you are in a company like that, you already know "what's next for your company." If not, the first step in understanding the next growth platform for your business is to identify your "strategic frontier."

Think of a strategic frontier as market, product, technology, or business process that lies just *beyond* your current corporate strategy and business model (see Figure 7-2). You probably have some reason to believe that moving to this strategic frontier could result in growth for your company, either because it works in other companies, because it addresses a problem you have, or because it addresses a need in the marketplace. However, you have never pursued this strategic frontier because it was always considered just outside your company's strategy. This was the case with the Pure-Touch product at Moen. While the company had preliminary designs in-house for a water filtration faucet, its development did not fit with the fast-follower strategy Moen was pursuing in the conventional faucet market at that time. When their exploration of the future marketplace identified a growing need for water filtration, that became the strategic frontier for Moen. As part of their new

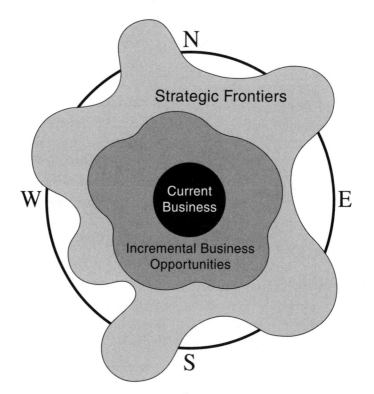

Figure 7-2. Strategic frontiers.

corporate strategy, the PureTouch concept was pulled out of moth-balls, developed, and introduced to the market.

A History of Frontiers: Terra Incognita

In the fifteenth century, mapmaking, or cartography, was anything but a science. Cartographers would gather the latest information from explorers returning from their journeys and update earlier maps by incorporating the new knowledge. Still, if you look at old European maps, you will see large sections to the west, north, and south labeled "terra incognita," or "unknown territories." These vast, empty expanses represented what the cartographers did not know. They were boundaries yet to be crossed or areas to be mapped by future explorers and cartographers.

Terra incognita or frontiers have played an important role in the development and growth of the United States. It was in 1803 that President Thomas Jefferson received congressional funding for the exploration of America's frontier at that time—the land west of the Mississippi River. Jefferson saw potential in that new frontier. In addition to any resources it may have contained, he had hoped that the frontier included a trade route to the Pacific Ocean. A "north-west passage" of inland waterways could eventually open up com-merce to Asia. So he appointed his personal secretary, Meriwether Lewis, to lead a reconnaissance group to explore and chart the U.S. frontier. Lewis teamed with William Clark, a captain in the U.S. Army, and the two of them assembled a team of thirty-one people and a dog for the trip. This group, referred to as the Corps of Dis-covery, spent almost two-and-a-half years exploring this frontier. Although this discovery team did not find a "northwest passage," their maps of the frontier and knowledge of the native people and plants proved invaluable to the explorers, traders, and settlers who followed them to open up the American West.

As long as we can perceive "places" we have not been, we will always have frontiers to explore.

Imagine that your corporate cartographer has been assigned the task of drawing and illustrating a map of your organization's future.

Where are the frontiers? Does the resulting map cause you to feel more or less secure regarding the future of your organization beyond today's business? How much of your corporate future map is labeled "terra incognita"?

Today's Frontiers

Whereas frontiers of the past often referred to land or geography, many of today's frontiers in the world of business are invisible to the human eye. As this book is being written, wireless communications, genomics, and nanotechnology are three of the most significant frontiers that are likely to dramatically change the world in the decades to come. However, a strategic frontier does not have to change the world to be of value to your company; it just has to advance or grow your business. A new product category, a new target audience, a new distribution channel, or a new manufacturing process can be viable strategic frontiers for your business. Anything that could add value to your customers and would also add value to your company is a strategic frontier you should be considering for the future.

When Craig Wynett, general manager of new growth opportunities for Procter & Gamble, thinks of strategic frontiers, he considers them at three different levels: new products, new projects, and new platforms. Each of these levels requires a different corporate response and level of commitment. Creating new products is the easiest level because much of it can take place within the company's current business infrastructure and current business model. New projects become more challenging for a company as they often involve new organizational forms or processes, such as different business units working together or new distribution channels being created. The most challenging strategic frontier for a company is in new business platforms, where new organizational forms and new metrics for success must be considered. Determining how to enter a new industry, leverage a new technology, or create a new market takes more time and requires more corporate flexibility and commitment.

Strategic frontiers span a wide spectrum of business opportunities (see Figure 7-3). They can be near-term, low-risk business opportunities that the company has been considering for a while but for which it never created an effective strategy for implementation. At the other end of the spectrum, strategic frontiers can be breakthrough, industry-changing business opportunities requiring substantial investments in time and resources. What a company selects as a strategic frontier will reflect their business philosophy, industry, and available resources. The important point is that each company know its strategic frontiers and commit to an exploration of those frontiers.

It is important to note that the "company-specific" frontiers noted in Figure 7-3 are aimed at elements of the company's business model. Those elements become frontiers only when the company considers major changes in those areas that will result in significant new value-creation and growth for the company. Mere *improvements* of those elements fall into a category of operational efficiency, not strategic frontiers. For example, identifying a new, lower-cost manufacturing source to boost operating margins would be operational efficiency, improving what already exists. On the other hand, considering the outsourcing of manufacturing so the company can focus its resources on sales and marketing only would be a strategic frontier, a major innovation in the business model that provides growth opportunities.

Company-Specific	Company-Generic	Marketplace
New product	*Franchising*	*Artificial intelligence*
New product category	*Globalization*	*Biotechnology*
New distribution channel	*JIT manufacturing*	*Genomics*
	Mass customization	*Internet*
New manufacturing process	*Outsourcing*	*Nanotechnology*
	Partnerships	*Smart materials*
New positioning	*Patent exploration*	*Wireless communications*
New sourcing strategy	*Services*	
New technology		*Automation*

Figure 7-3. Examples of strategic frontiers.

Managing the Core Business AND the Strategic Frontiers

There are times when senior management, because of market or corporate financial conditions, must be conservative in running the business. Investing in today's "core" business with incremental product improvements or lower-risk new business opportunities can be the most prudent financial strategy, reinforcing and building the company's profitable core. However, there will likely come a time when company growth beyond what is achievable in the core business is deemed necessary. What will that business be? It is the management of "today's core business" with the active pursuit of "tomorrow's core business" that may be the single most important relationship for senior management to monitor and shape. When these two priorities are constantly balanced in the management of a company, they create a strategic tension in the organization that results in a focused, dynamic path to future growth.

In the mid-1990s, Rubbermaid was selected as *Fortune* magazine's "Most Admired Company." This was due, in part, to the fact that Rubbermaid had developed a well-deserved reputation for balancing the growth of its core businesses with growth into new categories and industries, including playground toys, sidewalk refuse containers, platforms for changing a baby's diaper in airports, and numerous other products. The senior management of Rubbermaid had developed a process that assisted them in fostering this strategic tension between managing the core business and creating tomorrow's new growth.

Senior managers who place all of a company's resources on today's core business and ignore the future run the risk that changes in the marketplace will leave them unprepared to enter the markets of the future. On the other hand, a company that starves today's core business because its resources are placed as bets on "the next big thing" may find the cash cow running dry before the bets are ready to pay off. It is the balance of these two factors that is so critical to corporate success—advancing today's core while strategically exploring and capturing new markets on the strategic frontier.

Identifying Strategic Frontiers

The specific activities pursued in the next phase of the Discovery Process, the Exploring Phase, will be dependent on the strategic frontiers that are selected as the highest priority for this strategy innovation initiative. This is the primary objective of this Aligning Phase—the identification and alignment with senior management on strategic frontiers to explore.

Companies that have spent time considering markets of the future will likely have some sense of what represents a promising strategic frontier for them to consider. For those that have not yet done so, the Discovery Process offers a great opportunity to speculate on what those frontiers might be.

Focused Exploration vs. Open Exploration

Senior management may already know the strategic frontiers they would like the team to explore. Because of their knowledge of the business, strategic insights, or some evolution in the marketplace, they will be clear about where the next, new marketplace opportunities are likely to be found. When senior management communicates the frontiers to the Discovery team, the process becomes a "focused exploration." The team will be able to focus their planning and energies on this predetermined strategic frontier.

For companies that have not explored beyond their current markets and current business models, this idea of a strategic frontier will be a new concept. Senior management could randomly select a strategic frontier for the Discovery team to explore, but then the team would be constrained in their exploration to an area that might not hold the greatest potential for the company. Instead, we recommend that the Discovery team first be charged with identifying possible strategic frontiers for the company to consider. In this case, the process becomes an "open exploration" for the Discovery team, and the Aligning Phase of this process takes on a much more important role. It is the identification and alignment with senior management on the most appropriate strategic frontier(s) to explore that will be critical for the ultimate success of this strategic innovation initiative.

Focused Exploration

In a focused exploration, a Discovery team is assigned a strategic frontier selected by senior management. The purpose of the Aligning Phase then is for the Discovery team to be as clear as possible on the reasons why this frontier represents growth opportunities for the company and to understand management's perception of the frontier boundaries. When senior management is able to provide a thorough background and rationale for the attractiveness of the strategic frontier, then this communication may be all that is needed for the team to proceed to the Exploring Phase.

Occasionally, senior management will have a strategic frontier in mind as the focus of the Discovery Process but will still request that the Discovery team move through the steps of an open exploration. This enables management to test the rationale for its proposed frontier and to see whether it will "stand up" to the growth opportunities in other strategic frontiers that the team identifies. This is an approach we recommend for a number of reasons. First of all, it is valuable for senior management to understand how the Discovery team (who may be the next generation of senior management) views future growth opportunities for the company. Their different perspectives on the business could add significant insights and suggest new strategic possibilities. Secondly, when the Discovery team feels that they have contributed to the identification of the strategic frontier they will be exploring, they will feel a greater sense of "ownership" of the process. Rather than carrying out someone else's mission, they will be carrying out their mission in the Discovery Process. This shift in perceived ownership of the process will lead to greater involvement and commitment by the Discovery team.

Open Exploration

In an open exploration, the Discovery team is charged by senior management to survey the world of possible strategic frontiers and recommend those they would like to explore through the Discovery Process.

The Discovery team should begin their process by identifying a long list of possible strategic frontiers for their company. How long should the list be? Use the "Rule of 100," introduced in Chapter 6, as a minimum. Each frontier should represent some degree of future growth potential for the company. Remember, these are areas that deserve further study or exploration because they are likely to yield new business opportunities for your corporation. You begin by building a list of possible frontiers. As you build this frontier list, keep in mind the following:

Process Tip:

Resist the urge to prejudge the potential of strategic frontiers.

When hearing about a new frontier, people have a tendency to make a split-second decision on its attractiveness. What happens in that split second is that the form of a product or service on that frontier is assumed, a market potential is estimated, and a comparison to the company's hurdle rate for new businesses is made. Break that chain of thought! The idea at this stage is to identify the frontier and, on the basis of a thorough exploration of it later, identify a way to "change the rules of the game" on that frontier. That rule-changing innovation is impossible to determine prior to the frontier exploration.

- ◆ Do not overanalyze the frontier options you add to the list.

- ◆ Do not consider *how* that frontier would be implemented by your company, but assume that you could acquire whatever skills or resources you would need.

- ◆ Do not judge the growth potential for each frontier as you build the list, as most would be too difficult to determine at this point.

Both of these latter two issues—implementation and growth potential—will be important topics of the Exploring Phase. Rather than be concerned with them now, stretch your thinking and list any area that could possibly provide you with new business opportunities in the future.

How do you go about building a list of strategic frontiers? It starts with the Discovery team sharing their points of view. Grab an empty conference room and a flipchart and spend the morning speculating. See how long you can make the list. Following that exercise, use both internal and external sources to help expand the list.

Sources of Strategic Frontiers

After the Discovery team does an internal listing of potential strategic frontiers, they should then seek out other sources of frontier options, both internal and external to the company (see Figure 7-4).

Internal Sources for Strategic Frontiers

There are a variety of internal sources that the Discovery team can tap in search of potential strategic frontiers to explore.

Management Interviews

Senior managers, with their experience, systemic perception of the company, and responsibility for its strategy, often have ideas on how to grow the business. Discovery team members should con-

Internal Sources	**External Sources**
Management Interviews	*Trends Search*
Company Vision	*Technology Search*
Corporate Drawing Boards	*Business Model Search*
Redefine the Business	*Outside Experts*
Core Competence	
Intranet Survey	

Figure 7-4. Sources of strategic frontier ideas.

duct personal (one-on-one) interviews with all of the senior managers to identify their suggestions for viable strategic frontiers. The Discovery team sponsor can help set up these interviews. Listen to the responses of these senior managers but also listen for the assumptions and perceptions that are behind those responses, as they will help you understand the company's current view of the future.

In one Fortune 50 company where we were asked to conduct these interviews with the top fifteen executives, there was some concern that the appointments would be difficult to arrange and that, due to near-term pressures on the business, our reception might be a chilly one. We were pleased to discover that every executive willingly created the time; in most cases, the one-hour meeting extended to ninety minutes or more so that all their input could be captured. These executives were eager for the opportunity to influence the company's future focus by suggesting possible new frontiers to be explored.

Company Vision

Another critical input for the identification of strategic frontiers is the company's vision or mission statement. If it is a good one, the vision will be a proactive one that contains a focus for the company's efforts and some indication of what success looks like when the vision is fulfilled. What path to the future is suggested by the vision/mission? Is it a relatively broad path that encourages the pursuit of a goal in a variety of different ways? Or is it a relatively narrow path that minimizes the company's flexibility and possible strategic options?

Corporate Drawing Boards

Talk to the people in R&D, new product development, and marketing. Ask them if they have any new product ideas that were developed or submitted but not considered to be a good fit with the company's current product line. Are there elements of those products that would suggest a strategic frontier for further exploration? Do any of these new ideas contain materials, technologies, or functions that would broaden today's business or open up new market niches? If so, it could be a strategic frontier.

Redefine the Business

Chris Zook, in his book *Profit from the Core*, describes the importance of knowing the definition of your core business. "Defining the business accurately is a way of creating a logical hierarchy of territories in and around your core business that help you target wise investments . . ." As an example, Zook asks the question, "Is Coca-Cola in the cola business, the soft drink business, the beverage business, or some other business?"[1]

This is a good exercise for the Discovery team to help explore possible strategic frontiers. The team should first narrowly define the business they feel their company is in right now. As an example, if your company is currently in the business of manufacturing coffee cups, the Discovery team should then define a larger business of which the coffee cups business is some minor portion or share. Perhaps it is the "beverage container" market, which would also contain glassware, paper cups, etc. Keep going and define the next higher-level business of which "beverage containers" is a relatively small share. That might be the market for "liquid conveyance devices," which would include milk bottles, picnic jugs, and even tank trucks. Following these expanded definitions of a company's market could suggest a strategic frontier to consider.

Terry Tallis, one of the leaders of a successful strategy innovation initiative at Hewlett-Packard's Inkjet Supplies Business Unit, notes about that project, "We were creatures of our past. This experience raised us up so that we could see what had been invisible to us. We had thought we were in the 'printer' business. We discovered we were in the 'printing occasion' business. We had 50 percent of the printer business but less than 1 percent of the printing occasion business. That was key to the whole growth initiative."

Core Competence

A core competence of a company can, with some effort, be turned into a *core excellence*, creating new value for customers and growth for the company. Take a look at what your company does well and determine if significant advances in that area might represent a significant growth opportunity. Rather than just have your Industrial Design group designing great products for you to sell, can they provide design services directly for your clients (as BMW does)? Can your internal inventory tracking system be offered as a service to customers on an out-sourcing basis (as Mrs. Fields does)? If so, these are potential strategic frontiers for your company to consider.

Process Tip:

Core competencies and successful brands can be barriers to strategy innovation.

Often a logical starting point for the creation of new business opportunities is to leverage your current strengths, which frequently reside in core competencies and successful brands. However, core competencies and successful brands carry with them constraints or limits on how they can be used, so as to protect their "value" to the company. Be aware that these constraints may favor the incremental extensions of the current business over the pursuit of innovative new business opportunities.

Intranet Survey

Ask your employees if they have any ideas on how the company might grow. A quick question placed on the corporate intranet is an easy, efficient way to gather new ideas for strategic frontiers and provides a way for the employees to feel involved in the process. In 1999, P&G launched an intranet site called myidea.com, which attracted over 9,000 possible ways to grow the business. It followed that by fostering new connections among 18,000 engineers by linking them via its Innovation Net.

External Sources for Strategic Frontiers

Using internal sources for the identification of strategic frontiers will frequently reflect a corporate myopia about the business. If you have been with the company for more than a few years, you tend to believe that the way the company does business and the way the marketplace operates are "givens." If you were part of the company when many of the processes and infrastructure were established, you tend to believe that the company is already the best it can be. This makes it difficult to consider changes that could yield growth opportunities. It is important for the Discovery team to also explore external sources and perspectives in their search for potential strategic frontiers.

> **Process Tip:**
>
> *Visionary companies are seldom those that only talk to themselves.*
>
> **Visionary companies tend to be proactive companies. They are often driven by internal goals but guided by the marketplace. It is their constant measurement and connection with customers and experts outside their company that helps guide their strategy development. Get outside of your four walls and talk to those who envision, create, and measure the future.**

Many companies that have been in a business for a while, especially if they have been successful, consider themselves "experts" in the business. As experts, they believe that their opinions and perceptions of the market are superior to those of "outsiders," so that seeking outside perspectives is a waste of time. That may be true for managing today's business but it can be lethal in the pursuit of strategy innovation. The organizations that seek out new, outside perspectives as a stimulus to their strategic thinking tend to be the ones most prepared for dynamic shifts in their marketplace and the emergence of new frontiers. In the search for the next opportunity area, search outside the company.

Trends Search

Trends reflect changes that are taking place in the marketplace or in the world. Changes within any type of system disrupt its stability and create some imbalance, which is the source of potential opportunities. Organize a subgroup of the Discovery team to scour publications and the Internet for trends in various cultures or societies, lifestyles, or demographics. Do any of the trends, if they were to continue or increase in intensity, suggest new customer needs or some difficulty by current companies in meeting their needs? Think through the implications of the trends and all their potential outcomes.

We know of a London-based communications company that dedicated a portion of its quarterly executive meetings to a presentation of key industry trends to stimulate a future focus. Once the presentation was completed, the group invested time in assessing the possible importance of those trends and their implications for the organization. This type of input into a Discovery initiative is ideal.

Technology Search

Set up a "scout team" to search for technologies or new materials that your company might use to greatly increase customer value and satisfaction. Look for technologies that could be used in a product or in the making and selling of a product. Talk with suppliers, vendors, other companies, and scientists in laboratories. Technologies that offer any potential for stimulating growth in your company should be captured as a possible strategic frontier.

One European company used a "scout team" approach as a way of seeking out both promising technologies and promising alliances, partners, or acquisitions. They identified candidate companies where a visit might be mutually beneficial and set up site visits by the Discovery team. Even where a longer-term relationship did not play out, the Discovery team benefited from the new knowledge and insights gained in the exchange.

At the same time, assign this scout team the task of identifying any possible or probable technological "dislocations" in your industry. New frontiers can often be found on the other side of these technological disruptions in the marketplace.

Business Model Search

In addition to investigating trends and technologies, set up a third search team to explore the business literature for new ways of running a business. Business periodicals routinely profile companies that defy conventional business wisdom and meet with success. Is there something they do that, if applied to your business, could result in significant growth? Seeing what companies in other industries are doing to increase the value of their business model can provide important insights about strategy innovation possibilities.

Following this type of research, one media company assigned a team to identify all the possible component parts to a business model in their industry. Then, from all the parts, they built up a model for each market competitor and, from role-playing the competitor's position, evolved the model out five years. Now, with a possible (maybe probable) competitive business landscape looking out five years, they conceived from scratch the optimal business model for their company in that industry. This business model perspective assisted the team in identifying the areas to explore in order to migrate from today's business to the more-competitive-in-the-future business.

Outside Experts

Consider engaging the services of an outside expert for gathering strategic frontier options. Strategy consultants, venture capitalists, financial analysts, technology experts, and magazine editors are just some of the people who can add a valuable outside perspective to supplement the internal search for strategic frontiers.

One major German automobile manufacturer enlisted the help of three expert resources to develop a probable scenario for the global automobile industry in 2010. Each had a different focus for surfacing emerging trends: manufacturing processes, the Asian market, or the U.S. market. The strongest and best-supported trends of each study were combined into a single presentation and used to "provoke" new thinking on future frontiers among a gathering of global executives. The executive conference proved to be a powerful combination of the newest innovations in the production pipeline married to an introduction of future forces to stimulate new thinking for future innovations.

Thought leader panels can also be very effective in identifying appropriate strategic frontiers. For example, the first Moen thought leader panel, referred to as the "macro" panel, was intended to bring outside, expert opinions to the company to help define areas of future growth opportunities. Recruiting experts from a mix of disciplines for a two-day exploration of the future will provide your company with a proprietary view of the future and clarity around possible strategic frontiers. Details on the thought-leader-panel methodology can be found in Chapter 8.

Prioritize the Strategic Frontiers

The list of potential strategic frontiers should be long, inspiring, yet somewhat daunting to the Discovery team. How can the team explore the range of opportunities available in the depth that would be necessary to understand the frontier? The answer is, they cannot. A Discovery team can explore only one or two, possibly three (depending on the scale of the project) strategic frontiers at a time. Pursuing more than three frontiers will typically stretch the team's resources so thin that the resulting exploration is too cursory to identify specific business opportunities. Therefore, the next step is to prioritize the list of strategic frontiers to narrow the focus for the initiative (see Figure 7-5).

The Discovery team can use any process they are comfortable with to help narrow the list. Be sure to clarify the criteria you will use to prioritize the frontiers: size of opportunity, degree of innovation, fit with current strategy, consistency with today's core business, etc. One option is to understand how senior management might assess the potential of a strategic frontier. However, do not be afraid to use the team's energy or passion with a frontier as a basis for prioritizing, as an energized Discovery team will generally excel in this process.

The next step is to involve senior management in the prioritization process. Set up a meeting with senior management to review

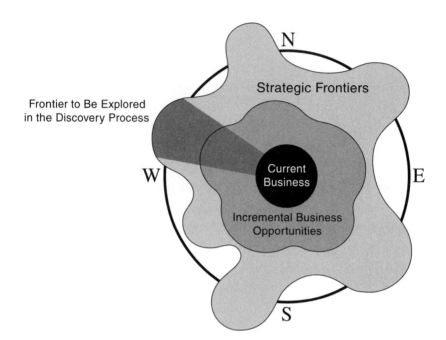

Figure 7-5. Strategic frontiers to be explored.

the strategic frontiers and share the Discovery team's prioritization efforts. Engage them in a dialogue about their views and priorities for these frontiers. Remind them that the exploration of this frontier will seek to understand how to create new value there. It will likely yield a range of short- to long-term opportunities, a range of low-risk to higher-risk businesses, and a range of conventional to innovative ideas. The objective of the meeting is to emerge with agreement on what strategic frontier(s) this Discovery team should explore in this Discovery Process. Keep in mind that this is not a commitment at this point to enter this area. It is only a commitment to explore its potential because of a belief that it may contain new growth opportunities.

This meeting with senior management is the first step in the all-important "alignment" that the team needs in order to keep the initiative relevant and to maximize the potential that their work can be implemented. Do not be surprised if the frontier decision takes more than one meeting. For many companies, this will be the first time that a proactive decision on the future has been made. It is an important strategic choice, so take whatever time is necessary to gain this early alignment.

Critical Role of Strategic Frontiers

The importance of this alignment of senior management and the Discovery team on the appropriate strategic frontiers for the company cannot be overstated. By authorizing this strategic initiative and focusing on strategic frontiers, senior management makes a commitment to the company's future. They agree to the challenge of managing today's core business while preparing for tomorrow's core business. It is much easier to focus on running today's business to satisfy short-term goals and let the future take care of itself. Being reactive about the future and what it will bring can be devastating to a company in a dynamic marketplace. Unexpected changes and shifts make a company vulnerable to new competitors, new technologies, and changes in customer behavior in a market. Being proactive about the future and creating the company's next growth platform will increase its chances of survival in a time of change.

Strategic Frontiers as a Corporate Vision

Much has been written about the positive role that a corporate vision can play in guiding the activities and development of a company. That compelling vision of an ideal future can motivate and influence employees as they make day-to-day decisions on behalf of the company. When we think of powerful visions, we think of how both Apple and Microsoft were purported to have been driven by the image of ubiquitous computers in the future. Corporate visions are particularly powerful for start-up ventures, but what about established companies? It is not easy to instill a new vision in an established company. Established companies cannot focus all their energies on creating a new company—they need to protect the ongoing business also.

Strategic frontiers are to established companies what corporate visions are to start-ups. A CEO of an established company can point to a previously unexplored strategic frontier and declare it to be the next growth area for the business. Distinct resources can be targeted to exploring and understanding that frontier while still maintaining the current business. Those resources can be guided in their search for business opportunities by the definition of that frontier.

When a company has both a current business *and* a strategic frontier, it is better able to balance the "current versus future" dilemma described in Chapter 2. Unless the future frontier is clearly identified, there is no reason for a company to dedicate attention and resources to the future. In fact, to allocate funding to a "fuzzy future" does not appear to be responsible spending. But allocating funds to a clearly delineated future frontier can make it a wise investment in the future. Senior management will be perceived by both employees and the investment community as leading the company, as taking a proactive stance.

> **Process Tip:**
>
> *Established companies should use strategic frontiers the same way that start-ups use corporate visions.*
>
> **The identification of a company's strategic frontiers will turn a "fuzzy future" into a more "focused future." By naming the next growth area, senior management makes a bold, proactive statement to both employees and the investment community that they are leading the company to an attractive future, while still maintaining the current business.**

The identification of a company's strategic frontiers will have other benefits also. It will provide a focus for the creative energies of the entire company by occupying some of the "mindshare" of the employees. If I am an employee and learn that wireless communication is our strategic frontier, everything that crosses my desk about wireless communication will now catch my attention, where it did not previously. If I am attending an electronics convention, I will wander by the wireless exhibits and booths. If I find a good article on wireless communication in a publication, I will share it with my colleagues. Identification of strategic frontiers can encourage employees to be more proactive and committed to the company's future. This results in a strong, intangible benefit to the company.

There is one more role that strategic frontiers can play in a company—the stimulus for change. Corporations are often quite resistant to the idea of change. It frequently requires a negative event, perhaps a major crisis or flirtation with bankruptcy, before change initiatives gain momentum. Strategic frontiers represent a positive stimulus for change in a corporation. Positioned by the senior managers as a challenge for the company that could have a very positive impact on its future, the successful penetration of a strategic frontier could provide a positive catalyst for corporate change.

Imagine, for a moment, the contrast between working for a company that is aligned on its future frontiers versus one that is clueless. Figure 7-6 illustrates some points of difference.

There is a choice. An organization can choose to wander into the future, letting today's events be the guide for their decision making.

Aligned on Near-Term Goals and Strategic Frontiers	Aligned on Near-Term Goals Only
Managing today's business with an eye on tomorrow	*Managing today's business only*
Sensitive to all changes in the business environment	*Optimizing today's competitive position*
Open to future perspectives	*Open to tactical perspectives*
Aware of evolving competitive landscapes	*Fixed on current competition*
Marketshare boundaries: dynamic	*Marketshare battle: Fractions of a percent*
Leadership: future focused	*Leadership: Wall Street–focused*
Innovation time horizon: long	*Innovation time horizon: short*
Future viewed as opportunity	*Future viewed as threat*
Organization's posture: proactive	*Organization's posture: reactive*

Figure 7-6. Impact of being aligned on strategic frontiers.

Or, an organization can choose to seize the future (carpe futurum!) by defining, exploring, and capturing the business growth opportunities on their strategic frontiers. It might take a few tries to identify the "right" strategic frontier for your company. Lewis and Clark did not discover the "northwest passage" they were hoping to find. But the mistake is in not starting this process, preferring to stay in your corporate comfort zone. If you are not searching your strategic frontiers, you will lose out to those who are.

Summary

- The importance of alignment in the Discovery Process comes from an inherent tension in any strategy innovation process, where creating something new can have value to a company but can also represent potential risks.

- In this process, the Discovery team will experience "discovery drift," where they embrace a series of small changes to the company's business model that lead to a major leap over the course of the initiative. In the meantime, senior management has not made that same mental shift, resulting in different expectations of the output of the initiative.

- Agreeing on the elements of the business model that will remain fixed, on the business assumptions to be tested, and on the strategic frontier for the Discovery team to explore will help align the goals and expectations with senior management.

- A strategic frontier is that unexplored area of potential growth that lies between today's business and tomorrow's opportunities. It is believed to have growth potential for a company but requires exploration by a reconnaissance group to determine if it is true.

- Strategic frontiers span a wide spectrum of business opportunities from near-term, low-risk business ventures to breakthrough, industry-changing new businesses.

- The identification of, and agreement on, the strategic frontiers to explore is the primary goal of this Aligning Phase. If senior management has not already identified that frontier, it is the role of the Discovery team to recommend options for them to consider.

♦ To identify potential strategic frontiers, the Discovery team should utilize a variety of internal and external resources for options.

♦ In addition to creating alignment between the Discovery team and senior management for the Discovery Process, the identification of a strategic frontier can play a significant role in the company by:

   ♦ Signifying a commitment to managing the business of the future

   ♦ Playing the role of a corporate vision within established companies

   ♦ Focusing the activities and "mindshare" of employees

   ♦ Providing a stimulus for corporate change, where necessary

♦ Established companies should use the identification and exploration of new business opportunities on a strategic frontier the same way that start-up companies use a vision statement: to focus the company's energy and efforts on the pursuit of a compelling future.

Endnote

1. Chris Zook, *Profit from the Core* (Boston: Harvard Business School Press, 2001).

Chapter 8

The Discovery Process

Exploring Phase

> Many companies take their industry's conditions as given and set strategy accordingly. Value innovators don't. No matter how the rest of the industry is faring, value innovators look for blockbuster ideas and quantum leaps in value.[1]
>
> —*W. Chan Kim and Renee Mauborgne*

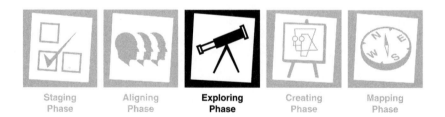

| Staging Phase | Aligning Phase | **Exploring Phase** | Creating Phase | Mapping Phase |

With strategic frontiers that align with the aspirations of senior management for this initiative, the Discovery team is ready to begin exploring those frontiers. Where do they start? Who do they talk to? What do they look for?

While the Exploring Phase is often the most intellectually stimulating, it is also the most time and energy-consuming phase of the Discovery Process. It consists of the following steps:

- ◆ Preparing to be an explorer
  - ◆ Adopting an exploratory mind-set
  - ◆ Aiming for visionary opportunities
- ◆ Planning the exploration route
  - ◆ Exploratory vectors
  - ◆ Immersions and interactions
- ◆ Selecting exploration activities
  - ◆ Customer value activities
  - ◆ Market dynamics activities
  - ◆ Business model innovation activities
- ◆ Discovering value on the frontier
  - ◆ New insights

Preparing to Be an Explorer

Former astronaut and United States senator John Glenn would qualify as a modern-day explorer and space pioneer. The first American to orbit the earth in 1962 aboard the Friendship 7 Mercury capsule, Glenn returned to space thirty-six years later, at seventy-seven years of age, to explore research on aging on a Space Shuttle Discovery mission. He told PBS, "The urge to explore the unknown is part of human nature and has led us to many of the most profound changes in our standard of living."[2] What does it take to be a good explorer in unknown areas? Glenn believes curiosity plays a key role. "This has been the real hallmark of what's made this country really good—the curiosity of how we can do things better, whether it's a door knob or a TV camera or better chairs. I hope we don't lose that curiosity."[3]

Ken Cox, a technologist and futurist at NASA's Johnson Space Center, agrees that curiosity is an important component of the exploratory mind-set of pioneers. But Cox would add a number of other requirements for those who venture into the unknown. He believes that good explorers need to be open-minded, fearless, and comfortable with ambiguity. He points out that new information discovered in the unexplored frontier does not always fit into our old ways of thinking. As a result, an important skill for the explorer is to be able to discern new patterns in the new information being collected on the frontier. It is the identification of new patterns that often leads to the thrilling "eureka" response made famous by Archimedes.

Discovery team explorers will benefit greatly in this Exploring Phase by adopting these same attributes. As you look to learn more about customers, the emerging market, and new business models, be curious, open-minded, and fearless in your pursuit. Then, recognize that it might take some time to discern the new patterns in the new information, but keep at it because the discovery can be quite thrilling.

Adopting an Exploratory Mind-Set

Just as NASA rockets need to escape the earth's gravitational field to reach new planets, the Discovery team must escape the force of "corporate gravity" in order to discover new business opportunities. Corporate gravity is an invisible force that prevents employees from venturing too far from the current business model. As managers in charge of maintaining the integrity of the company's current operations, you spend most of your working days protecting the business model from anything that would have a negative impact on those operations. As a result of many years of doing this, you develop a knee-jerk reaction to anything that does not fit the current business model. The process is quite quick—you see something new, assess its fit with the current business model, and accept or reject it based on your expectations of its fit. If it would affect your efficiency or lower your ROI, you reject it. If it requires an infrastructure change, you reject it. If you can't quantify it, you reject it. This is corporate gravity. It acts as a filter for your perspective so that only corporate-friendly observations get through.

The Discovery team must first recognize this phenomenon of corporate gravity and then take steps to escape beyond it. One way

Process Tip:

In order to see more opportunities in the Exploring Phase, adopt the role of an independent, venture-backed entrepreneur.

Corporate managers often assimilate a shared view of the marketplace that helps streamline and coordinate their efforts. For example, most agree on what comprises a good (or bad) business opportunity, how customers behave, and what it takes to get a product to market. These shared assumptions, while promoting efficiency, can prevent the discovery of innovative (break the rules) new business opportunities. In order to minimize the impact of these corporate filters, team members should look at the market through the eyes of an entrepreneur. What would an entrepreneur trying to break into this market see in this Exploring Phase?

to do this is to adopt the perspective of a start-up entrepreneur, as outlined in the Staging Phase discussion in Chapter 6. By ignoring the constraints and restrictions imposed by your current corporate business model, you are free to perceive and consider new things in this Exploring Phase. Anything can inspire a potential business opportunity to a start-up entrepreneur. That is the mindset necessary for the Discovery team in this Exploring Phase.

Another way to escape the force of corporate gravity is to ignore any information you receive that is too "comfortable" for you. When you hear someone say that they are happy with the product that your company makes, politely ignore them. Instead, focus your energies on those who find it ineffective, too expensive, or too fragile—that is where the new business opportunities are located. If people tell you that the industry is healthy and stable, challenge them. Look for surprises, exceptions to the rule, possible market dislocations, and growing markets on the very fringes of the industry. If the corporate side of you would find it irrelevant or uncomfortable, the entrepreneur side of you would embrace it as the link to a potential opportunity. Practice being a contrarian with a mission.

Being a contrarian was a favorite ploy of Bob Galvin when he was running Motorola. He admired counterintuitive thinkers, claiming that "common wisdom holds back uncommon wisdom." When Motorola had big decisions to be made, Galvin would often look for the opposite approach.

> Frequently I would listen to my very intelligent associates to see how they were thinking out an idea. If they did a good job, we would go with it. If it were a very significant decision, the opposite thinking would often be the right approach. One of the consequences is that ultimately, the position that is right is a minority position—it is new and different. Most of us are not comfortable with the new and different. It takes courage to be a minority thinker to push it through. Every major Motorola decision when I was there were initially minority positions.

Aiming for Visionary Opportunities on the Strategic Opportunity Spectrum

The strategic frontier you identify will turn out to be an area containing a wide range of new business opportunities. Some opportunities will be short-term, some longer-term. Some will have large growth potential, others will be more modest. The way the Discovery team decides to explore the strategic frontier and the amount of time and effort put into the exploration will determine the number and variety of opportunities and variations they will discover. Achieving both a breadth and a quantity of options prior to making strategic decisions is a cornerstone of this Discovery Process. To ensure that the Discovery team aims for breadth and quantity, we suggest that they target their search to cover the entire Strategic Opportunity Spectrum (SOS) within each strategic frontier.

The Strategic Opportunity Spectrum is a method of categorizing the business opportunities you discover on your strategic frontiers (see Figure 8-1). On the left end of the spectrum are those business opportunities that are closest to today's core business. We call them "visible" opportunities because you probably know about them already and may have even considered them at some point. With a few minor changes in the current business model you can achieve a new growth opportunity on this frontier.

Visible opportunities, successfully brought to market, are all around us. John Deere's extension from professional-grade agricultural tractors to riding lawnmowers for the weekend farmer wannabe was a visible opportunity for them. Reese's Peanut Butter Cups have mined their "visible" boundaries from ice cream to breakfast cereal (after the Pieces and the Sticks). Zip-Loc used to mean airtight "bags" but now, with the introduction of reusable, hard plastic containers, it means airtight "containment."

Because the changes required to the corporate business model are relatively minor, the pursuit of visible opportunities is usually shorter-term and usually lower-risk. Markets for these products or services often exist already, customers are known, and the manufacturing and distribution infrastructure may have been established. These opportunities are the low-hanging fruit, easiest to harvest for your business. However, the existence of the market and the relatively low barriers to entry in that market often make visible opportunities lower-volume opportunities also. If someone else got to that market first, they probably captured the significant share of the revenue and profit potential.

"Visible" or not, we understand that senior management of some companies will quiver at the prospect of strategically extending beyond the most incremental of business innovations. What

Figure 8-1. Strategic Opportunity Spectrum.

might be the impact on the base business? Diet colas were a visible opportunity for many years in the beverage category before a company made the leap to bring them into the fold. Remember Tab, the first commercially marketed diet cola? Coca Cola was so concerned that it might cannibalize Coke's market share that Tab's "flavor notes" were designed to not taste very good. You had to really, really want the diet benefit to tolerate the strange taste created for Tab. Of course, history has shown that the "diet innovation" of Diet Coke actually did not significantly cannibalize Coke's market share. It caused the category to greatly expand by attracting new weight-conscious consumers to the soft drink category.

On the other end of the spectrum lie the visionary opportunities. Visionary opportunities are typically based on the inspired imagination of the Discovery team. Markets, customers, and infrastructure for visionary opportunities do not currently exist, they must be imagined. We often see visionary opportunities arise in companies that are looking to fulfill a mission or cause in the marketplace. A visionary opportunity is often an "idealized" scenario of how a customer's needs can be fulfilled, based on a strongly held conviction that drives the company. Fred Smith of Federal Express dared to imagine a visionary opportunity of delivering mail overnight, and Apple's Steve Jobs imagined a computer in every home, based on his conviction of the value it would ultimately deliver. Both of these visionary company founders dared to dream of meeting customer needs in a new and unique way, even though the markets did not yet exist.

Visionary opportunities are not, however, exclusive to start-up companies. Motorola, originally a manufacturer of automobile radios, attained leadership in multiple "visionary" frontiers over the years, from televisions to wireless communications to microchips. And even though their early inventions were test-and-measurement devices, William Hewlett and David Packard committed their company to a vision of excellence in engineering that is both leading-edge and socially responsible. Because of this broad vision, Hewlett-Packard is now playing a leadership role in the once-visionary opportunities in computing, printing, and imaging industries, among others. 3M had humble beginnings as a mining venture that did not "pan out." It has been more successful replicating its innovation formula thousands of times into both "visible" and "visionary" frontiers, in industries ranging from sandpaper to pharmaceuticals.

Visionary opportunities are longer-term opportunities because they usually require the development of technologies, infrastructure, and customers that do not yet exist. From this standpoint, they also carry a higher risk compared to visible opportunities. However, visionary opportunities typically contain the possibility of *very* high rewards, both financially and psychologically, to those willing to take the risk.

The majority of new business opportunities identified in the Discovery Process lie somewhere between the two ends of the Strategic Opportunity Spectrum. They are opportunities that add value to customers in some way and require varying degrees of change and market development by the company in order to meet those needs. Opportunities in this middle range vary in the size of the market and revenue potential.

The Strategic Opportunity Spectrum is introduced here because the way the Discovery team thinks about the opportunities they will develop has a significant impact on the ultimate success of this process. Setting a goal of identifying a number of visible opportunities for your company will result in finding a few visible opportunities, but probably not much more. However, setting a goal

> **Process Tip:**
>
> *If you stretch your thinking to identify visionary opportunities, you will also identify opportunities all along the Strategic Opportunity Spectrum.*
>
> **Incremental thinking will produce, at best, incremental ideas. Stretch thinking that pursues the "big idea" in any marketplace will produce a large quantity of ideas, ranging from world-changing new industries down to incremental product improvements.**

of identifying a number of visionary opportunities will provide not only the visionary opportunities the team is looking for but also a large quantity of opportunities that fall all along the spectrum, including visible opportunities. It is the "stretch" in the thinking required by visionary opportunities that reveals the greatest quantity of new opportunities of all types (see Figure 8-2).

The *pursuit* of opportunities at the visionary end of the spectrum will establish the open-minded, anything-is-possible attitudes necessary for the team to "see" new opportunities everywhere. Often the visionary ideas they find will contain within them some element that the company can use today to improve their business. The process does not, however, work in reverse. Teams that are interested only in identifying short-term, visible opportunities close to their current core business are not likely to identify bigger, longer-term opportunities. Their desire to focus short-term prevents them from entertaining ideas that might fall to the right side of the spectrum, and they end up with a much smaller quantity of opportunities.

It does not matter whether senior management is seeking a visionary opportunity as part of their strategic portfolio or not. Even when the company will only consider developing the shorter-term, lower-risk, visible opportunities, it is important that the Discovery team aims to stretch their thinking and exploration to identify opportunities that lie on the visionary end of this spectrum.

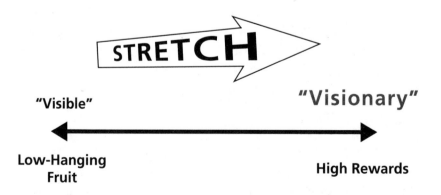

Figure 8-2. Strategic Opportunity Spectrum: Setting stretch goals.

Some visionary opportunities are slow to be recognized or are missed entirely. All the major television networks missed the dedicated news network opportunity that Ted Turner developed in CNN. IBM missed the importance of software. Microsoft was slow to recognize the Internet. Motorola possessed the capability, but failed to see the market opportunity in inkjet printing.

Planning the Exploration Route

Like most explorations, the Exploring Phase of the Discovery Process is done "away from home." To gain new perspectives and discover new ways to think about your future business, the Exploring Phase must begin with an "external" exploration. It does not begin with an understanding of what a company does well (core competencies) or what it is currently able to do—that would be a capability in search of a market. The Discovery Process is a market-centric process that *begins* with an understanding of the emerging market and its needs, and then proceeds to a search for how the company might go about meeting those needs. This is an "outside-in" process for the Discovery team.

This is not an exercise to be conducted from your cubicle with a Web browser. The Exploring Phase will require the Discovery team to travel, meet with people, see what they see, and walk in their shoes. If yours is a regional business with local clients, the travel will be less. If yours is a global company, pack your bags and grab your passport.

There is no one formula or linear sequence of steps for the Discovery team to take in this Exploring Phase. Every industry is different, and every Discovery team will differ on how and where it finally chooses to explore. But where should they start?

Mapping the Route Along Exploration Vectors

To think about a starting point for the exploration process, take a step back and think for a moment about what business is all about. Business is about creating value for someone (a customer) and, in delivering that value, creating value for yourself. So identifying new business opportunities should focus on value—what it is and how it can be delivered or enhanced.

Where do you look for that value? Consider that a business transaction takes place between a customer and a company, in a marketplace. Therefore, the search for value should include explorations of the customer (customer value), the company (business model innovation), and the marketplace (market dynamics). We describe these three areas as exploration vectors, the pathways that a Discovery team should take to understand and identify value-creating opportunities on the company's strategic frontier (see Figure 8-3).

Customer Value Vector

Businesses do not exist without customers. Customers do not purchase goods and services unless those goods and services deliver value. Therefore, a logical starting point for exploring new business opportunities is to meet with potential customers and understand their perception of value. It is the new insights gained around emerging customer needs and their perception of value that can be the basis of exciting new business opportunities. Companies that are very customer-centric, and those that aspire to be, often begin the Exploring Phase with work in the customer value area.

Market Dynamics Vector

If strategy innovation is about creating the company's future, it should not be based on today's markets, today's products, or to-

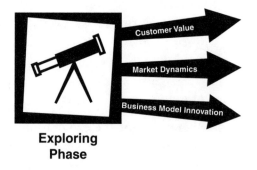

**Exploring
Phase**

Figure 8-3. Exploration vectors.

day's customers. You need to understand the world of tomorrow and use those insights to drive the strategy innovation process.

In a stable world, the markets of tomorrow look a lot like the markets of today, minimizing the value to be gained by studying the future. In a dynamic world, changes in any aspect of the marketplace can have a ripple effect through not only that market, but all other markets that touch it. When world oil prices rise, sales at the local drive-thru restaurant can fall. Studying the future and the forces that affect markets will reveal the possibilities of change. Change is a two-sided coin (pun intended). On one side, it will have a negative effect on those who are vested in the old way of doing business. On the other side, it will cause market disruption and imbalances, opening up new business opportunities for those who are prepared to participate. Therefore, we strongly recommend that the Discovery team include market foresight in their exploration plan. Companies that feel they have a core competence to leverage and are very marketplace-centric often begin with the vector of market dynamics.

Business Model Innovation Vector

Many recent examples of strategy innovation have involved changes in the traditional business model used in those markets. Furniture was expensive and sold in showrooms until IKEA designed a line of inexpensive, Scandinavian-style, assemble-it-yourself home furnishings to be sold in large retail outlets to young buyers. Southwest Airlines rejected the standard hub-and-spoke system of air travel and concentrated on low-cost, local, point-to-point travel. A Belgian movie theater owner defied the industry logic of multiple-screen econo-boxes and built a hugely successful megaplex consisting of twenty-five screens and over 7,000 luxury seats. New business opportunities can come from old businesses, where changes in the traditional ways of doing business results in greater customer value and growth for the company.

This was the case with Cemex, an international cement company located in Mexico. They developed a sophisticated communications network and a strategically placed distribution system to be able to offer their customers on-demand cement delivery, within twenty minutes of the contractor's call. In his book *Value Migration: How to Think Several Moves Ahead of the Competition*, Adrian Slywotzky writes, "Value migrates from outmoded business designs to ones that are better able to satisfy customers' most important priorities."[4]

We recommend that you spend some exploration time examining the potential for new growth that comes from changing elements of your current business model. Companies that recognize their need to change or feel that the creation of new businesses is one of their core competences are often those who first explore business model innovation.

Setting Up New Activities

It is likely that your company has spent some time exploring customers, markets, and business models in the past, such as interviews or focus groups with your customers. In the Staging Phase, we mentioned that it is valuable to review old research to provide everyone on the team with an understanding of today's core business. However, *do not* use any previous work for the Exploring Phase. The reason is that the previous work was probably done to provide information for a specific reason, usually to support some aspect of the current business. For example, you may have used previous focus groups with current customers to test their reaction to a new line extension or new promotional materials. Chances are good that you talked to the types of customers you usually talk to and asked them some standard questions in order to get that information. This process was helpful for the core business at that time but it won't help you identify new business opportunities. The goal of strategy innovation on the frontier is to discover *new ways* of doing business. You cannot ask the same people the same questions and expect to learn something new. Instead, the Discovery team should concentrate their efforts on setting up new activities designed specifically for this initiative. Create new and unique events where you ask different questions of the same people, the

Process Tip:

To see things differently, you need to do things differently.

There are probably very good reasons why you take the same route to commute to work every day. However, if you ever get tired of the same old scenery, you won't be satisfied until you change your route. Looking for new business opportunities in the same places you have always found them will produce the same types of opportunities you have always found. To innovate, look elsewhere. Try different approaches.

same questions of different people, or different questions of different people.

The Discovery team should consider less conventional ways of doing their explorations in the Discovery Process. If the normal process for interacting with your customers is to watch a discussion from the other side of a one-way mirror in a focus group facility, consider meeting with customers on their turf—in their homes or in their offices. Or "immerse" yourself in their lives—follow them around for a day or night, to learn about their lifestyle, their needs, and the factors that influence them. By approaching them in different ways and/or asking them different questions, you'll gain new insights that could lead to exciting new business opportunities.

There are many marketing research and consulting companies that offer unique ways of exploring customers and the marketplace in search of insights for new business opportunities. The appropriateness of a technique will depend on the industry in which you work as well as the quality and experience of the company offering the technique. Searching books, journals, and Internet sites, as well as networking with colleagues, are the best ways to identify these exploratory techniques.

As an additional corporate benefit, this "fresh" look at customers, markets, and business models causes organizations to have new perspectives on their existing customers, markets, and business models. As a consequence of the Discovery Process, there is an infusion of "fresh thinking" into an enterprise for current, as well as future, growth. This is often a catalyst to an increased vitality felt throughout the organization and confidence about its prospects for the future. We have observed this even in organizations that specialize in visionary or innovation services. Become too static, and your products and your organization become "stale." Instead, challenge yourself to see new things in new ways, and the whole organization benefits from an infusion of fresh perspective.

The Goal: Identify Insights to the Creation of Value

Regardless of which activities the Discovery team uses in the Exploring Phase, the goal for all activities is to identify anything that could *create or enhance value.* In the customer value vector, it is learning what customers value, what is important to them and could cause them to take action. In the market dynamics vector, it is learning how the market will likely evolve and what technologies, market shifts, or emerging environments will create needs that will have value to those who are prepared for it. In the business model innovations vector, it is learning how new ways of configuring your business model can create greater value for both you and your customers (see Figure 8-4).

The identification of current, underlying, or emerging value is a good way to state the goal of the Exploring Phase. However, people do not usually talk directly about what has value to them or what would create value in the marketplace. When people behave or act

Vector	Focus
1. Customer Value	*Customer Needs*
2. Market Dynamics	*Emerging Marketplace (foresight)*
3. Business Model Innovation	*Company Structure/Processes*

Figure 8-4. Discovery Process exploration vectors.

in a certain way, they are often not aware of the values that cause them to act—they just act. And when you ask them why, sometimes they cannot articulate why. Therefore, it is often the goal of the Discovery team in these explorations to identify "hidden value." The Discovery team must become "detectives" to find evidence or clues in what they hear and see that could point to a cache of hidden value.

The Discovery team must focus on generating a large quantity of "insights" during the Exploring Phase. Insights are any new understandings about customers, market dynamics, or business models that could reflect some hidden value. When team members learn something new that *could* have some value potential, they should write it down as a new insight gained. It is *not* important that team members clearly know what that value potential is, how it could be delivered, or whether it would be worth pursuing. At the time they hear it, they should capture it as something that is new and different and has the *potential* for some value.

Team members should fight the urge to derive implications and conclusions from the insights gained. In their book *Radical Innovation*, authors Richard Leifer and colleagues speak to this issue:

> Ideas evolve, and they don't always evolve in predictable ways. Psychologists call the activities associated with idea development "loose associative thinking" processes. Associative logic is not sequential. It's jumpy. For a time, the maintenance of uncertainty is important. Closure is a killer, it strangles associative thinking in favor of arriving at "an answer." Early in the process, leveraging uncertainty, riding it, and valuing it are critical to developing robust ideas.[5]

The goal of the Exploring Phase is to generate a very long list of insights. Generating a large *quantity* of insights will result in more high *quality* insights, which are more likely to inspire innovative ideas.

Selecting the Exploration Activities

For each frontier being explored, your Discovery team will want to consider creating one or more activities in each of the three exploration vectors as a way to gain new insights. Setting up a worksheet, such as the one depicted in Figure 8-5, will help start the planning of the exploration activities.

This section is designed to share some of the techniques we have used with teams in previous initiatives. See Figure 8-6 for an overview of those techniques. It is by no means a complete listing of what is possible to do in the search for new insights! However, it may suggest ways in which your team can create its own exploration activities that fit your industry.

Process Tip:

Savor the insights you find and fight the urge to jump to product conclusions.

On hearing a customer express a need, just note the need they have. That is the insight. We all have a mental tendency to jump immediately to what product might fulfill that need, how large the market might be for that product, and whether our company would be interested in that market. All of that thinking happens within milliseconds, resulting in an unjustified judgment concerning the value of that insight. Fight the urge to assume, assess, and conclude—just focus on the insight. A month from now you might find a unique way to address that need.

Exploration Vectors

	Customer Value	Market Dynamics	Business Model Innovation
Strategic Frontier A			
Strategic Frontier B			

Figure 8-5. Exploration activities worksheet.

Exploratory Vectors

	Customer Value	Market Dynamics	Business Model Innovation
Interactions	ValueProbes Specialists	Thought leader panels	Benchmark calls Thought leader panels
Immersions	Safaris Lifestyle experiences Stake-outs	Experiments Conferences Guided journeys	Benchmark visits

Figure 8-6. Examples of Exploring Phase activities.

Interactions and Immersions

For each of the exploratory vectors, divide the exploratory activities into interactions and immersions. Think of interactions as "events" that are set up for the exchange of information. Any type of interview or meeting would be an interaction. If the Discovery team sets up group discussions with customers, interviews with marketplace experts, or telephone discussions with people in other companies to discuss their business model, think of them as *interacting* with others. Interactions are fairly standard means of gathering information and are very appropriate for this Exploring Phase. Interactions can be creatively tailored to produce either routine, baseline information in an unfamiliar area or advanced knowledge in a familiar one, determined by the Discovery team's needs in the Exploring Phase.

Another method of gathering insights to the exploratory vectors is for team members to "immerse" themselves in an environment of interest. Immersions allow the Discovery team to make *observations* in the various challenge areas, which can reveal insights or information that customers would not mention in a typical interaction. Instead of setting up a meeting with customers, an immersion might consist of spending a day with a customer, observing the customer in his/her own environment. In such a customer immersion, for example, team members might notice that the customer is working in a crowded office situation. Your company's product is seen buried under stacks of paper and is not easily accessible to the customer. This observation could lead to a redesign of your product line to minimize the product's "footprint," or perhaps introduce wireless remote access so that the product can be used more easily even when hidden behind stacks of paper. These are things that customers might not think to mention in a typical customer interaction (such as interviews or focus groups) but that can be identified in a customer immersion.

Customer Value Vector Activities

There will be a tendency on the part of the Discovery team to consider the current customers to be the customers of the future. This is one of the underlying assumptions of businesses that have been following a strategy of incremental improvements every year. It makes up part of the "corporate gravity" described earlier in this chapter.

Who Is the Customer of the Future?

Strategy innovation invites teams to question who the customer of the future is. Current customers remain an option but so are others. Perhaps there is an opportunity to sell your product to an underserved population, such as college students or customers in other countries. Perhaps there is an opportunity to turn nonusers of a product into users. Perhaps there is an opportunity to grow a small, niche market at the periphery of the business into a larger, more mainstream market. Spend time thinking about who on your strategic frontier represents a potential customer and be sure to include them in this Exploring Phase.

Unarticulated Needs: The Holy Grail of Consumer Value

It seems as if it should be an easy process to identify new business opportunities. Just go to customers, ask them what they want, and give them what they ask for. There are some industries where this approach can still be effective. Talking to customers will almost always yield important information that can be used to help enhance a company's business in some way.

However, customer interactions frequently lead to changes that are more incremental in nature, not innovative. The reason for this is that customers have a relatively narrow frame of reference, based primarily on what they have experienced in the past. They can usually tell you what they like and do not like about your current product and how that compares to other products they have experienced. They will tell you they want the buttons on your product to be a little larger and easier to push. This will lead to some incremental product improvements for your next "new and improved model" but will usually not lead you to the new business platform that will drive company growth in the future. Terry Tallis, a former business manager with H-P, makes a similar point using the example of a Siberian ditch digger. If you talk to the ditch digger and ask him what products can improve his work, he will not likely mention a heavy-duty, diesel-powered, hydraulic-lift backhoe—because all he has ever known is a shovel.

Most customers are also more reactive than proactive. Show them a new product you have designed and they will react to it, giving you helpful feedback. However, they are unable to *speculate* on what innovative new products or services will better suit their needs than today's products. There is a tendency for people to want to ask customers to describe their "ideal" product. Again, that is a speculative exercise that might provide some incremental product improvements but seldom innovations. They will not be able to tell you, for example, that they want artificial intelligence built into your product so that it will adjust its performance as it is taken into different usage environments. You will have to figure that out for yourself. They will also not be able to tell you what products or services are *missing* from their lives, waiting for a company to invent them and make them wildly happy. In short, you cannot rely on customers to tell you what innovative products or services they would like to see created that will meet their needs. They will not design innovative new products for you.

Because most customers cannot describe the next-generation products you are looking to develop, the holy grail of the customer value vector is understanding their "unarticulated needs." What product or service would customers find valuable but, because they are not able to proactively describe it, remains unarticulated in most customer interviews? It is clear from sales figures over the past decades that customers have a need for a Sony Walkman, a Dodge Caravan, or a Starbucks grande latte. However, it is highly unlikely that, prior to their introductions, customers would have said they needed a portable stereo, minivan, or espresso with steamed milk. If companies are able to discern these unarticulated needs of customers, they can create significant new business opportunities.

Because of the importance of unarticulated needs to the creation of innovative products and services, it is worthwhile considering what they are and how they might be discerned. An unarticulated need can be considered something that has *value* to a customer. The early purchasers of a Sony Walkman were probably people who valued listening to good music. Prior to the Walkman, they accepted the fact that good, stereophonic music had to come from large components that took up a considerable amount of shelf space in the den. As a result, they planned their quality music experiences around being stationary in the den, where the stereo was located. That is the way things were in those days, and music lovers were satisfied with that arrangement because alternatives did not exist. They did not know any better; they did not have any idea of what was becoming possible with electronics. However, there was also something else that these customers valued—being mobile. If you had a traditional focus group on stereo music back in those days, chances are that customers would not have thought to mention their interest in going places and being mobile in their lives. After all, this was a focus group on stereo music, which had nothing to do with mobility in their lives. Therefore, the need for mobility would have remained unarticulated in that research venue. Had it been revealed in a discussion session, observers would have noted that the value of good music was in conflict with another value of customers, that of being mobile. This insight would have identified a conflict, which, if addressed, would have created greater value for the customer. Addressing this unarticulated need for mobility while listening to quality music created a new industry of the portable stereo (see Figure 8-7).

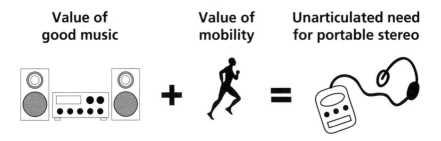

Value of   **Value of**   **Unarticulated need**
good music   **mobility**   **for portable stereo**

Figure 8-7. Unarticulated needs.

To identify unarticulated needs of customers, it is important to pursue an understanding of what they value. This pursuit of value must not be limited to current products or markets, as people tend to accept products and markets as they are, not speculate on how they can be. Finding new ways to explore customer values should be the focus of your exploratory efforts with customers.

Large-scale quantitative surveys of customers will *not* produce valuable insights into unarticulated customer needs. A survey is designed to get everyone to answer the same questions into precategorized answers, with little or no flexibility of responses allowed. It is often the exceptions to the questions or the subtle nuances of responses that can contain new insights that are so valuable for new business development. Quantitative surveys will not provide these new insights, but they do play an important role in the Creating and Mapping Phases, when metrics are required to evaluate the market opportunities and plan their implementation. The search for customer insights in the Exploring Phase should be personal, face-to-face encounters with customers.

Customer Value Vector: Interactions

The Discovery team should consider staging interactions with customers. The forms the interactions take can be traditional forms, perhaps one-on-one interviews, or group interviews, such as found in a focus group format. However, if you want to find new insights into customer needs and values, make sure that the line of questioning in those interactions is very nontraditional. Rather than just asking customers to react to current products and services in a market, extend the scope of the discussion to include an exploration of *what they value*. For example, if your business consists of selling widgets to small companies, don't spend time discussing only the widget market, the widget pricing, and widget delivery times. Also explore that customer's current business environment, how it is changing over time, and what they hope to do about it. Learning about the customer's customers, recent horror stories they have experienced, company priorities, and aspirations for the future all provide a valuable understanding of the context in which widget decisions are made. This broader line of questioning provides insights into what that customer values, helping you to see how you might redefine your widget business to provide greater value to your customers than it does now. That is the ultimate goal of the Discovery team—to redefine your business to provide the customer with greater value than you are now.

ValueProbes

One type of customer interaction we call ValueProbes (see Figure 8-8). They are discussion sessions aimed at exploring customer perception of what is valuable to them, to help them to articulate some of their unarticulated needs. By using a less traditional line of questioning or special, creative techniques, customers will articulate some of their previously unarticulated needs or opinions they might be reticent to express in a traditional interview setting. The key is to ask a different set of questions or use different techniques—not straight Q&A. There are many different techniques that can be used to foster these discussions, such as projective techniques, storytelling, role-playing, and photo-taking. When asked to express themselves in different ways from what they are used to doing, customers will sometimes reveal information that would

Exploratory Vectors

	Customer Value	Market Dynamics	Business Model Innovation
Interactions	ValueProbes Specialists		
Immersions			

Figure 8-8. Exploring Phase activities: Customer value interactions.

otherwise remain unconsidered and unspoken in the standard interview format.

In our work in the customer value vector, we have successfully used a technique of drawing combined with metaphors. For example, we have asked business customers to draw their company as a vehicle of some type, noting its important features that cause it to be better or worse than the "vehicles" of its competitors. We have seen organizations identify significant competitive weaknesses or threats, new target markets, the importance of new technologies, or ways to take advantage of a discontinuity using this indirect, creative technique. In any situation it can be helpful to know what, metaphorically, is an organization's steering wheel, its accelerator, its brakes, its power source, or its hood ornament. What is the road ahead like—a washboard surface of a dirt road or the smooth-banked turns of an autobahn? Are there any obstacles in the road? What is the weather like and what might it be like in the future? We have seen organizations, using this technique, depict themselves as Ferraris and, in one instance, a "parked Model T." How do you think today's customers would describe your organization using this vehicle metaphor? How would you like them to describe your company in the future? These nontraditional questioning techniques cause participants to think in new ways, often revealing new insights and values/needs that had previously been unarticulated.

Another tip for the identification of "hidden value" with customers is to zero in on the *emotions* that accompany their words. If you think about it, our emotions often reflect some underlying value that we have. If I am angry or frustrated when I describe using your product, it is probably because I value something different from what you are providing. If I am effusive in my praise of your product, it is because you have exceeded my expectations and delivered more value to me than others have ever done. If my emotions result from the difference between what I have and what I want, then they reflect what I value. Therefore, if you want to learn what is important to me, follow the trail of my emotions. Listen for my expressions of joy, anger, surprise, fear, excitement, and disappointment. Underneath may be a value that I have not articulated before.

One example of an exercise we have successfully used to identify emotions is to have customers draw their "emotional EKG" during a certain activity. For example, if your business is a restaurant, ask customers to reflect on a recent experience in your restaurant on a moment-by-moment basis. Have customers start from the moment they decided to go to the restaurant and continue to the moment they arrived back home again. Thinking about the emotional highs and lows of that experience, ask customers to represent those feelings as if they were generating a readout of their EKG. Then ask them to describe the output. What was your feeling when you decided to go to the restaurant? What caused the blip up when you first entered the front door? Why did your emotions dive when you were seated? The re-creation of this experience, using the emotional EKG metaphor, is a good way for customers to express their opinions and underlying values (see Figure 8-9).

Traditional focus groups spend a significant amount of time discussing *products* with customers, probing how they are used, likes and dislikes, and possible improvements. In a ValueProbe discussion, consider exploring the *environment* in which a product is used rather than the product itself. For example, let's say you sold sewing machines. Instead of asking customers about their sewing ma-

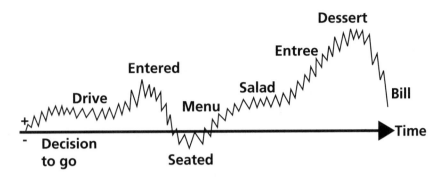

Figure 8-9. Emotional EKG: Restaurant visit.

chines, ask them about the act of sewing and the environment in which they do their sewing. Why do they sew? What role does sewing play in their lives? What are the "rewards" they get for sewing? When they think about sewing, what comes to mind? Where and when do they do most of their sewing? Where and when would they prefer to do their sewing? What do they aspire to sew some day? What is frustrating about the sewing process? What do they currently have to give up or sacrifice in order to sew? What are the most thrilling or magical moments in sewing? What would they put into their Sewing Hall of Fame? Questions like these help reveal the emotions and underlying values that surround the use of a product. That is the value to be gained by talking to customers, because they are the only ones who can talk about those values. Don't ask them to design a new sewing machine for you. But find out what problems, frustrations, or unfulfilled wishes they have, and then design the product or service that meets those needs and delivers them value. It is up to the Discovery team to connect the insights gained from customers to product or service features that will provide a new benefit or value.

Specialists

A second interactive approach in the customer value vector is the use of specialists. Instead of conducting these discussions yourself or with a trained facilitator, hire a specialist trained in a particular discipline to run them. A good psychologist or behaviorist leading these discussions, for example, can provide interesting new insights into how customers perceive a situation, why they act, or where and how they find value. In some work we did for a suitcase manufacturer, a psychologist revealed a series of customer needs around anxieties that customers encountered while traveling. With innovative products designed to allay these anxieties, customers perceived greater value in them.

The Periscope team from Moen successfully used a specialist interaction in their Exploring Phase. As described in Chapter 5, they had an anthropologist visit a number of people in their homes and observe the ways in which water was used and how it was valued by people. The anthropologist explored various uses of water in the home and some of the underlying symbolism and meaning of these acts. According to Dan Buchner, "What came out was fascinating. It opened people's minds and helped spotlight some myths we believed in terms of water use. We found that people really didn't care about things we thought they cared about."

Customer interactions can provide new insights to the perception of value if the questioning process employs new approaches or techniques. The techniques should be aimed at exploring customer value in new ways, attempting to get them to articulate what otherwise, using more conventional techniques, would probably remain unarticulated.

Customer Value Vector: Immersions

Whereas customer interactions typically rely on *discussions with* customers, immersions rely more on *observations of* customers. Immersions become a critically important component of the Discovery Process when the Discovery team agrees that innovative new business opportunities will likely be based on customers' unarticulated needs. Observations do not attempt to get customers to articulate their unarticulated needs. By entering the environment of your customers, you will *see* the context in which customers make their decisions and exercise their values. You walk in their shoes, see with their eyes. With these observations, you can better understand their needs and what could comprise value to them in new products and services (see Figure 8-10).

Maureen Wenmoth, director of marketing services at Moen, described how the Periscope project helped them focus more on observational research. "Now, when people come to me saying they want to do focus groups, we tell them we don't do that anymore." Instead, Moen sets up "real life laboratories where we can understand how people live and what they do." Video cameras set up in the homes of customers provide digital observations of people using Moen products in real-life, at-home situations. These tapes are then coded for the activities portrayed on the tape, such as hand-washing, use of the sink sprayer, or double-showering. When a team at Moen begins the development of a new product, they have instant access to videos of in-home use situations, which provides actual customer usage information that can help drive the creation of new and innovative product designs.

Safaris

The growing field of observational research is sometimes referred to as "ethnography," a term first used to describe a research method in the field of cultural anthropology. It refers to observing subjects in their own environments and attempting to understand

Exploratory Vectors

	Customer Value	Market Dynamics	Business Model Innovation
Interactions			
Immersions	Safaris Lifestyle experiences Stake-outs		

Figure 8-10. Exploring Phase activities: Customer value immersions.

their perceptual frameworks in order to understand their behavior. In its most basic form, the Discovery team could arrange to do ethnographic research via customer visits. Customer visits, which we often call "safaris," provide a more intimate understanding of customers than focus groups or interviews because they reveal insights of both the customers and their environments. Safaris also eliminate other problems typically encountered in traditional focus group discussions, such as customers forgetting (or overlooking) things or being embarrassed to mention something with other customers in the room.

When you sell to consumer households, it means setting up safaris to the homes of your customers. There are many market research companies that can set those visits up for you. Plan ahead what you hope to observe in these visits. Watch carefully how customers use (or misuse) your product. Note where it is stored. See what other products they are using in conjunction with yours. What can you learn about your customers from observing where and how they live? Can you get an idea of what is important to them? Can you determine what they value? As Yogi Berra is purported to have said, "You can observe a lot just by watching."

If your product is sold to other businesses, the Discovery team should arrange to visit customers in those business locations. Ask for a tour to see how your products are being used. Similar to home visits, note where the products in a business setting are being used, how they are stored, how they are tracked, when and how they are reordered. Also note the operating environment, the context in which the product is used. What is the space like? How many people are sharing the product? Have they made any adjustments to the product to make it work or fit better? Are your competitors' products there also? Are other products combined with yours to enhance performance?

When doing customer safaris, be sure to ask about things you find unusual or intriguing. It is like the story of the woman who cut the end off a pot roast before cooking it. When asked why she did it, she said that was the way her mother and grandmother before her had always cooked pot roast. A check with her grandmother revealed that she cut the end off because the cooking pan she had when she first got married was too small to hold an entire pot roast. In spite of changing conditions, some behaviors stay the same. Therefore, it is important to find out what drives behavior—a need, a perception, or a merely a habit carried over from the past.

Lifestyle Experiences

A second type of customer immersion is a lifestyle experience. Rather than visit the customer in one specific environment, observers "live" with their customers over the course of a day (or more). Go where they go, do what they do. Understand their world, what drives them, how they make decisions, what they value, how they are influenced. Ford Motor Company executives and designers visited malls, nightclubs, and other hangouts of young adults to understand their lifestyles and their needs in the design of their Focus model. Harley Davidson executives take to the road each summer to attend motorcycle rallies and spend time listening to their customers in their world.

Stake-Outs

A third type of immersion experience that the Discovery team should consider is what we refer to as "stake-outs." According to the strategic frontier you are exploring, identify where you can observe people using, considering, or buying products of interest to you. If your product is sold at retail, consider a stake-out in the store. Hang out in the store aisle and watch as people make their purchase decisions. Or, there are companies that will set up cameras in cooperating stores so that you can videotape this purchase-decision activity over a longer period of time. Better yet, see if you can work in a store for a week to gain a greater understanding of your customers and their shopping experiences.

Another stake-out option is to spend time observing your product being used in a public setting. For example, executives from a Honda U.S. design team spent time in the parking lot of Disneyland watching families there unload and load their vehicles. After watching people lift heavy cargo into the trunks of their cars, Honda redesigned their trunk so that it was lower and easier to load.[6]

A relatively new way to "observe" customer behavior is a stakeout via the Internet. People interact on the Internet, share opinions, and express their values there. You can have each member of the Discovery team log on to bulletin boards or take part in online chats. What is the focus of the discussions that you hear? Do people online have different perspectives about your product category? What can you learn from their complaints? We recently ran across a company that has developed software to monitor discussions about various product categories in chatrooms and bulletin boards on the Internet. The software will categorize the nature of those discussions and provide insights to trends, questions, and problems that are being discussed.

Customer immersion experiences will provide more of a "real-life" understanding of customers than interactive experiences will typically provide. However, the immersions tend to be more complex and time-consuming to implement than more standard interactions. The Discovery team must decide what mix of interactions and immersions with customers are likely to reveal the types of insights that will drive the creation of new business opportunities on your strategic frontiers.

Market Dynamics Vector Activities

The future cannot be predicted with a high degree of accuracy. There are always unforeseen forces that create "discontinuities" in the marketplace, causing current trends to accelerate or decelerate from expectations. However, there is tremendous value to be gained by understanding the forces that exist and that are likely to have an impact on the market.

In Search of Foresight

Bob Galvin, former CEO of Motorola, tells of learning the importance of anticipating the market from his father, the company's founder. "In the late 1930s, my father went to Germany and could tell that at some point we would be going to war. You didn't have to be a genius to see that something was going to happen. We knew something was going to happen, and we did something about it." What they did was develop some wireless technologies for the Army's Signal Corps. Even though the Army did not purchase their product initially, it gave Motorola a technology they would apply in World War II and quite profitably in future years. Galvin added, "A lot of the future is observable or guessable, but will anybody do anything about it? It takes the application of resources to make it happen—that is strategy."

Moen was also interested in market foresight. Tim O'Brien, vice president of technical innovation at Moen, explained that the Periscope team in their Exploring Phase was interested in determining which forces were likely to have the greatest impact on their market as it evolved to the future. Also of interest were the possible discontinuities, as being aware of them would help them in their planning process. O'Brien noted, "We need to make our boat watertight in case of future storms or hurricanes, even though we can't predict when they will actually happen." Recall that one of the potential dislocations identified by Moen in their Exploring Phase work (back in 1995) was the possibility of terrorists poisoning municipal water supplies. That predicted possibility has taken on new importance in the past few years.

Another company that has embraced the power of foresight in the creation of strategy is 3M. In the mid-1990s, they created the company's first corporate foresight division. In a recent interview with William Coyne, former senior vice president of R&D at 3M, he said, "We now have three people to do corporate foresight—not looking at today but just focused on the future and trends in technology, consumers, and geography. They then look at the business plans and find the disconnects with the future."

By market foresight, we mean gaining a better understanding of the emerging marketplace, your market of the future. What factors will likely drive its growth? How could technology change the dynamics of the market? How might globalization represent both an opportunity and a threat to your company's future? What impact will demographics have on usage and purchasing patterns? What new scientific discoveries are on the horizon? To make future plans without understanding the potential context of the emerging market is a risk to a company's financial health, and perhaps its survival.

Market Dynamics Vector: Interactions

Of all the market foresight work we have done for clients over the years, none has been more effective than a market interaction process we call thought leader panels (TLP).

Thought Leader Panels

These two-to-three-day meetings provide a very rich understanding of the evolving marketplace from a panel of "experts" recruited from a variety of different disciplines. The variety of their future views and the reconciling of their differences create among observers a shared understanding and appreciation of future forces and possible discontinuities. What emerges from this exercise is a proprietary view of the future that is shared by all in attendance, typically the Discovery team, the Extended Discovery team, and other senior management executives (see Figure 8-11).

In the case of Moen as outlined in Chapter 5, the Periscope team

Exploratory Vectors

	Customer Value	Market Dynamics	Business Model Innovation
Interactions		Thought leader panels	
Immersions			

Figure 8-11. Exploring Phase activities: Market dynamics interactions.

conducted two thought leader panels as part of their Exploring Phase. As Dan Buchner recalled:

> The thought leader panels worked well. We did two of them—one a high-level group and one more focused on implementation issues. We really needed the high-level view, the context in which we existed. We were a very tactically oriented company, and some people thought they would "put up with" the first (higher-level) panel in order to get to the more tactical one. However, we learned a lot from the first panel that caused us to change some of our thinking.

One of the important discoveries in this first panel was an understanding that the faucet business was undergoing a fundamental change in the 1990s, requiring Moen to reconsider its overall strategy. Buchner explained, "The thought leader panel allowed an open dialogue to take place around this issue. We explored the changes going on and discussed the myths that existed in our company with people who were outside our company. We agreed that these thought leaders were experts in the field so we had to listen to them. It allowed people to ask the hard questions and then believe what they heard. It wasn't about politics anymore, it was about a group making decisions together."

To conduct a thought leader panel, it is important that the Discovery team first identify the topics from the strategic frontier they feel are important to explore and understand in more detail. Topics usually consist of those areas that might have an impact on the development of future markets on the strategic frontier. Although every panel will differ, based on the issues within each industry, some common industry-wide topics frequently emerge, including technology, demographics, environmentalism, globalization, government regulation, retailing trends, and materials science. Panel topics can also focus on company issues related to the future, including marketing strategies, infrastructure expansion, technology development, retail channels, and human resource development. An ideal number of topics for a TLP would be five or six.

Once those topics have been identified, the next step is to recruit "experts" to represent each topic. Often, members of the Discovery team have some idea of who might be a good candidate to speak to the future of that topic. If not, searching books, periodicals, the Internet, and networking are the best ways to identify candidates. Telephone discussions with the candidates will reveal their qualifications and interest in participating. Other thought leaders could include demographers, magazine writers/editors, newsletter publishers, general futurists, representatives from similar companies in different industries, people who formerly held key positions, academics, authors, corporate leaders, psychologists, cultural anthropologists, Wall Street analysts, and government officials.

Don't be afraid to invite a "wild card" expert to your panel. A wild card expert is someone who has a perspective or skill set that is only indirectly related to your business but could help stimulate ideas. We have used a science fiction writer to help think about future scenarios, a database developer to help conceive of new market segmentation approaches, and an artist to help make intangible ideas visible. Another approach to consider is to invite someone who has "learned from experience." In one thought leader panel, a representative from a major company that had recently gone bankrupt provided very valuable insights into what a company should not do.

Experts from within your own industry should be used with extreme caution. They frequently work under the same assumptions and business model constraints as you do, restricting their abilities to conceive of new and innovative ways to create value in that industry. If you must include an industry expert, invite one who is focused on the future, has a good "big picture" perspective, or understands a part of the business that you do not.

Thought leaders should be asked to play the role of "provocateur" in the TLPs, not a consultant role. A consultant will sift through the possibilities of the future and, based on an understanding of the company's needs, offer the most appropriate "answer"

Process Tip:

No expert can adequately define a proprietary future for your company.

Your company is a unique blend of people, processes, culture, and spirit. No matter how knowledgeable they are, thought leaders or anyone else outside your company should not determine the future of your organization. Gather all the best insights you can from others but be sure that your future has been created by people inside your company. This makes it a proprietary future, one owned by your company because it reflects your interests, skills, values, and vision.

for a client. Thought leader panels are different. They focus more on creating the long list of possibilities for the future, not just a few answers that someone else feels is most appropriate for your company. In the language of the creative process, it is a "divergent" exercise aimed at exploring lots of options and possibilities. Toward the end of the panel, the Discovery team and Extended Discovery team will work to synthesize the list and identify the proprietary future that is most attractive to the company.

The thought leaders are asked to share their views of the evolving future in their areas of expertise, highlighting important trends and discontinuities that are possible. Subsequent interactions between the thought leaders usually reveal a deeper level of understanding about the future and the interaction of forces that could create it. Then sharing specific company issues with the thought leaders provides an opportunity for both thought leaders and company participants to imagine a future customized to the interests of the company. It is then up to the members of the Discovery team and the Extended Discovery team to craft a proprietary company future from the combined input and interactions of all of the thought leaders in the panel.

The proprietary future that emerges from a market interaction such as a thought leader panel is a powerful means to gain management alignment around the future. The outside expertise of the thought leaders provides a credible, objective, external view of the topics of interest on the strategic frontier. Attendees learn and react together to future possibilities, creating a common framework for internal strategic discussions. Bob LaPerle, a former director of business planning in the photographic products group at Kodak, observed, "The team members sitting with the experts and writing scenarios was very interesting and helpful to us. We had never done detailed scenarios before. They were plausible and had enough substance for new product generation. It was definitely a landmark event for the company."

At Moen, management decisions on the development of new products in the early 1990s were frequently based on personal opinions and available resources in the necessary departments. The thought leader panel's work with the Periscope project revealed a future where "water filtration" would be an important strategic frontier for Moen to consider. After that TLP, management decisions on new products shifted to this common framework. Said Tim O'Brien, "After Periscope, there was agreement on the trends so we needed to make decisions on products that were consistent with the trends. No longer could you put projects on the back burner for no good reason. If you wanted to cancel a product, you had to argue why that view of the future was no longer something worth believing in. The future became an arbiter and guide for our decisions."

Market Dynamics Vector: Immersions

Understanding the marketplace and its possible evolution can also be done with an immersion exercise. These immersions can take the form of "experiments" in the market, which are then monitored for their impact (see Figure 8-12).

Experiments

Immersion into a marketplace to understand its dynamics is more complex than many of the other processes outlined in this section.

Exploratory Vectors

	Customer Value	Market Dynamics	Business Model Innovation
Interactions			
Immersions		Experiments Conferences Guided journeys	

Figure 8-12. Exploring Phase activities: Market dynamics immersions.

The Discovery team needs to spend time at those places where the market is in action. For companies whose products are sold at retail, it may mean setting up your own retail experiment. If you are in the apparel industry, purchase or set up your own clothing store. Then experiment with leading-edge programs: new products, new methods of merchandising, new technology, new store layouts, and new marketing programs. Staff the store with people who are very customer-friendly and learn as much as you can about customers and their needs (customer immersion also). What you can learn from this experiment are valuable insights as to what the future may hold for that industry.

There are prototype stores in Japan called antenna shops that serve a similar experimental immersion function. Companies that manufacture products will open antenna shops to show prototypes of new, innovative products currently in development. Product design and marketing personnel interact with customers and learn their reactions to the prototypes before they go into production. Antenna shops provide customer insights on product innovations in the marketplace.

Conferences

Another immersion method to generate market foresight would be for the Discovery team to attend a variety of conferences on the topics of interest. If the conference has a future orientation to it, attendees can learn how that topic might evolve over time, key factors in that evolution, and the organizations that will play critical roles in that future.

Conferences require less of a cost and time commitment for the Discovery team than other methods of market foresight. However, the insights gained from conference attendance are generally fewer and less customized than the other methods mentioned here.

Guided Journeys

Guided journeys are useful when a Discovery team desires fast learning in a focused area of potential opportunity. The technique requires defining the area of opportunity as tightly as possible. Then a "guide," from inside or outside the company, is recruited to design and lead an immersion experience whereby the Discovery team experiences the key current problems, challenges, and forces that are likely to influence how the future of that area might unfold. On the basis of this experience, the team then speculates on what the emerging opportunities might be in that area. The experience can then be debriefed in the presence of "experts" who can affirm or challenge the learnings and insights.

One European company was interested in exploring the U.S. market for home security. Their team decided on a guided journey to gather market insights and spent a day touring residences in New York City. In the morning the team was led by a "beat cop" from Times Square, who directed them through the different boroughs of the city. From the Upper East Side to Harlem, the Discovery team saw examples of how New York City homeowners were at risk and, from a policeman's perspective, the simple steps that might be taken to reduce that risk. The afternoon was spent at New York City Police Headquarters, hearing firsthand from some of the department leaders what they considered to be the current and emerging threats to residents of the "Big Apple."

The Discovery team spent the next half-day debriefing its new learnings, surprises, and insights from their Guided Journey. They then used these insights as catalysts to generate innovative new opportunities for the home security market. The Discovery team then went on to explore several other frontiers in a similar fashion.

Business Model Innovation Vector Activities

The third exploratory vector for the Discovery team to consider including in the Exploring Phase is business model innovations. As mentioned previously, there are many examples in the business press about companies that have identified innovative new ways to conduct business in an established market. For example, Dell Computer pioneered a new business model in the established category of personal computers, serving as an example of the power of strategy innovation at the business model level. Instead of producing a line of computers for sale in a retail store, Michael Dell chose to offer custom-designed computers via the Internet. He then configured the rest of his business model to minimize the supply of parts on hand, the turnaround time for delivery, and the need for customer service. The result was an extremely efficient business model that produced handsome profits for many years.

Thinking About Remodeling

If you were an entrepreneur just entering your marketplace now, how would you structure your business to create greater value for customers and for your company? Which functions or business structures have you carried over from doing business in the past that are now draining cash from your bottom line and could be eliminated? Would customers respond to a new product configuration or sales process if it meant greater value for them?

Strategy innovation at the business model level can be scary for organizations because it implies changes to the organization, where change implies risk. As a result, it is usually only considered as a strategy of last resort. However, if there is *value to be gained* by an organization through the creation of a new business model, market dynamics suggest that it will eventually happen. Our capitalist system and the efficiency of financial markets dictate that unrealized value will eventually be realized. Therefore, it is important for companies to understand what is possible in this area and at least have a strategy ready for when that entrepreneur finally enters your market with a new way of doing business.

It should be noted here that many of the business opportunities identified in the other vectors (customer value and market dynamics) will also require some change in the company's business model. For example, learning that there is a market for your products in China will force you to consider the creation of a new element of your business model—a distribution network in China. It is a rare situation when a Discovery team identifies a great new business opportunity that requires no adjustment or change to the current business model.

The types of business model innovations we are talking about here are ways to reconfigure the system of functions and processes that make up your current means of doing business, rather than ways to increase the efficiency of your current processes. As pointed out by Harvard strategy professor Michael Porter, operational effectiveness is different from strategy. Operational effectiveness in the manufacturing area, for example, might mean finding ways to cut production time or costs. Business model innovation in the manufacturing area might mean asking the question of whether manufacturing should be outsourced completely or determining if there is some component of the manufacturing process that could be delegated to customers, such as having them assemble the parts at home. These innovations might help open up new markets or new distribution opportunities that would not be feasible under the current business model. Again, strategy innovation is about doing different things to create new value, not doing the same things a little better than before.

Houses built in previous centuries contained parlors, sitting rooms, and formal living rooms because those living spaces reflected how people relaxed and entertained in those eras. Does that floor plan fit the way families of today live? It can be difficult putting the large-screen television with surround sound in a parlor. Today's families need larger common rooms, kitchens for entertaining, outdoor living space—a different house design that fits the changing needs of today's lifestyles.

Is your current business model a relic from a previous business era? Are your current systems and departmental structures based on "the way we have always done things here"? Did they evolve over time based on corporate personalities or is it the best way to deliver value to your customers? Dare to look at your current business model and ask, "What if . . ."

Business Model Innovations Vector: Interactions

For most employees, the company's business model is invisible. They accept the processes, structures, and norms that shape their daily behavior and do not stop to think about whether it is the best way to achieve the company's objectives. The first step in considering strategy innovation at the business model level is to make it visible to the Discovery team. A good way to do that is to understand how other companies do business. Read business publications on how companies accomplished turnarounds, reengineered their processes, or cut costs dramatically compared to competition. Find out who those companies are and learn from them (see Figure 8-13).

Exploratory Vectors

	Customer Value	Market Dynamics	Business Model Innovation
Interactions			Benchmark calls Thought leader panels
Immersions			

Figure 8-13. Exploring Phase activities: Business model innovation interactions.

Benchmark Calls

The best way for the Discovery team to start exploring the possibilities of business model innovation is to contact companies that have done it before. Searching the business press for articles and stories of business model successes and failures will highlight companies that have attempted to do something that your team finds intriguing or a possible strategic frontier for your company. Call representatives of those companies and ask to learn more about the process. What worked and what did not? If they were to do it again, how would they do it differently? How did they handle the creation of the new business model so that it did not destroy the value still being created by the old one? Benchmarking calls like this will provide valuable insights into the attractiveness of business model innovation for your company.

Thought Leader Panels

Another, more powerful process for exploring business model innovation is to convene a thought leader panel (TLP). As discussed in more detail earlier in this chapter, TLPs consist of "experts" in a topic of interest attending a two-to-three-day meeting with the Discovery team and the Extended Discovery team plus senior management. Thought leaders in the business model innovation area would be representatives of companies that underwent a business model innovation. They would be asked to share their stories and what they learned from the creation of a new way of doing business.

The H-P Inkject Business Unit (IJBU) conducted two thought leader panels in their Exploring Phase that were aimed at building their business model. In their case, they were not interested in understanding how the *market* for inkjet printers would evolve, as they knew it would become a huge business, very quickly. Their challenge was to determine how to create the right business model and infrastructure to prepare for that growth and manage it for long-term success. Their first thought leader panel focused on the topic of "high market share." They recruited experts from major corporations, such as Coca-Cola, Intel, DuPont, and others, to share their stories of developing and maintaining a high share in the marketplace. From this panel, their team created a business vision and strategic plan for managing high market share in the inkjet printer market.

Shortly after that first thought leader panel, the team arranged for a second panel. Whereas the first one was aimed at marketplace activities that the company should undertake, the second had more of an internal focus. Called the "hypergrowth" panel, it also consisted of experts from major corporations (Cisco Systems, Microsoft, and Conner Peripherals, among others) that had to deal with the internal management of rapid corporate growth. From this panel, the team learned how to create systems and process strategies, as well as culture and infrastructure strategies, for handling rapid growth.

Terry Tallis, business planning manager for H-P, said, "We were intrigued with the idea of thought leader panels because they were so different from how we worked with other experts in the past." He said that the benefit of the thought leaders enabled IJBU to gain new perspectives, which in turn created a shared view of these new perspectives that ultimately altered their strategy. It was this new, shared view that ultimately led to the creation of a consensus strategy. According to Tallis:

> For the first time, the core team all had a common base of understanding. In our staff meetings, we would get information from different groups but it would all be filtered information. That did not happen with the thought leader panels, where we all heard everything at once. Thought leaders would ask insightful, naïve questions that were not politically motivated, such as, "Have you thought about it this way?" This was particularly helpful in the breakout sessions, as it really opened our eyes to new options. Later, people who attended the panels would recall quotes and advice from the thought leaders, instead of focusing on internal battles of who ought to be doing what.

Attendees at a business model thought leader panel will be able to make an assessment of the opportunities and risks involved with business model innovations. As with the market dynamics thought leader panels, the output of this work is an awareness of the variety of different ways that business model innovation can be done and an alignment by the senior management team on how it could work best within your company.

Business Model Innovation Vector: Immersions

Benchmarking Visits

Understanding business model innovations at a deeper level might consist of benchmarking innovative companies by visiting their operations (see Figure 8-14). Many companies will agree to provide tours or visits to other companies interested in benchmarking their operations. The advantage of an immersion (visit) over an interaction (telephone call) would be the opportunity to observe the operations, rather than just hear about them. As with the immersion visits with customers described earlier, Discovery team members should discuss ahead of time what information would be most valuable to obtain in a benchmarking visit. Note anything in the visit that could help your company understand the implications and implementation issues that might be associated with innovations in your current business model.

Exploratory Vectors

	Customer Value	*Market Dynamics*	*Business Model Innovation*
Interactions			
Immersions			Benchmark visits

Figure 8-14. Exploring Phase activities: Business model innovation immersions.

Discovering Value on the Frontier

The experiences you create in the Exploring Phase will expose your Discovery team to new ideas, new perspectives, new assumptions, and new mind-sets. Every one of these new understandings is potentially useful as the basis for the development of a new business opportunity. The key determination of its usefulness is its ability to create value for the customer and, as a result, value for your company.

The Discovery team should gather and record these new understandings during its exploration of the strategic frontier. After each interaction or immersion, conduct a debriefing session where team members share what they heard, what was new, what impressed them, and what surprised them (see Figure 8-15). We refer to all of these as insights gained from the exploration. There are no rules about what is, and what is not, an insight, so don't spend time debating what qualifies

Process Tip:

Insights are perishable, so share them in a debriefing session while they are fresh.

Immediately following any Exploring Phase activity, team members involved in that activity should plan a formal debriefing process. Create a list of what you learned, what has value, and what you consider at that point to be possible implications of what you learned. Writing down memorable quotes from the activity tends to extend their shelf life.

Insight		Implication
Convenience drives the purchase process.	→	*Make our product more accessible.*
The reward is a child's smile.	→	*Test it with children first.*
"I often spill it while opening."	→	*Consider a chewable version.*
All products are alike.	→	*Look into co-branding.*

Figure 8-15. Debriefing exercise.

as an insight. If it is new and thought to potentially have value in the marketplace, record it on a flip chart. Try to identify a long list of insights from each interaction or immersion—at least twenty from an individual customer interview, at least fifty from a Value-Probe session, and at least one hundred from a thought leader panel. These quantities of insights will force the team to listen and think carefully about all of what they heard and experienced.

As the team will eventually narrow this list of insights at a later time, it is a good idea to note during the debriefing session any possible *implications* for each insight generated. In that way, the implications will serve as a reminder of the potential value of that insight when used in the Creating Phase.

Summary

- ◆ To be able to perceive new opportunities on the strategic frontier, the Discovery team must escape "corporate gravity" through entrepreneurial and contrarian thinking.

- ◆ The Strategic Opportunity Spectrum (SOS) is a method of categorizing the business opportunities you discover on your strategic frontiers from "visible" opportunities to "visionary" opportunities.

- ◆ Stretch your thinking to identify visionary opportunities, and you will identify opportunities all along the Strategic Opportunity Spectrum.

- ◆ Business is about creating value for someone (a customer) and, in delivering that value, creating value for yourself. So identifying new business opportunities should focus on value—what it is and how it can be delivered or enhanced.

- ◆ Pathways for exploring for value on the strategic frontier can be found along three "vectors"—the customer value vector, the market dynamics vector, and the business model innovation vector.

- ◆ To gain a fresh perspective and unique insights, the Discovery team should consider less conventional ways of doing their exploration activities in this Exploring Phase. To see things differently, you need to do things differently.

♦ Exploration activities can be categorized as interactions or immersions. Interactions are events set up for the exchange of information while immersions are entering an environment in order to make observations.

♦ In the customer value vector, the goal is to identify unarticulated customer needs. To do that, consider interactions such as Value-Probes and specialists, and immersions such as safaris, lifestyle experiences, and stake-outs.

♦ In the market dynamics vector, there is tremendous value to be gained by understanding the forces that exist that may have an impact on future markets. To gain that understanding, consider interactions such as thought leader panels, and immersions such as experiments, conferences, and guided journeys.

♦ In the business model innovation vector, there is much to be learned about how other companies created a unique business model to capture greater value in the marketplace. To learn how to do that, consider interactions such as benchmark calls and thought leader panels, and immersions such as benchmark visits.

♦ Conduct a debriefing session immediately following every exploration activity so that team members can identify and share the insights gained from that effort.

Endnotes

1. W. Chan Kim and Renee Mauborgne, "Value Innovation: The Strategic Logic of High Growth," *Harvard Business Review*, January/February 1997.
2. John Glenn, www.pbs.org/kcet/johnglenn/rightstuff/faq/exploration.htm, January 2003.
3. John Glenn, www.floridatoday.com/space/explore/stories/1998b/102998k.htm, January 2003.
4. Adrian Slywotzky, *Value Migration: How to Think Several Moves Ahead of the Competition* (Boston: Harvard Business School Press, 1997).

5. Richard Leifer, et al., *Radical Innovation* (Boston: Harvard Business School Press, 2000).

6. Robert L. Shook, *Honda: An American Success Story* (New York: Prentice-Hall, 1988).

CHAPTER 9

THE DISCOVERY PROCESS

Creating Phase

> The purpose of divergent thinking is to define the possibilities and propose a promising solution that can be validated to the point of creating a business plan that will attract external investors.[1]
>
> —*RICHARD FOSTER AND SARAH KAPLAN*

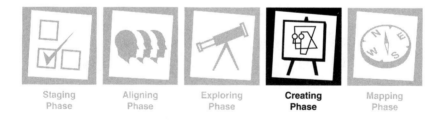

| Staging Phase | Aligning Phase | Exploring Phase | **Creating Phase** | Mapping Phase |

Your explorations have ended. No more arranging of appointments and schedules. No more eating M&Ms in the viewing room of a marketing research facility. No more long lines at airport security. Your Discovery team may be weary, but their interactions and immersions over the past several months have provided them with a deep understanding of customers and what they value, the emerging marketplace of the future, and the potential for business model innovations. They have collected experiences and valuable insights that now can be used to create the business opportunities of the future.

The Creating Phase is, as you might guess, a creative activity where imagination is used to envision and define businesses of the future. It consists of the following:

- ◆ Establishing the right environment
  - ◆ Creative
  - ◆ Collaborative
  - ◆ Entrepreneurial
- ◆ Collecting the necessary tools
  - ◆ Insights
  - ◆ Opportunity format
  - ◆ "Rough" evaluation criteria
- ◆ The creative process
  - ◆ Divergent phase: Identification of beginning ideas
  - ◆ Convergent phase: Concept development and evaluation

Establishing the Right Environment

Discovery team members will enter the Creating Phase as artists enter their studios. Their rich experiences in the Exploring Phase have helped them conceive of new opportunities that exist on the strategic frontier. Sometimes it is a specific, vivid image that only needs a medium and the time to recreate the image in their heads. In other cases, team members envision certain elements of the opportunities but cannot yet envision it in its entirety. In the Creating Phase, the artists of the Discovery team will give expression to these ideas.

Artists are usually very particular about the environments in which they work. Some prefer a rather plain, quiet studio so as not to be distracted by outside influences. Others prefer more stimulating, vibrant surroundings to feed and reinforce their creative impulses. The environment for the Creating Phase is a very important consideration. In order to facilitate the right interaction of team members and maximize the output of quality business opportunities, the working environment for the Creating Phase must be:

◆ Creative

◆ Collaborative

◆ Entrepreneurial

Creative

As described in Chapter 6, the Discovery Process is based on the principles of creativity applied in a business environment. Perhaps the creative element that is most useful to business is the two-step approach to identifying new ideas (see Figure 9-1). The first step, the "divergent phase," is the unbridled, unencumbered identification of a wide range of options to consider. Most people recognize it as a "brainstorming" type of activity. Without regard to practicality, feasibility, efficiency, or effectiveness, team members first identify a large quantity of ideas and options that could be used to run a business. It is through this divergent activity that participants "wander" beyond current constraints, ignore previous assumptions

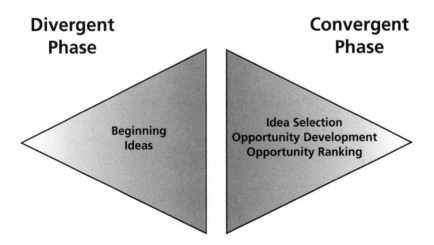

Figure 9-1. The Creating Phase.

about the business and discover new ways of doing business. When they do that, innovative ideas emerge. Without this permission to wander, speculate, and dream, options are few and tend to reflect old thinking patterns.

A senior manager of a large chemical company wondered why the room went suddenly quiet when, after challenging his team with an important problem, he exclaimed, "Now, everyone give me all your GOOD ideas!" He was oblivious to the importance of inviting all ideas without prematurely assessing whether they were good or not. As a result, each person in the room hesitated to offer any ideas, not knowing for sure how the manager would be distinguishing a "good" idea from a "bad" idea. The premature insistence on practical ideas led to a stifling of all ideas.

Because all business decisions must ultimately be practical, feasible, efficient, and effective, there is a second step to the creative process for business called the "convergent phase." This phase can be viewed as a "filtering" phase, as the great quantity of options identified in the divergent phase are filtered by the important business criteria. The team's options then converge on those ideas that make the most sense for the business.

Discovery team members are either extremely comfortable in the Creating Phase or they are somewhat uncomfortable. Inspired by the thrill of discovery they experienced in the Exploring Phase, some team members are easily convinced to continue this open-ended, anything-is-possible way of working. They will be eager to speculate and dream in the divergent phase about new business opportunities that could possibly exist. Other team members are anxious to take what they have discovered and identify the specific, practical, short-term implications for the current business. They do not want to think about new ways of doing business. They are ready to take action, to make specific recommendations to senior management. This latter group could be uncomfortable in the beginning of the Creating Phase. They must be patient, as their interests and skills will be used later in the Creating Phase and into the Mapping Phase, after a large quantity of new business opportunities have been created.

Collaborative

The new business opportunities that emerge from this Discovery Process must be viewed as being created by the entire Discovery team, not by particular members of the team. This is an important distinction to take into the Creating Phase because it establishes the most effective working environment for the team. The Discovery team will be "building" the opportunities together. It is a highly collaborative effort where all team member interactions are aimed at the same objective, creating the best future business opportunities possible from the insights gathered.

Think of the process of the Creating Phase as similar to the Discovery team creating clay sculptures together. While everyone will be asked to do the initial design and formation of their own sculpture, each will then spend time enhancing in some way the sculptures of all of the other team members. The sculptures are continuously evolving during the Creating Phase, with team members offering their insights that could lead to valuable refinements and revisions. Because the clay remains malleable until it is fired in the kiln, the team can decide when it is good enough, when it needs more work, or when it needs to be destroyed and the process started all over again. What emerges is a large quantity of works-of-art that everyone on the team supports, because everyone on the team has played some role in developing them. This is collaboration at its best.

To keep this spirit of collaboration alive in meetings, the Discovery team needs to adopt a new vocabulary. When someone on the team offers an idea and you see a way to enhance it, say, "I would like to build on that idea" and offer your addition. This acknowledges that what you heard was valuable and that you would like to contribute to its development—rather than your statement being perceived as a criticism or evaluation of what you heard. While it sounds subtle, we have found that using this "building" language enhances the team collaboration and incentive to maximize the business opportunities.

The synergy produced through collaboration is the most powerful approach for achieving high levels of team creativity. Of all the ideation tools and techniques we have used or heard about, none match the effectiveness of an inspired team collaborating toward a common challenge. From the many different perspectives represented on the team, they are able to identify ways to "build" and strengthen an idea by addressing collaboratively its gaps and points of weakness. You will recognize when your team achieves this level of teamwork by how the credit for an idea is given to the team, rather than to the individual. The individual egos become fused into one "team" ego. It is not dissimilar from the level of teamwork observed in many championship teams. In the 2001 NFL Super Bowl, the New England Patriots, heavy underdogs but the eventual winner, refused the traditional individual player introductions at the beginning of the game. Instead, they entered the field as one motivated mass of bobbing unity, recognizing that their strength was in the collaborative effort and not in superior individual performances.

Entrepreneurial

Using the insights gained about customers, the marketplace, and business models, the Discovery team will be identifying *business opportunities that will exist in the future*. The Discovery team is *not identifying business opportunities that your company should consider*. When you think only about opportunities for your company, you are unconsciously trying to "fit" a new insight into an old way of doing business. In doing so, you may be compromising the value inherent in the opportunity because of your company's current constraints or shortcomings. It is not difficult to imagine that in the years before Federal Express, the U.S. Postal Service could have identified the need for overnight mail service but expressed it as a one-day service because they were not set up for or capable of delivering overnight service. The need (and value) of the opportunity was for overnight service, not one-day service.

In assuming that someone else will be responsible for implementing the plan, adopt the mind-set of an entrepreneur. Assume

Process Tip:

You only dream to the level of your perceived implementation capabilities.

Try as hard as you want, it is very difficult to "think big" if you perceive that you will be the one responsible for implementing that big plan. Your subconscious concern of your ability to execute the plan will prevent you from ever articulating it in the first place. To create truly great and innovative business opportunities that will effectively deliver the value you envision, you have to assume for this Creating Phase that "someone else" will be responsible for implementing the plan.

that the capital, the skills, the partners, and the knowledge needed to fulfill that marketplace need will immediately become available as soon as you are able to "dream" it. Express the business opportunity in that way so that everyone is made aware of the opportunities that exist now or will exist in the future. It is then a separate strategic question to be addressed later of whether your company is willing to pursue that opportunity (and the resources required) or whether it is an opportunity that you will cede to another company.

One of our favorite ways to assist teams in adopting this entrepreneurial approach is to challenge them to become entrepreneurs for a fictitious company called Hurricane, Inc. Hurricane, Inc., is in the imagined business of providing emergency support to communities immediately following a storm of hurricane force. The company can assist a community in recovering from the aftermath of a storm's damage by supplying energy, food, water, and temporary housing. The team's challenge, as the Discovery team for Hurricane, Inc., is to identify new opportunities for new growth for the company.

Among a number of things, this imaginary challenge to the team helps determine whether the team is more comfortable "creating" at safe, near-term levels or at big-idea, breakthrough levels. Not surprisingly, all teams begin generating opportunities for Hurricane, Inc., that might be classified as visible opportunities on the Strategic Opportunity Spectrum—disaster insurance, home construction or reconstruction, and home meal delivery. Some teams are more aggressive in their strategy innovation, with ideas that extend disaster relief beyond just hurricanes, to include tornadoes and typhoons, or, a little further out, earthquakes, volcanic events, and avalanches. Teams that achieve a visionary level might identify opportunities such as a GPS–driven natural disaster forecasting, a warning and tracking service, or a systemic disaster-relief holding company that includes an integrated, cost-effective package of prevention planning, broad insurance coverage, and guaranteed property restoration.

When offering this type of creative challenge to a team, it is one thing to work with adults, it is quite something else to work with children. When the Hurricane, Inc., challenge was given to a class of fourth- fifth- and sixth-graders at Thacher Montessori School in Milton, Massachusetts, they generated a representative number of the above-mentioned ideas from visible to visionary. However, these children, unconstrained by the realities of business and eager to find "value" in a new situation, then stepped beyond to create two new spin-off opportunities for Hurricane, Inc.:

1. Hurricane Energy, Inc., is in the business of capturing and storing a portion of the megawatts produced as a hurricane moves through an area. This energy is then provided back to the community for emergency power or is sold to other parts of the country to help fund the recovery.

2. Hurricane Entertainment, Inc., is in the business of setting up "amusement parks" that harness a hurricane's force for purposes of recreational fun. Imagine a theme park with an area the size of a basketball court enclosed by netting rising thirty feet in height. Inside are rubber "bubbles," large enough for a large child or adult to get into. The stronger the hurricane winds, the wilder the experience for this "bumper cars in the air" amusement ride.

When you think you have reached visionary levels with your innovative, entrepreneurial thinking, remember how these children responded and push yourself to find what ideas are beyond those you have already.

Fresh Perspectives

As mentioned previously, consider inviting new team members to help identify new business opportunities in the Creating Phase. Someone from outside the company could provide a fresh perspective for the team. In addition, an outsider will not be affected by your "corporate gravity" and will be more likely to create business opportunities that fit the customer need, not the company's current business model. One company invited a science fiction writer to the Creating Phase for this purpose. Another enlisted a retired venture capitalist, who provided a breadth of business-model experience that was quite helpful.

When considering new team members, also consider internal employees, even senior management. Using our adage of "people support what they help create," you will want someone on the senior management team of your company to support the new business opportunities you create, so why not include him or her in their creation. One caveat to the involvement of senior executives, however, is that they must adopt the role of an "equal" to the other team members and abide by the rules of creativity and collaboration. If they prefer to play an advisory or evaluative role as "higher ranking" officials, the dynamics of the team and the process would be too compromised, and productivity would plummet.

Another outside perspective that can contribute significantly in this phase is that of a "visual illuminator." A visual illuminator is an artist who can bring to life the ideas being shared by the team. At this point in the process, ideas are intangible, incomplete, and fragile, as they have not yet been subjected to the critical scrutiny that further shapes and improves them. When a visual illuminator portrays that idea on paper, it takes on reality and becomes a tangible expression of what team members have created. They are now better able to understand it and to communicate it to others. We asked Harvey Ehrlich, a veteran visual illuminator, to describe the role that he plays in the Creating Phase for teams. He told us:

> In business, new ideas, whether they are tactile in nature or only philosophical, become easier to grasp and understand when, in addition to a carefully crafted verbal construct, a visual image is used. Visual illumination can cut through verbal camouflage and present an idea by means of a visual metaphor that can elegantly communicate. I have also found that humor, attached to both the visual and verbal images, embeds these ideas in the minds of the team much better than a verbal presentation can. The brain relishes what makes it laugh. To say more about visual illumination would require an image.

Collecting the Necessary Tools

With the appropriate working environment established, the Discovery team must then gather their tools for the Creating Phase. Unlike the myriad tools that artists have to provide expression to their ideas, there are only three "tools" necessary for this exercise: the lists of insights gathered from the Exploring Phase, an opportunity format, and some "rough" evaluation criteria.

Lists of Insights

As noted in the Exploring Phase, insights are new understandings of customers, markets, or business models that have the potential to create value for both the customer and the company. Insights from the Exploring Phase are the building blocks of the new business opportunities developed in the Creating Phase.

The Discovery team will have identified and recorded the new insights they gained in the various interactions and immersions of the Exploring Phase. A debriefing session immediately following each activity will have highlighted the insights gained and potential implications (way to create value) for each insight. With many hun-

Process Tip:

Add a visual dimension to your Creating Phase.

Invite an artist, cartoonist, or visual illuminator to join you in the creating process. It is not a frivolous expenditure. A talented (fast-working) artist can add a visual, tangible dimension to the creation of ideas and concepts that often has a dramatic effect on the team. Ideas come to life, color stimulates the environment, and humor can help the team think in new directions. The artist's output can also help dramatically in the communication of the new opportunities to the rest of the organization.

dreds of new insights identified by the team, the first step is to review them and identify which ones appear to have the most potential for further development into a new business opportunity.

Any process can be used to filter or converge around the most promising insights for your team to consider in the Creating Phase. We have successfully used a two-step sorting process based on the 3 Cs (clarity, confidence, and conviction) and an insight's value potential.

3 Cs

Using notes from all of the debriefing sessions, ask team members to first identify those insights on which, after all of the interactions and immersions, they have the most "clarity, confidence, and conviction." Either because of the frequency with which they were heard, the passion by which they were expressed, or the credibility of the source, some insights will emerge as creating a higher level of clarity, confidence, and conviction than others. The first step is to review the hundreds of the gathered insights and note which are selected by team members on this dimension and the frequency with which those insights appear within the team. The result will be a range of insights on the team's 3-C dimension.

Value Potential

A second filter is based on the team's perception of the potential value of a particular insight. Some insights may be able to generate only a slight, incremental value in the market, such as a new color option for a product. Other insights may indicate the potential for an entirely new product category or distribution system, creating significant value by reaching underserved customers. Sorting the insights that emerged from the 3-C filter into those with higher value potential and those with lower value potential will provide a matrix of insights for the team to consider (see Figure 9-2).

The insights that fall into the team's upper-right quadrant are those that, according to the team, have the most clarity, confidence, and conviction, as well as the greatest value potential in the market. This is one way for the team to narrow the number of insights so they can focus their energies on the Creating Phase.

Wild Cards

We believe that everyone on the team should have a wild card option in all sorting and voting activities in the Creating Phase. The purpose of the wild card is to allow everyone to pursue something that intrigues them or about which they have considerable passion,

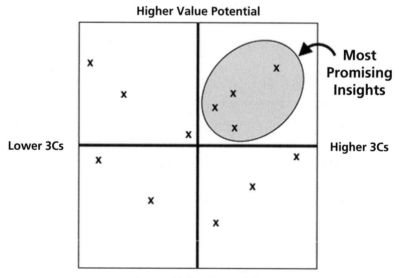

Figure 9-2. Value graph for insights.

even if it does not satisfy the sorting requirements or criteria the team establishes. For example, you may recall an isolated comment from a customer interview that you found particularly intriguing. Because you only heard it once, you don't yet have clarity, confidence, and conviction about this insight. So it technically would not pass your first sorting of the insights. However, you believe that this idea may have tremendous value potential if you could figure out a way to do it. In this case, you could use your wild card option to keep the insight under consideration by the team until you can further develop its possibilities later.

Opportunity Format

The second tool necessary for the Creating Phase is a format for the development of the new business opportunities. The purpose of the format is twofold. First, it helps guide Discovery team members in the creation of a new business concept. Because the team comes from a cross-section of the organization, there will be a number of members who have never had to describe a new business before. The format will take them step-by-step through the thinking process necessary to define the business opportunity. By filling out the format, they will have covered the important considerations of the business.

The second purpose of the opportunity format is to add a degree of standardization to what is created. This will be very important later in this phase when the team is asked to evaluate the opportunities. Having a common format makes cross-opportunity comparisons considerably easier. Standardization will also enhance the presentation of the new business opportunities to senior management at the end of the Discovery Process.

Every opportunity format is different. The nature of the industry will have the largest impact on what is important in the description of a business. The description of a new business opportunity in the restaurant business will include elements that are vastly different from the description of a new business opportunity in the biotech industry. The goal of the opportunity format is to consider the primary elements of the business model in that industry and the process requirements for its development. In restaurants, the focus could be on the theme, customers, ambiance, food, and service. In biotech, it could be the targeted disease and population, underlying science, clinical trials, regulatory issues, and partnerships.

Figure 9-3 illustrates a "generic" format that could be used as a starting point for the creation of a more customized format for your Discovery team.

Other elements that could be included in the opportunity format are unique point of differentiation, proprietary elements, current assets leveraged, reinforcing trends, conflicting forces, major internal constraints, major external constraints, and resources available. In addition, some industries may have critical success factors that should be included in the opportunity format. Keep the number of items included on the opportunity format to eight or ten so that the task does not appear too ominous to team members.

There are a variety of ways to create these business opportunities. Team members can develop them individually, in pair teams, or in small groups (of three or four people). When teams create the opportunities individually, they generate more opportunities overall and allow team

Process Tip:

Think BIG—but in phases and segments.

Team members often have difficulty describing the bold, ideal future they are asked to depict in these business opportunities. Because their day jobs consist of managing systems and assets of the company, they innately want to create realistic and feasible ideas that the company can implement. Tell team members not to think of big ideas as having to be implemented all at once, to all markets immediately. Instead, encourage them to describe that big, bold, ideal future but to break up its implementation into manageable phases and/or segments.

Your Name:

New Business Opportunity Format

1. **Code Name:**
   Strategic Frontier:
   Key Insight:

2. **Description of Opportunity:**
   (In 25 words or fewer, what is it and how does it create value?)

3. **Target Audience:**
   (Who is the primary target audience? Secondary audience?)

4. **Key Benefit(s) to Customers:**
   (What are the key benefits to customers in the opportunity? How will it help improve their lives?)

5. **Important Elements of the Opportunity:**
   (What are the products and/or services involved? Describe the elements that make it unique, useful to customers.)

6. **Competitive Advantage:**
   (How will your opportunity provide a competitive advantage over what competitors could offer?)

7. **Resources Required:**
   (What resources would be necessary to develop this opportunity—technology, budgets, parnerships, skill sets, etc?)

8. **Additional Information Required:**
   (What additional information will be necessary before the opportunity can be further developed?)

Figure 9-3. Opportunity format.

members to express their own points of view. In pair teams, every-body gets a teammate to help craft and refine the opportunity, each acting as a sounding board for the partner. Small group develop-ment of the opportunities is appropriate when the opportunities are quite complex, but it will cut down the total output because of the added time for groupthink and consensus-making. We recom-mend using opportunity development by individuals and pair teams wherever possible.

As team members craft these new business opportunities, remind them to develop them not to fit the capabilities of your company, but to fit the needs of the customer. Attempts to make them feasible for your company may compromise the business opportunity that exists. Instead, encourage team members to be bold and to envision how the opportunity could look at that point in the future when all the elements are in place and customers are being served. Using the Strategic Opportunity Spectrum concept presented in Chapter 7, the Discovery team should aim for creating visionary ideas, which will result in opportunities ranging from visible to visionary.

"Rough" Evaluation Criteria

Prior to the start of the Creating Phase, the Discovery team should know how they will go about screening or filtering the quantity of new business opportunities they create in this phase. The criteria they use will be based on the overall objectives of the strategy inno-vation initiative. They are just "rough" screening criteria at this point—used mostly for rank-ordering the ideas created and not for purposes of making market go/no go decisions. For example, if se-nior management and the Discovery team sponsor determine that the company needs a series of mid-term (over the next two to four years) opportunities that leverage a certain core competence and have the potential to eventually be a $30 million business, then those are the "rough" evaluation criteria that will be used to rank the opportunities created.

As with the opportunity format mentioned earlier, the rough evaluation criteria will be different for every company. Typically we would use three to five criteria for this initial screening. Some of the criteria to be used are:

- Time to market (specifying short-term, mid-term, long-term)
- Revenue potential
- Leverages a particular core competence, in-house technology, or brand profile
- Is unique in the market
- Will provide a proprietary advantage
- Leverages a customer or market trend

The identification of rough evaluation criteria just prior to the Creating Phase is a double-edged sword for the Discovery team. On the positive side, the criteria provide a focus for the development of new business opportunities and, when they are part of the team's objectives, increase the likelihood that the opportunities developed will be strategically valuable to the company. On the negative side, the evaluation criteria can diminish the latitude that the team feels in developing the best opportunities possible and could result in ideas that are less innovative.

As an example of the potentially constraining role that the criteria play, let's say that the Discovery team identifies an insight in the Exploring Phase that suggests a strong market opportunity for customized music CDs. Without any evaluation criteria to guide them, the team may develop the business opportunity to include an automated digital recording system connected to a Web site, where customers order their new CDs from their homes, and download the finished CD. However, if the evaluation criteria say that the new business should leverage the company's current retail distribution system, the customized music business opportunity that is created by the team will end up looking very different. It would likely involve a much more complex ordering process (at the store), less convenient for customers, and potentially a more expensive product. The point here is that evaluation criteria that are too stringent will prevent the team from identifying business opportunities that provide the greatest value for customers.

How do you deal with the *need* for evaluation criteria but the potentially constraining impact that the criteria could have on the process? Make the Discovery team *aware* of the evaluation criteria that will be used but at the same time make sure that they don't feel constrained by them in the creation of the new business opportunities. If a business opportunity, such as the Web-based CD system, is ultimately filtered by the evaluation criteria, the Discovery team can also use its wild card option to keep the idea alive for further consideration.

Innovation vs. Feasibility

The goal of a strategy innovation initiative is to identify innovative new business opportunities for a company to consider. However, highly innovative ideas, conceived as they are here outside the constraints of practical business considerations, could end up being impossible to implement or not financially viable. Thus, the need for innovation in these opportunities can be at odds with the company's need for feasibility. So how do you manage to keep ideas both innovative and feasible at the same time?

When faced with this innovation/feasibility trade-off, always go for the innovative. This was a principle of innovation used in early work at Synectics. Ideas will never be more innovative than they are during this Creating Phase. Free from the practical considerations of business and being encouraged to dream and think big, team members will be more likely now than at any other time to dream up innovative ideas.

At the same time, there is a natural, unconscious tendency for people in business to want to take new and innovative ideas and find ways to make them more "practical" or more feasible, quickly. They will say in response to an innovative idea, "Great idea—how can we implement it today rather than waiting for two years." These invisible *feasibility forces* will look for ways to refine the innovative ideas by substituting shorter-term, more feasible options.

Process Tip:

It is easier to build feasibility into an innovative idea than to build innovation into a feasible idea.

In the Discovery Process, "feasibility happens." Faced with a highly innovative idea, people in business naturally try to find a way to make it more feasible so as to be able to use that idea. However, it is very difficult to take an idea that is already feasible and give it a booster shot of innovation. Therefore, the team should focus on creating the most innovative ideas possible instead of the most feasible, knowing that the feasibility forces will work their invisible magic.

The result is that longer-term, highly innovative ideas are usually refined and revised to become shorter-term and more feasible as they are further considered.

On the other hand, it is very difficult to build innovation into a feasible idea. If someone on the team suggests a feasible idea for a new business, chances are that it is more of an incremental product improvement than an innovation capable of changing the basis of competition in the marketplace. People are comfortable with its feasibility already and are reluctant to add innovative elements to it that will make the idea a less feasible, longer-term idea. In other words, there are usually no invisible *innovation forces* that will go to work and make a feasible idea more innovative.

Understanding this important mix between innovation and feasibility is important to keep in mind in the Creating Phase.

The Creative Process

Unlike the Exploring Phase, which can last from weeks to months, the Creating Phase is typically a two-day offsite meeting of the Discovery team (plus any other invitees). Another option for the team to consider is to start the Creating Phase during the Exploring Phase. For example, if your team is traveling to ValueProbe sessions in another city, you can debrief the insights gained from the sessions immediately after the sessions. Then, the next day, the team could meet again to begin to turn the insights into new business opportunities—while the insights and their implications are fresh in their minds. Whether you do it that way (create opportunities following each exploring event) or set aside a two-day session following all of the Exploring Phase work is up to the team. The process for the creating session is the same.

The Creative Process: Divergent Phase

The best way to describe the two-phased creative process used by the team to develop the new business opportunities is to think of it metaphorically as a funnel. The first phase, called the "divergent" phase, consists of filling up the funnel with a large quantity of "beginning ideas." A beginning idea is a small piece or portion of a business opportunity. It is not a finished description of the business opportunity. Do not attempt to move from an insight gained in the Exploring Phase directly to a completed new business description! For example, perhaps an insight gained in the Exploring Phase was "customers want their customer service problems resolved quickly." Rather than moving directly to the redesign of your customer call center or installing a new CRM system, create some *beginning ideas* based on that insight. One beginning idea from that insight might be, "Create an Internet-based customer service capability." Another might be, "Create the customer service equivalent of an emergency room triage system." Still another beginning idea off this same insight might be, "Assign an ombudsman to each customer when they call."

Don't spend time thinking through the implications, cost factors, or feasibility of a beginning idea. Just note the idea as a beginning idea, "throw it into the top of the funnel," and move on quickly to the next beginning idea. Go for quantity. Remember the Rule of 100, because eventually you will want several hundred beginning ideas in your funnel. Use a rapid-fire, brainstorming-like process for collecting these beginning ideas. Some will be very good ideas, some will be terrible ideas, and a lot will be in-between. Do not stop to judge any of the ideas. Judgment in this divergent phase will not only slow the process, it will dampen enthusiasm and drain creative energy from the team. Encourage dreaming, wishing, and rampant speculation. Ideas offered by one member of the team will usually inspire someone else to think of an opportunity. Allow this free-flowing interaction to take place. What are the many ways to create value in the marketplace?

The divergent phase should last into the afternoon of the first day. When the tsunami of beginning ideas becomes a ripple on the shore at low-tide, it is time to move to the second phase of this creative process, the convergent phase.

The Creative Process: Convergent Phase

Bob Galvin, former CEO of Motorola and great advocate of using creativity in business, described the creative process as, "Most ideas are grunt work, first getting a quantity of ideas and then looking for the quality ideas in there." The convergent phase is all about sorting through the quantity of the ideas you inserted into the funnel and finding the highest-quality ones.

At this point in the Creating Phase, you should have hundreds of beginning ideas written on flip chart paper and hung on the walls around the room. In the convergent part of this process, the team will go through the following steps to turn hundreds of beginning ideas into five to ten potentially viable business opportunities:

1. Select the most promising beginning ideas
2. Develop those ideas into concepts or opportunities
3. Rank-order the opportunities

Select the Most Promising Beginning Ideas

Any process can be used to narrow the list of beginning ideas to a more manageable number. One idea is to give out a quantity of colored adhesive circles—what we call "energy dots"—that team members can stick next to the beginning ideas they find "most intriguing." Don't use more stringent criteria at this point because beginning ideas are not yet ready to be evaluated by the evaluation criteria. They are not yet developed as business opportunities and thus cannot be expected to live up to the criteria for those opportunities. So for this first converging step, you could use the criteria of what the Discovery team finds interesting or intriguing. They have been close to consumers and market experts in the Exploring Phase and have developed a good idea of what would create value in the marketplace. It is also important for the team to feel some level of interest (or potentially, passion) about the beginning ideas. They will be the ones presenting their business opportunities to senior management and may have to defend them at some point.

Use this first convergent exercise to identify as many as thirty to fifty beginning ideas (if using the energy dots, list those that get at least one "dot" from the long list) that the team believes deserve more consideration and further development.

Develop Those Ideas into Concepts or Opportunities

The second convergent step is developing the most "intriguing" beginning ideas into business concepts. We call these concepts "business opportunities" and use the opportunity format presented earlier in this chapter as the basis of the exercise. Have Discovery team members select which of the beginning ideas they want to advance or more fully develop into business opportunities that can be evaluated. These opportunities can be new products or services, new target audiences, or new elements of a company's business model. Using the format and some quiet time, have team members think through what it might take for a company (not just *their* company but any company) to create value in the marketplace with the beginning idea they selected. What would it look like? How would it work? Who are the customers and why would customers like it?

A Discovery team will typically create between twenty and forty new business opportunities in a two-day Creating Phase session. Each idea is developed by either an individual or, at most, a pair team. It is much more efficient to develop the opportunities by individual or pair teams than in a large group. Managing who develops which beginning ideas will avoid duplication of effort and maximize the number of different opportunities created.

After the opportunity formats are completed, team members are asked to present their opportunities to the rest of the team. Following each presentation, team members can offer "builds" or suggestions on how to refine the opportunity to make it even stronger. It is a good idea to collect the builds and suggestions for improvement from the team and ask the authors of the business opportunities to then refine them as they see fit. It is the prerogative of the author to determine which builds are incorporated to create the refined business opportunity.

Rank-Order the Opportunities

The twenty to forty refined, new business opportunities are then ready for a screening process, the final convergent step in this process. Using the rough evaluation criteria identified earlier, the Discovery team will rate or rank all of the business opportunities they developed to provide a prioritization of those opportunities.

It is important to note here that this prioritization is not a go/no go decision for that idea. Many team members are disappointed when their concepts do not make the cut and mistakenly believe that they have failed because their opportunities have been rejected. This is not the case. That opportunity has been developed and should become part of a database or archive for this initiative. At any time, anyone can continue to work on that idea, refining it in ways that will better align with the evaluation criteria established or with the needs of a business. The creative process is an iterative process, where you can create, learn, and refine ad nauseam. Therefore, the screening out of an opportunity at this phase is not a "no go" decision, but merely a "not yet" decision on the part of the team.

Any process can be used for screening the business opportunities using the rough evaluation criteria. Some teams will very carefully evaluate every opportunity for every individual evaluation criterion, using complex, weighted, quantitative techniques and rating scales.

Other teams will just keep the criteria in mind as they select the three to five opportunities from the list that they like best. Whatever technique you use, the intent for this evaluation is to determine which of the twenty to forty opportunities are most aligned with the evaluation criteria that were established. Typically following this evaluation step, five to ten opportunities will emerge at the top of the ranking list as having the most potential for further consideration and development.

Don't forget the wild card option. Discovery team members, after evaluating the developed opportunities, may find that their favorite opportunities were far down the rankings. Perhaps an opportunity is very strong on most of the criteria but fell short in one area. The team needs a way to keep one or more ideas alive, if they have the passion for them. Let team members vote for one wild card opportunity they would like to keep in the running, based more on their passion for it than the evaluation criteria. Passion is a powerful, contagious force in innovation. A champion (or, better yet, a team of champions) with passion for an idea can build consensus and create momentum that will cause the organization to change.

At the conclusion of the Creating Phase, the Discovery team should have five to ten business opportunities that show some promise for the company. These opportunities are:

- ◆ Grounded in insights discovered in the Exploring Phase
- ◆ Part of a long list of beginning ideas
- ◆ Selected as "intriguing" or promising by one or more team members
- ◆ Developed by an individual (or pair team)
- ◆ Refined by suggestions from the entire Discovery team
- ◆ Screened by the rough evaluation criteria established earlier in the process

At this point, the team decides how many of the five to ten opportunities they want to move to the Mapping Phase, where they are placed on a time line and given a strategic context that will be important for their final evaluation stages.

Tim O'Brien from Moen noted the importance of this entire convergence process (which he referred to as synthesis) in the Periscope project. As he observed, "Synthesis must be a group activity, where the more people involved with it, the better, because you have that many more people making that many more connections. This synthesis resulted in management alignment on what we needed to move ahead."

Summary

- The Creating Phase is a time for Discovery team members to turn the insights gained in the Exploring Phase into new business opportunities.

- Establish the right working environment, one that is creative, collaborative, and entrepreneurial.

- Identify the business opportunities that will exist in the future, based on the insights gained in the Exploring Phase. Do not identify only those opportunities that fit your company's current capabilities. If the opportunity is attractive enough, you will find a way for your company to implement it.

- The only tools necessary for this creating process are the lists of insights gathered from the Exploring Phase, an opportunity format, and some "rough" evaluation criteria.

- Think of this process as moving through a metaphorical funnel. Begin by offering a large quantity of "beginning ideas," based on the insights gained, into the top of the funnel. This is the divergent phase of the creative process where the quantity of ideas is more important than the quality of each one. Innovation takes precedence over feasibility.

- Move the most promising of the beginning ideas "down the funnel" by selecting them and further developing them into concepts, using the opportunity format.

◆ The final step is to rank-order the opportunities using the rough evaluation criteria, allowing the strongest to emerge from the funnel for further consideration in the Mapping Phase.

Endnote

1. Richard Foster and Sarah Kaplan, *Creative Destruction* (New York: Currency/Doubleday, 2001).

CHAPTER 10

THE DISCOVERY PROCESS

Mapping Phase

> Make no little plans; they have no magic to stir men's blood and probably themselves will not be realized. Make big plans; aim high in hope and work, remembering that a noble, logical diagram, once recorded, will not die.
>
> —*DANIEL BURNHAM*

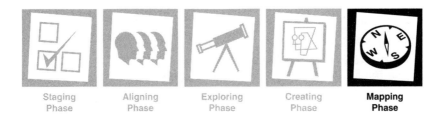

| Staging Phase | Aligning Phase | Exploring Phase | Creating Phase | **Mapping Phase** |

Your team has created a series of new business opportunities based on new insights about customers, foresight about the emerging marketplace of the future, and/or ways of reconfiguring existing business models in the market to increase value to customers and companies. These opportunities have been through a "rough" evaluation process that suggests that they may fulfill the needs outlined by senior management.

The Mapping Phase is the final step in the Discovery Process. It is a planning process for the implementation of the new business opportunity and consists of the following steps:

- ◆ Identify the critical strategic sectors
- ◆ Create road maps for each sector
  - ◆ Action items
  - ◆ Trends
  - ◆ Discontinuities
  - ◆ Milestones
- ◆ Develop measurement tools
- ◆ Present to senior management

A Strategic Road Map

Following the completion of this five-phased Discovery Process, senior management will have a portfolio of new business opportunities that can be found or created on their strategic frontiers. They must then consider how the company should respond to those opportunities. To do this, senior management will need information that will help them make those decisions.

Frequently the first piece of information that management will want is the market viability and potential revenue impact of these opportunities. Nearly every company has a means in place of estimating the potential size and profitability of new business opportunities. To be considered, a new business must pass certain hurdle rates, usually related to sales potential, margin requirements, or financial return requirements. We consider this fine-tuned, sharpen-the-pencil evaluation phase to be the next step that companies take *following* the Discovery Process. Because each industry and company differs in how they assess the viability of a new business opportunity, we do not believe that a "universal" evaluation process is possible within this process.

Beyond the internal financial implications, senior management will need to understand the marketplace in which these decisions will be made. What changes are on the horizon that could affect if, when, and why a business opportunity should be pursued? In a dynamic marketplace, this information is crucial to all strategic decisions that are made. To help management make these strategic decisions, the Discovery team should prepare a strategic road map for the frontier(s) they explored, as the final phase of the Discovery Process.

The Mapping Phase is so named as it engages in the preparation of a strategic road map for the company. This road map is a time line into the future that contains critical activities, milestones, and marketplace events that must take place for the new business opportunities to succeed. With a new business opportunity that appears viable and attractive to the company, the "big picture" view of the implementation plan provided by the strategic road map will uncover key issues that must be addressed. For example, a Discovery team might have been given a charge to identify a new business opportunity for introduction by the company in the next two to four years. In the Exploring Phase, they discovered a consumer need for a new medical device. It is in the mapping process that they learn that a clinical trial with patients must be conducted before the device will obtain government approval. That clinical trial may need to last for three years to prove efficacy and safety issues. Placing the three-year clinical trial on a two-to-four-year time line will very clearly indicate the timing necessary for the company to develop and implement this business opportunity. It uncovers potential conflicts, barriers, and constraints that the Discovery team will need to address, even by refining the business opportunity concept itself.

Dan Buchner, one of the team captains for the Moen Periscope project, describes the role of the strategic road map for Moen. "We took the output from the thought leader panels and built future maps, which we made part of our planning. They were quite detailed, helped us focus, and made it much more apparent what the difficult decisions were that had to be made. We had been trying to do everything in the marketplace, but the maps helped us focus our attention and our efforts." His boss, Bruce Carbonari, former CEO of Moen, added, "The nice thing about the maps is that everyone learned that the world is bigger than just Moen, and there are lots of things that cause other things to happen."

One of the important benefits of a strategic road map is that it makes tangible the company's proprietary future. No company can possibly monitor or manage all of the trends that will create the future. Instead, companies should focus on those areas and trends that are most relevant to *their* futures, the ones to be found on their strategic frontiers. The creation of a strategic road map captures the most relevant areas of their emerging futures and makes them available for the entire company to understand and track.

Another value of the strategic road map created by the Discovery team is that it provides a consensus "plan" from which all departments and functions in the company can operate. Recall that this was one of the primary reasons for creating a cross-functional Discovery team with people who will help implement the opportunity. The Discovery team is the ideal group to create this strategic road map for the organization because they understand the business opportunity (they created), and they understand what it would take for the organization to implement it. When this road map is created collaboratively by all members of the team, it provides the alignment necessary across all functional areas to quickly and effectively begin implementation.

If your company has a process for strategic mapping, we encourage integrating the findings from the Discovery Process to date in that process. For those companies that do not regularly map their future, we offer our model for the development of a strategic road map here.

Identify the Critical Strategic Sectors

The strategic road map offered here is a time line that consists of many bands or strata that represent important "sectors" that must be considered in the development of the business opportunity. As with most of the "tools" introduced in this Discovery Process, it must be customized to fit the specific industry and opportunity identified.

The first area of customization is the time line itself. It should be segmented by the relevant planning periods for operating in that industry. For highly dynamic industries such as electronics, the relevant time segments are probably in quarter years, if not months. In biotechnology, it will be years or perhaps decades. For many businesses, six-month intervals that stretch out over three to five years will often be an appropriate time line for the strategic roadmap.

In a mapping meeting, you can create time lines by taping together a number of flip chart pages and drawing the time line across the bottom (see Figure 10-1).

Identifying the critical strategic sectors is next. The team, using what they learned in the Exploring Phase, will determine the various areas that must be considered when developing, introducing, and competing in the marketplace of the future. Thought leader panels, described in the Exploring Phase, are extremely valuable in understanding the forces that will have an impact on the emerging marketplace. Some of the more common sectors that apply across many different industries include the following:

- Opportunity development (internal)
- Consumer/society
- Customer/marketplace
- Competition
- Technology
- Government/regulatory

Each industry may also have unique and important sectors to include on the strategic road map.

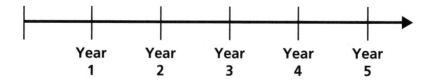

Figure 10-1. Time line.

The Discovery team should select those sectors that will likely play a role in developing the new business opportunity. If a sector can have an impact, either positively or negatively, it should be included in the strategic road map. In a mapping meeting, you can draw a series of "bands" on the flip chart paper just above the time line, labeling them with the sector names. An example can be seen in Figure 10-2.

Opportunity Development Sector

The opportunity development sector is the internal time line showing how your organization will develop the products, services, or new business processes that will take advantage of the new business opportunity identified. Included in this sector are the critical steps to be taken in the key functional areas of the company. Product development and R&D will show developmental milestones, testing processes, and intellectual property considerations. Marketing and sales will outline the key steps for advertising, packaging, promotions, sales, and merchandising strategies. Operations will identify a plan for manufacturing the product. Human resources, legal, and finance departments will indicate where and when they will play a

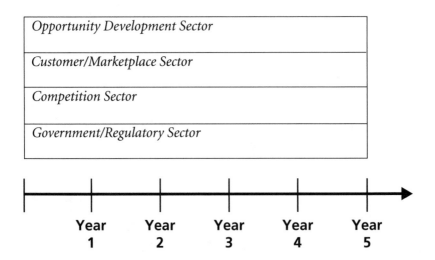

Figure 10-2. Strategic road map sectors.

role. Figure 10-3 shows the opportunity development sector broken out into these key areas that should contribute to this sector.

The Discovery team should include only the *critical* elements on the opportunity development sector, as too much detail makes the maps confusing and difficult to use. Each functional area should later develop a separate, more detailed time line for their internal planning purposes.

Consumer/Society Sector

The consumer/society sector of the strategy road map will consist of a variety of trends that are taking place in demographics, society, or lifestyles. If your customers are consumers, include those consumer trends that will have the greatest impact on the need, awareness, or acceptance of your business opportunity.

Customer/Marketplace Sector

Technology, globalization, and economic conditions are just some of the many factors that could have a dramatic impact on the marketplace in which you compete. It is important to try to predict

Opportunity Development Sector

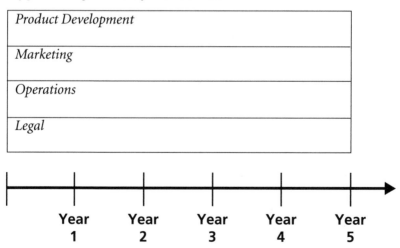

Figure 10-3. Strategic road map opportunity development sector.

how these forces might affect your market and customer base over the time frame of your strategic roadmap. Anticipating changes in distribution channels, sourcing options, supplier networks, and economic conditions could be critical for the success of your new business opportunity.

Competition Sector

In the dynamic marketplaces of the twenty-first century, it is unlikely that strategic actions by one company would not cause some reactions by its competitors. Faced with the possibility of losing business and/or customers, competitors will typically look to respond to new business introductions. Anticipating their responses and estimating their response times provides valuable information for the strategic road map. It establishes a "window" of time where competitive pressures are minimized and your company can maximize its market penetration. Think about which company will introduce a competing product and when. Which company will lower their prices? Which competitors will go out of business? Also think about what competitor (or new entrant to the market) might leapfrog your new product with a next-generation offering. All of these competitor reactions should be included, along with appropriate statistics, on the strategic road map.

Technology Sector

Because of the importance of technology for many new business opportunities, this sector is often one of the more critical ones on the strategic road map. It should highlight key trends in technology, availability dates of new technologies and capabilities, and dates of anticipated price drops in established technologies. Where one technology has not yet emerged as a standard, multiple technologies should be identified and tracked. Note which companies or organizations are developing and/or supporting these technological developments and anticipate any strategic moves they could make.

Government/Regulatory Sector

In many industries, there are government or regulatory issues that must be included on the strategic road map. It may be the testing process to satisfy the FDA, a wavelength licensing issue with the FCC, or a special ruling required from the EPA. In some cases, the process necessary is understood, and time frames are predictable. In others, decisions are heavily influenced by leaders and political considerations, which are less predictable. In either case, it is important to record on the strategic road map the factors and activities in this regulatory area that could have an influence on the development and introduction of your new business opportunity.

Create Road Maps for Each Sector

Following the identification of key sectors for the strategic road map, the Discovery team will focus on developing a road map within each sector. These sector road maps should include the following:

- ◆ Action items
- ◆ Trends
- ◆ Discontinuities
- ◆ Milestones

Action Items

Put the most critical action items in each of the sectors on the road map. Indicate items such as when the R&D group needs to apply for a patent, when the market research test begins and ends, and when manufacturing turns out the first production units. Also include on the strategic road map whatever actions trigger the commitment of resources or represent critical decision points in the development of the opportunity.

Action items can also be action taken by others. The anticipated response of competitors to your new business will take the form of action items to be included on the map.

Trends

It is also valuable to identify key trends on the road maps. If a trend is expected to have either a positive or negative impact on the development of the opportunity, it should remain visible to the team by being placed on the map. It is a good idea to quantify the trends by estimating their progress over time. For example, if a key trend for your business opportunity involves the use of DVDs in the home, estimate the household penetration level for DVD players at several different points on your time line.

Discontinuities

In addition to trends, the sectors of the strategy road map should also include any discontinuities that are possible. Discontinuities are those events that radically change the "normal" progression to the future because they quickly change perceptions and/or behaviors in society or the marketplace. The terrorist attacks of September 11, 2001, were the most significant, recent discontinuity that altered the emerging future of many, if not most, businesses. However, the introduction of the transistor, the home computer, and the growth of the Internet could also be considered discontinuities because they all caused shifts in how people lived or worked. Some discontinuities, such as new technologies, can often be anticipated, while others, such as major natural disasters or changes in governments, are much less predictable. If you know of the possibility of discontinuities, build them into the sector road maps.

Milestones

The strategic road map should also include milestones that mark progress. The timing of the identification of a strategic partner, for example, would be a milestone to include on the road map. You may also want to include go/no go decision points along the way or the points at which key financial decisions must be made (see Figure 10-4).

The best way we have found to build the sector road maps is to write the action items, trends, discontinuities, and milestones on Post-it Notes and apply them in the sector bands in the appropriate place over the time line. In this way, the elements can be shifted when the team discovers that their original timing estimates need to be adjusted. There will be a fair amount of adjusting and refining of the road maps as conflicts and sequence issues are discovered.

Work Backward

When creating the sector road maps and considering timing for various activities, we recommend working backward. Start with the launch date for the business, when you would like to be in the market. Then take the final steps and plot them on the road map, followed by the steps that precede them (in the development process). This will help the team create a more aggressive schedule and one more likely to hit the hoped-for market introduction. Otherwise, there is a tendency for team members to be conservative in

Opportunity Development		*Select Manufacturing* *Partner*		
Finalize *Product* *Specifications*	*Prototype Available* *In-Home Testing* *Patent Filing*	*Assign Ad Agency*	*National Sales* *Convention*	*PRODUCT* *LAUNCH*

Customer/Marketplace			
Target Market *Reaches 3 million*	*Excess Production Capacity*	*Pricing War*	*Industry Consolidation*

Competition	*GHInc. Introduces*		
ABCorp. *Introduces* *New Website*	*New Product Line*	*JKLtd. Enters* *US Markets*	

Government/Regulatory			
Legal *Review*	*New EPA* *Regulation Due*	*Federal* *Elections*	*Advertising* *Claims Review*

| Year 1 | Year 2 | Year 3 | Year 4 | Year 5 |

Figure 10-4. Strategic road map.

their estimates or even "pad" them for unexpected problems, which can extend significantly the timing of the development.

Develop Measurement Tools

What are the elements of this new business opportunity that are most crucial for its success? Perhaps it is a target audience of a certain size. Perhaps it is product cost under a certain target. Perhaps it is a global distribution network. Whatever the elements are that make the financial projections a viable business opportunity, those elements should be closely monitored during the development stages.

Along with identifying these key elements, we recommend creating a measurement tool to track those elements. A regularly scheduled market research survey can track key customer trends, behaviors, or attitudes. A phone call to the engineering department can update the latest product cost estimates. A new line item added to an existing monthly sales report can be used to track distribution progress. Put these measures in place so that results can be compared to the estimates placed on the strategic road map. It will highlight progress made and, more importantly, provide an ongoing assessment of the market potential for the business.

Strategic Road Maps as a Planning Tool

The process of creating a strategic road map will identify implementation issues that will need to be addressed for the development of a new business opportunity. Any issues that present significant hurdles to the process should be included on this road map for senior management, as they will need that information in their work of defining the corporate strategy.

In many cases, this strategic road map represents the "launching" of the first phase of development for the new business opportunity. With key action items and milestones available, people can be assigned to this new project, and work can begin.

It is important to consider the strategic road map to be a "living" document that changes and evolves along with the business development process. According to Moen's Maureen Wenmoth, "We used the future map for years, worked it as a tool. We updated it frequently as we found that some things happened faster than we predicted."

Presentation to Senior Management

With a portfolio of new business opportunities and a strategic road map, the Discovery team is ready for a presentation of their output to senior management. The Discovery team's sponsor can play an important role in this presentation by helping to guide its development. The sponsor can provide insights to the Discovery team on the following topics:

◆ How do the new business opportunities "fit" into the current thinking of management?

◆ What is the best way of explaining the insights that drove the development of these opportunities?

◆ How developed should the opportunities appear?

◆ Will senior management want to play a role in helping to refine the opportunities?

◆ Are there certain strategic options being considered that would make some of the opportunities more attractive to management than others?

◆ How aggressive is management feeling about new ventures?

◆ What level of risk is currently considered tolerable?

◆ What is the best way to introduce the visionary opportunities?

This presentation needs to be factual and accurate in the information shared, but special attention does need to be paid to making it engaging for senior management. The Discovery team has been through an intense and transformative process. They have learned a lot about customers, the future, and innovative ideas. They have points of view and, perhaps, even passion about these ideas. It is important to portray these elements in the presentation. Don't reduce your ideas to a few PowerPoint slides. Think of innovative and novel ways to communicate these opportunities. Identify a theme that runs through the presentation. Use video clips, bring in thought leaders or market experts (or get them on a conference call). Make sure that senior management feels the energy that was produced by the Discovery Process and the opportunities that exist for the future.

We recommend that the presentation to senior management include all members of the Discovery team and all members of the senior management team. The environment created for this meeting should be similar to that of the Discovery team in the creation process: creative, collaborative, and entrepreneurial. The business opportunities are not yet fully developed, as they have not been through the important financial evaluation process and refinements that may accompany their development. Therefore, the opportunities are not ready for senior management to provide a go/no go decision. The purpose of this meeting is to present to senior management the findings of the Discovery Process and begin to create some alignment around interesting new business opportunities that could lead to possible new corporate strategies.

Senior management should understand that they are being presented with business opportunities discovered on the company's strategic frontier, which the team believes will create value in the marketplace and value for the company (should they decide to pursue them). The business opportunities will not yet contain a detailed plan for how the company would implement them or the impact of the opportunity on the company's infrastructure or systems. We believe it is the role of senior management to identify how the company's business systems could be employed to implement a new business opportunity and to remove any internal barriers for its development. Decisions regarding the allocation of resources and redeployment of corporate assets to take advantage of market opportunities—the essence of corporate strategy—should be the primary role of the senior management team.

We favor a fairly structured process for the meeting with senior management but some teams prefer a more relaxed and informal interaction. In a more structured process, members of the Discovery team present the business opportunities, one at a time. Following each presentation, the senior management team is asked to first identify things they like about the opportunity, creating a list that is recorded on a flip chart. They are then asked to note issues and concerns they see with that business opportunity (or their perceived ability to implement the opportunity). Finally, senior managers are asked to identify "builds" or enhancements that might help address some of the issues and concerns they identified. This three-part process flow is used for each of the business opportunities presented.

At the end of the meeting, the senior management team provides direction for the next steps for the Discovery team. One possibility is that the team will be asked to further refine the opportunities, based on the feedback provided by the senior management team. Another is that the opportunities are sufficiently attractive to move to the next step, the evaluation stage.

Beyond the Discovery Process: The Evaluation Stage

The output from the Discovery Process is a portfolio of new business opportunities and the strategic road map based on the exploration of the strategic frontier. The strategy innovation process ends at this point, and the strategic planning process begins. Senior management will typically determine which of the business opportunities warrant moving to the evaluation phase. In the evaluation phase, market forecasts are made, revenue flows are determined, costs are estimated, and a quantitative business plan is crafted. The resulting key measures are compared to company hurdle rates for new businesses, and the attractiveness of the opportunities are determined.

Because every industry is dependent on different variables for success, and every business has a different evaluation system, it is impossible to suggest a best approach in this area. Some companies do this analysis internally, while others turn their new portfolio over to external consulting companies for help in evaluating and crafting strategic options.

Summary

- The Mapping Phase gets its name from the creation of a strategic road map for the company, making the proprietary view of the company's future tangible for all to see.

- A strategic road map is a time line into the future that contains critical activities and milestones that must take place for the business opportunity to succeed. The "big picture" view of the implementation plan provided by the strategic road map will uncover key issues that must be addressed.

- Begin the mapping by laying out the relevant time frame (often five years) and identifying the important sectors, such as the opportunity development, consumer/society, customer/marketplace, competition, technology, and government/regulatory sectors.

- For each sector, identify and place on the time line the action items, trends, discontinuities, and milestones that will play a role in the development of that business opportunity (or a portfolio of opportunities).

- Develop measurement tools to track the key elements placed on the strategic road map so that progress can be noted and actions taken.

- As the final step in the Discovery Process, present the portfolio of business opportunities and a strategic road map to senior management for their consideration. Frequently, these business opportunities will then undergo a quantitative assessment of their potential for the corporation, using in-house standards and evaluation criteria.

PART THREE

ADVANCED
STRATEGY
INNOVATION

CHAPTER 11

Maximizing the Discovery Process

> Whenever you are asked if you can do a job, tell 'em, "Certainly I can!" Then get busy and find out how to do it.
>
> —*Theodore Roosevelt*

The preceding chapters described the basics of the Discovery Process—with sufficient detail to get you started. This chapter contains the answers to some additional questions we have been asked concerning the process.

Discovery Process and the Corporate Vision

Q. *What role does a corporate vision play in the Discovery Process?*

A. Vision statements in many corporations are ineffective because they are created to describe the current way of doing business rather than being an aspirational view of a desired future. Think about many of the vision statements you have seen. Nearly all of them talk about the same things:

We will strive to:

- Produce the highest-quality, most dependable products in the markets in which we compete

- Provide the highest level of service to satisfy the needs of our customers

- Be dedicated to the belief that our people are our most important asset

- Conduct our affairs in a manner consistent with the highest ethical standards

- Provide a fair, consistent rate of return to our shareholders.

What do these statements say? They say that the company is dedicated to doing the things that will help them stay in business. It is the equivalent of a person saying that their goal in life is to keep breathing. Too often vision statements are descriptions of how the company will be run, not a vision of where it is heading.

To be effective, a vision should describe some "future state" that is so appealing that the company stakeholders will be motivated and dedicated to the journey. And it needs to be more than "be number one in our industry" or "double our return on investment." Measures of this type are *by-products* of doing something else well, not a statement of what you want to do well. Investors may like financial measures as visions but most employees are not motivated by the prospect of making someone else wealthy.

The goal of a vision should be to identify what the company would like to achieve that will somehow have an important impact. Think of the purported early vision of Apple Computer, with a computer in every home (at a time when no one knew what a personal computer could do). Merck wants to eliminate diseases. Marriott wants every guest to leave satisfied. These are aspirational future states that have value. Moving toward these worthy goals can be very motivating. It stimulates our behavior by first engaging our emotions, our passions. Perhaps the real goal should be to have every corporation produce a passion statement, so that it is more likely to motivate.

So the question about a vision and the Discovery Process hinges on whether the company has a vision of a compelling future state or if it has a description of how it runs its business. If it is a vision of a compelling future state, it dovetails nicely into the Discovery Process. The future state will clearly identify the end goal for the company, making it much easier to define its next strategic frontier. If Merck wants to eliminate diseases, then assessing where diseases are right now versus the goal of "no diseases" will clearly outline what needs to be addressed in the near future. If Marriott has any unsatisfied customers, they can find out where their next strategic frontier needs to be on the way to their vision. When you know that the top of the mountain is your goal, you can usually tell where you need to go next as long as the peak is in sight.

If the corporate vision statement is not an ideal future state but merely a statement of how the company will operate, then it will not provide effective guidance to the selection of a strategic frontier. In fact, in these types of companies, it is the exercise of identifying the strategic frontier that helps the company gain a vision of where they are heading. Often it is the first time that management has looked up from their quarterly reports and balance sheets to think about where the company is headed next. The teams we have worked with are usually energized by thinking about and exploring the company's future, its next strategic frontier. It stimulates their thinking and engages their passions, just as a vision should. So, use the identification of your corporate strategic frontier as a worthy substitute for an ineffective vision statement.

Case in Point: Carl Zeiss

A different way to answer this question is to say that the Discovery Process can be used by a corporation to help identify its corporate vision. Carl Zeiss, a 150-year-old company headquartered in Ober-kochen, Germany, is known as a pioneer in the field of precision optics. Their expertise in this area spawned a variety of new businesses over the years, including ophthalmic products, microscopes, photographic lenses, laser optics, and many more. Toward the end of the twentieth century, Zeiss was a global, 13,000-employee company consisting of six business units, all of which were the number one or two brand in their different industries. The business was quite strong in 2000, when a new board chair and CEO, Dieter Kurz, was appointed.

It was Kurz's assessment that the thriving business units were all pursuing different strategic paths in their respective industries and that there was decreasing value in being part of the Zeiss family of businesses, except for the brand name. As a result, he committed to the alignment of these distinct businesses on a single corporate vision and to create an opportunity road map to help guide corporate growth through the year 2010.

Outside the company's board of management, there was some skepticism of this initiative. The business units were thriving, the future looked positive, and managers were not convinced that dedicating resources to an effort that did not have a direct, bottom-line impact was a worthwhile expenditure.

Consistent with the Discovery Process, teams were formed for this initiative. They included the top three corporate officers, who committed a significant amount of their time as active steering committee members. Because of their involvement, there was no need for further management alignment, and the team moved quickly to the Exploring Phase.

The core team determined that the insights necessary to drive the creation of a corporate vision were not business-based, but value-based. Corporate values are taken very seriously at Carl Zeiss. This initiative first sought to understand the company values across all of the business units. Many employees were engaged in this assessment, which represented something of a turning point for the initiative. These interactions drew the company together as they discussed common values, obsolete values, and aspirational values as they looked to their futures.

With an understanding of key corporate values for the future, the core team sought to better understand the emerging global marketplace for their businesses. A thought leader panel was conducted to explore cutting-edge trends in demographics, technologies, lifestyles, globalization, and brands. Insights were generated, organized, and used to develop a series of scenarios out over the next decade. Managers from across the Zeiss business units were becoming clearer, both individually and collectively, on the forces most likely to influence their businesses. This consensus was an important foundation for the development of the corporate vision.

The vision team then gathered all of the values and marketplace insights and drafted a vision statement for Carl Zeiss. They worked through the benefits and impact of the vision on a wide range of stakeholders. They fine-tuned the statement through discussions with employees around the world, as well as with the help of experts in vision creation and communication. They also developed a future map, illustrating the key milestones on the way to an envisioned Carl Zeiss of 2010. The vision statement and the map were then presented at the first annual executive vision forum for the top 300 company executives. There, the board of management played the role of the primary presenters and proceeded to enlist everyone in the communication and implementation of the vision throughout the organization. Their new unifying vision is led by the charge, "We make it visible."

Staging Phase

Q. *While I agree that "people support what they help create," how can we possibly get enough people involved so that support is widespread? Our company has offices all over the world.*

A. Global companies can present something of a logistical challenge to the Discovery Process. The secret to creating broad involvement is in creating an infrastructure of teams, all with different responsibilities in the process. That was the case with Schott Glas, a one-hundred-plus-year-old manufacturer of high-quality specialty glass products, and a sister company of Carl Zeiss. Headquartered in Germany, the company's 18,000 employees are distributed over forty countries worldwide.

The objective of the initiative was to create a corporate vision for the company that would guide their strategy out through the year 2010. The sponsors of the initiative insisted that the new corporate vision be embraced by all of the company's offices, as the basis for new growth initiatives in the future.

The first step was to form a core team of four senior Schott executives, who would provide overall guidance for the initiative. Next, ten additional teams were formed, representing geographical, functional, and/or special interests within the organization. Each team participated in a two-and-a-half-day team workshop, held at six different locations around the world. In all, about 150 Schott employees from a wide range of levels within the company directly participated in the initiative, including representatives from all of the major offices.

Following the workshops, the captains of each team joined the Schott core team to form a new group called the visioning team. This visioning team met for three days to consolidate and integrate the work of the ten teams into a vision document. The document was then shared with an operating group within Schott's headquarters plus a thought leader panel of experts from other large corporations, providing valuable insights for clarification and refinement.

The unveiling of the new corporate vision, called Vision 2010, was made at a two-day worldwide annual conference of 200 of Schott's most senior managers. Conference attendees were also given a chance to provide feedback and refinements, extending the involvement of this key group in the creation of the vision. Because people support what they help create, take the time to involve as many people as makes sense in a strategy innovation initiative. Build in a variety of teams and a variety of events for providing input and feedback, but keep the "creation" element to a smaller core group.

Aligning Phase

Q. *We are having trouble focusing on one strategic frontier that we want to explore for the future. Any suggestions?*

A. Like many processes, the Discovery Process needs to find the right trade-off between breadth and depth of exploration. If you decide that you do not need a breadth of information (for example, one frontier), you can afford to explore it in more depth and detail. If you decide that you need more breadth in your search (more frontiers), then you may not be able to explore those multiple frontiers to the same depth and detail as you could with one frontier.

Although we have suggested that teams focus on one frontier, the process will also be successful with several (up to three) frontiers. The Discovery Process is a creative process, and creativity thrives on the ambiguity that results when focus cannot be attained. In fact, there can be value in pursuing multiple frontiers simultaneously and letting the explorations interact with each other. Often it is the intermingling of unlike things that causes people to make new connections among those things, resulting in innovative new concepts.

A popular exercise in creativity sessions is to ask people to intermingle unlike things. One way to get people to create innovative products is to tell them to combine their product (let's say, a flashlight) with another, random product (such as dental floss). What new product is suggested by the hybrid of these very different categories? Is it a flashlight on a rope, dental floss that glows in the dark, or perhaps a narrow flashlight that can be used and stored in tight places? New ways of thinking are sparked when unlike ideas are intermingled and forced to coexist. It is almost as if the human mind tries to give meaning to this unusual combination and finds a way for the items to make sense together. So take advantage of the variety of your strategic frontiers and explore several or all of them at the same time. As a result, you may identify a new hybrid product category that could make an interesting new business opportunity.

We experienced something similar in a strategy innovation session with a division of 3M in the mid-1990s. At that time, 3M was requiring all business units to identify new business platforms for their future.

This task of identifying large, new business platforms was particularly challenging to one of 3M's divisions, Electrical Specialties. Located in Austin, Texas, the Electrical Specialties Division (ESD) had a rather eclectic mix of products in its line. It sold electrical and thermal insulating tape, electrical connectors, cable ties, and electrical diagnostic and detection equipment for the electrical trade. It also sold static protection, and heat and conduction devices for use in integrated circuit manufacturing. Finally, its method of treating steel reinforcing bars (rebar) to resist corrosion made it a supplier to large construction companies involved in concrete building projects.

With such a diverse mix of products and technologies, how could it focus its exploration efforts for a large, new business opportunity platform? Which of the customer segments should it address? Which of the technologies should it leverage? Which market should it explore?

A cross-functional team was formed to help address these questions in the pursuit of new business platforms. The team decided to pursue a two-pronged attack. The first was to meet with customers in all three of their strategic business areas—electrical supply companies, circuit board manufacturers, and large construction companies. The team identified key customers in each group, split into teams of two to four people each, and made personal visits to each of these companies. While these meetings were helpful and identified a number of customer insights that helped ESD improve their customer relations and product lines, they did not identify any breakthrough insights that could lead to a robust new business platform.

The second part of the initiative was to gain market foresight. Where would these markets be going in the future? What market forces were in place that would affect product sales, distribution channels, competition, and technologies? How could ESD get "in front of the curve" and create the products their customers would need before competition?

To gain market foresight, ESD decided to conduct a thought leader panel. The panel would consist of six "experts" who could provide an understanding of market dynamics and potential future scenarios. But how do you conduct the thought leader panel with three diverse strategic business areas—one panel for each area? That would be a time-consuming and expensive effort, as each panel can take four to six weeks to plan and recruit. Selecting only one of the strategic business areas, however, would be the equivalent to making the decision on the future of the company. How should the thought leader panel be set up to provide the market foresight that ESD needed?

The team made the decision to include a thought leader from each of the three strategic business areas on the same panel: electrical, corrosion protection, and electronics. They also added thought leaders from three *other* areas they felt might have an impact on their future business: wireless transmission, power supply management, and environmental issues. Would this eclectic mix of thought leaders provide anything valuable to the ESD team? Would their selection of "breadth" of topics over "depth" of topics give them enough understanding of their future? How would the panel ever be able to focus its conversations?

As you might guess, the panel was a big success (otherwise we would not have included it here). The thought leaders presented their areas of expertise and then began to interact with each other. In these interactions, they discovered how their fields might intersect and affect each other. Many started looking, almost unconsciously, for synergies across the areas. The result was the identification of "smart materials" as a wave of the future. One of the thought leaders offered the idea that in the not-too-distant future, when a concrete-reinforcing steel bar in a bridge cracked, it would break a low-grade electrical current running through it, which would trigger the automatic notification of authorities by a wireless telephone call.

Innovations often result from combining things that have never been combined before. In the Exploring Phase, be sure to include variety in your explorations. Go for breadth over depth. Spice things up by intentionally introducing some ambiguity.

Always add a wild card thinker to every panel, someone who can act as a catalyst for fresh perspectives, new approaches, different ways of looking at the world. Experts in an area tend to gravitate toward "groupthink" unless there is someone to help them broaden their thinking.

Q. *Why can't you just do a traditional market analysis to determine whether a strategic frontier is attractive to your company?*

A. If the strategic frontier you selected is an established market with established products and an established way of doing business, doing a traditional market analysis may be helpful background information for the team to have. However, if that analysis goes from being background information for the team to the "rules" by which the team will identify new business opportunities, you will be abandoning the goal of identifying "innovative" business opportunities. By adopting the "established" nature of the market and its current rules, you are more likely to identify business opportunities in that market that use traditional products sold to traditional customers in a traditional manner. The ultimate potential for strategy innovation is finding a *new* way to enter that market, delivering new or greater value to customers than current competitors. Strategy innovation needs to break the current rules, not follow them.

Looking at the size of an established market may not be a good indication of its potential as a strategic frontier. A market analysis for transistor radios in the early 1960s, for example, would not have been a good measure of the market potential for a Walkman—because the Walkman broke the rules for the transistor radio market and greatly expanded it. If you assume that you will find a way to add new value to customers or bring more customers to the market, then a current market analysis may not accurately reflect the potential.

We suggest you be very careful with traditional market analyses in this Discovery Process. You run the risk that your team will begin to think conventionally about the market, rather than look for innovative breakthroughs and ways to change the rules. If successful in that, the size of the current market may not be indicative of the size of the potential market. With better products, different customers, different distribution channels, or lower costs, you can impact the market in a way that a traditional market analysis cannot anticipate.

Exploring Phase

Q. *It seems like there are so many activities to consider for the Exploring Phase, how should we decide which ones to use?*

A. Start with the strategic frontier selected for the initiative and the three exploratory vectors: customer value, market dynamics, and business model innovation. First decide which of the vectors would be appropriate for the strategic frontier. Would customer insights be critical to a business opportunity that your company might consider on that strategic frontier? If so, plan to do some activity on the customer value vector. Customer insight would be critical on the frontier of online shopping, for example, but not as critical on the frontier of biotechnology.

Do the same thing for the other vectors also. Will changes in the marketplace have an impact on your frontier? If so, plan a market dynamics activity. Is there a likelihood that making changes to your company's business model would allow you to experience an increase in value? If so, look into business model innovation activities.

Once you have determined which exploration vectors apply to your strategic frontier, then decide what type of activity in those vectors would likely yield you *new* insights. Try several different activities. For example, in customer value, do some ValueProbes to listen to people talk about their interests and values concerning a product category, but also set up some in-home visits to observe how they actually use those products. Also try to do something very different from what you normally do, such as interviewing people on the street or visiting online chatrooms.

On an ongoing basis, the Discovery Team should be identifying what it is that they don't know about the frontier—and wish they did. By debriefing after every exploration activity, the team can assess what they learned, what additional questions were raised, and what other information might be valuable to know. Let this information drive the decision on what other activities to do. If you have the luxury of time, you can make some of these decisions sequentially. This is the true spirit of exploration.

Keep adding activities until you are overwhelmed with fresh insights or have run out of time or money.

Q. *What are some of the things you do in a thought leader panel?*

A. We usually start out with individual presentations by each of the thought leaders, to allow them to share their perspectives and views of the future. Following that, we often engage the thought leaders in a panel discussion, asking them to respond to specific questions and issues from the members of the audience.

One of our favorite exercises is the business assumption test. Give each of the thought leaders an 8½-by-11 inch drawing of a fist with a thumb protruding from it. Then read to them a business assumption currently held by the company with regards to the future. For example, you might say, "The trend among adults for healthier eating will accelerate in the next five years." The thought leaders would then hold up their drawing in a thumbs-up "I agree" mode or a thumbs-down "I disagree" mode. No sideways thumb is allowed. Each thought leader would then be invited to share the thinking that contributed to his or her response.

As cited in Chapter 7, the identification of business assumptions for the future is a powerful way for the Discovery Team to align with senior management and to focus their exploration efforts. With the right thought leaders on the panel, this exercise can be one of the most powerful means of influencing Discovery Teams and their management as to the issues that lie between their current business and future opportunities. The key is being clear on the expertise best suited to play the role of sounding board.

The team must believe the thought leaders to be credible with regard to their future business assumptions. What is the right expertise for the panel? Can you benefit most from senior officers or board members from a parallel but noncompetitive industry? What if you could attract thought leaders who had successfully traveled a strategic path similar to the one you are on now? Or, what if you could find thought leaders who were unsuccessful in one of their ventures so that you could learn their hard-earned lessons before going down that path? We have been impressed with the value of this exercise and the willingness of world-class experts to play the role of sounding board for the future of other companies.

The results of this business assumption test are surprisingly predictable. Some of the assumptions are affirmed, often in new ways that gives management an even deeper conviction about staying the course. Some assumptions are challenged, often causing management to revise their assumptions to account for the new insights shared. And finally, some assumptions are outright rejected by the thought leaders as obsolete in a dynamic world.

Creating Phase

Q. *How can we identify more visionary opportunities?*

A. It sometimes takes a while (or a push) to get team members to think big and identify visionary new business opportunities. The strength of corporate gravity and the belief that ideas offered should be practical will keep team members from offering any "wild" ideas. Therefore, you need a way to force wild thinking.

A common approach is to ask people to define business opportunities that would appear far in the future. The nice thing about thinking in the future is that it contains none of the constraints that are felt so strongly today. With the idea that future technology will allow many things to happen that cannot happen today, people are usually more willing to offer more speculative and more visionary ideas.

Another way to get people to stretch their thinking is to go the opposite direction and actually *increase* the pressure of constraints. Tell your team you want ideas for a new widget that costs half of what today's widgets cost. This will require team members to abandon the current method of making widgets and rethink the entire process. In other words, unrealistic constraints will often force blank-page, innovative thinking to occur.

Finally, the work done by Clayton Christensen and colleagues on "disruptive" innovations can be a very effective stimulus for getting team members to identify more visionary opportunities for their companies. Christensen posits that most innovations are sustaining innovations, which are improvements to current products or services aimed at current customers in that market.[1] His work shows that disruptive technologies can have an even greater impact because they create new markets. The way that many disruptive technologies work is to provide a somewhat inferior but cost-effective product to people who are not currently customers in that market. By creating a business model that can sustain this new, lower-cost product, the disrupter will gain an important foothold in the market, dominate its segment, and be protected from its larger, cost-bloated rivals. Expose team members to some of Christensen's work, and they will be stretched in their thinking.

Q. *Do you have any examples of creating a new business model innovation?*

A. We were privileged to be part of a very important strategy innovation initiative with IBM Research in the 1990s. From its inception, IBM Research had been and nurtured for the purpose of pure research. For decades, their corporate parent was an arm's-length sponsor, proud of the Nobel Prize–winning efforts of its scientists. This relationship between IBM and IBM Research resulted in breakthrough discoveries in science, but was never expected to show a direct linkage with the corporation's bottom line.

That relationship was tested in the early 1990s when IBM fell on hard times. In 1992 and 1993, IBM lost over \$13 billion, and in the prior three years, it had lost close to 50 percent of its mainframe market share. These losses led to layoffs of 45,000 IBM employees while red ink flowed and its market value sank. Seeking help, IBM brought in a new CEO, Louis V. Gerstner, Jr.

His first day on the job, Gerstner boarded a helicopter and flew to Yorktown, New York, to meet with Jim McGroddy, vice president of IBM Research at the T.J. Watson Research Center. "If there was a soul of IBM, this lab was it,"[2] noted Gerstner, who was uncertain at the time whether IBM Research should continue as part of the corporation.

The visit proved to Gerstner that there was marketable "value" to be mined from the intellectual property at IBM Research, and later he convinced McGroddy that Research was in need of a new "value model" in its relationship with the corporation. Research could no longer produce only science for the sake of science. The corporate parent wanted a return on its investment.

So, McGroddy challenged his organization to identify strategies that would enable IBM Research to double its value to IBM within one year. To address this challenge, McGroddy chartered a global team of ten fast-track researchers to create a blueprint for "Doubling the Value" of IBM Research. This cross-functional team, representing each major lab from around the world, gathered insights and data from its current and potential corporate customers. The team adopted a "guerilla" approach to the initiative—doing whatever it would take to create value-generating new concepts in a very limited amount of time. They planned to present their findings to McGroddy at a meeting of the global research council, less than a week away. Hours were long and meals, if any, were taken during working sessions. This working style galvanized the passion and commitment of the team to their goal.

The final phase of the process involved a multiday team immersion behind locked doors in San Jose, California, where the team focused on a continuous iteration of the proposed strategies. A pair team of scientists would advance a concept as far as possible and then, in round-robin fashion, pass it on to the next pair team. Each "Doubling Value" concept was iterated a half dozen times or more. All team members were able to add their fingerprints to every concept, multiple times. An artist was enlisted to bring visual life to each concept. The presentation was rehearsed and rerehearsed.

The output consisted of a series of novel and unique solutions in areas such as metrics for new patents and technology licensing, to be implemented by McGroddy and his executive staff. This new strategic direction also dovetailed nicely with Gerstner's view that "the IBM Research Division was far more fertile and creative than our ability to commercialize all of its discoveries. We were underutilizing a tremendous asset."[3]

Today, with Paul Horn having taken the leadership baton from Jim McGroddy in 1996, IBM Research has dramatically increased its tangible value to IBM. In 1999, IBM was able to generate $1.7 billion in patent licensing fees alone, and this vital revenue stream has continued to grow.[4] IBM Research created a radically different "business model" than the one originally envisioned by Thomas Watson, one that links leading-edge science to the corporation's financial vitality and new shareholder wealth.

Mapping Phase

Q. *Coming up with new business opportunities is not the problem in our company—implementing them effectively is our problem. Why doesn't the Discovery Process include an implementing phase?*

A. For many companies, the challenge of effective implementation of an innovation is more difficult than the identification of the innovation. We did not include an implementing phase in this process because we have found that it varies significantly by industry and by company within industries. Any implementing phase that we could develop would need to be generic enough to apply across industries and would probably not be specific enough to meet the needs of individual companies.

However, we have had experience successfully using elements of this process on implementation issues. One example is with the Hewlett-Packard Inkjet Business Unit (IJBU). This HP business unit designs, manufactures, and markets inkjet print cartridges for the HP family of printers, faxes, and large format plotters. In the early 1990s, the significant growth of HP printers for personal computers resulted in a 63 percent compound annual growth rate over five years. However, the next five years promised even greater growth, with revenues projected to increase from $1 billion to $6 billion by the year 2000. In the meantime, competitive companies were overcoming technological barriers and threatening to step into this market and benefit from this surge in demand.

In 1994, the IJBU was faced with a positive, but daunting, challenge—to keep up with the tremendous growth prospects in the market and maintain their dominant market position in a competitively charged environment. Dana Seccomb, general manager of IJBU at that time, recalled the challenge of moving a 10,000-employee company in one focused, strategic direction amidst the chaos of phenomenal growth. At one point, his management team had received fifty-six different proposals from the various functional groups on what needed to be done to grow the business.

Seccomb formed a team of ten of his direct reports to identify an implementation plan for the next five years. The team identified two key areas that would be critical to their success. The first was the development of their relatively weak marketing function so that they could remain competitive and hold on to their share as new companies entered the ink cartridge market. The second area was to create a plan for expanding the company's infrastructure and assimilating the new employees that would be required.

With the key areas identified, the IJBU team sought outside expertise in the form of two different thought leader panels. The first was a panel of experts in marketing at companies such as Coca-Cola, Kraft, Intel, and DuPont. A month later, the team held the second thought leader panel, addressing the issue of "hypergrowth," with experts from companies such as Cisco Systems, Microsoft, Atari, and Conner Peripherals. Each thought leader panel consisted of presentations by the experts and interactions between the experts and the IJBU team. These sessions were followed by debriefing sessions with the team to distill key learnings and insights and to align around next steps.

Using the insights from the experts who had lived through similar marketing and hypergrowth conditions, the IJBU management team established four strategic opportunity areas that they would develop to drive the business planning. Subteams were created for these four areas, and a total of eight "bridge strategies" were developed to move the company from a $1 billion business to a $6 billion business over the next five years. They included such things as the communication of the business vision, the expansion plans of each of the company's key business processes, and the communication and training vehicles to assimilate new hires into the distinctive HP culture.

These bridge strategies, the implementation plan, became the strategic road map for the IJBU. They were tracked quarterly by the management team and were reviewed and revised at each yearly strategic planning session.

Endnotes

1. Clayton M Christensen, Mark W. Johnson, and Darrell K. Rigby, "Foundations for Growth," *Sloan Management Review*, Spring 2002.
2. Louis V. Gerstner, Jr., *Who Says Elephants Can't Dance? Inside IBM's Historic Turnaround* (New York: HarperCollins, 2002).
3. Ibid.
4. "Eureka! Laboratories that Produce Profits: IBM Masters the Way to Make Research Pay Off Now," *The New York Times*, September 9, 2001, Section 3, p. 1.

CHAPTER 12

FORMALIZING A STRATEGY INNOVATION SYSTEM

> Your system is perfectly designed to give you the results that you get.
>
> —W. EDWARDS DEMING

For some companies, the pursuit of strategy innovation can be done on an as-needed, ad hoc basis. Pulling a Discovery team together periodically to explore the future of the market and customer needs will yield a portfolio of new business opportunities that could keep internal development teams busy for a couple of years.

However, there are many other companies where the intermittent pursuit of new opportunities is not enough. Industries that feature a new product line every year rely heavily on understanding their evolving market and customers. Companies that pursue a corporate strategy of market leadership and the commitment to innovation in their markets will need a more regular infusion of customer insights and market foresight to fulfill their goals. Companies in a turn-around situation will need to be constantly identifying and exploring their strategic frontiers for new business opportunities that will lead to their survival.

We believe that every company in the future will have strategy innovation as one of their core capabilities. Because most companies in the future will have access to information, technology, capital, manufacturing capabilities, and markets, it is the capability of a corporation to construct an innovative value proposition and a profitable business model that will determine success. And success will be fleeting, as competitors will attempt to replicate that success.

If your company could benefit from having innovation as a core competence, you should consider the *formalization of a strategy innovation system.* When strategy innovation is formalized, it has a home. Someone is accountable for it. People know where to go with questions, suggestions, or information needs. They also know where to go for results.

Hewlett-Packard's Inkjet Supplies Business Unit perceived the need to formalize strategy innovation after their initiative. Terry Tallis, business planning manager, said, "We tried to make it a process internally because the euphoria of the project can wear off rapidly. How do you get it ingrained in your day-to-day activity? Who do you go to for a new road map, a new strategy? What happens if the financial environment changes? Who owns responsibility for tracking these changes?"

The formalization of strategy innovation in an organization also contributes significantly to the culture of that organization. The number of companies that list "innovation" as one of their core values is mind-boggling. Everybody says they value innovation, and everybody wants their companies to pursue innovative ideas. However, very few companies to date have made a commitment to innovation by formalizing it, building it into the structure and the day-to-day operation of the business. Employees "hear" a lot from their senior management on how the company should behave. It is what they "see" from senior management that lets them know when they are serious and committed to what they say. A company with an ongoing, formalized practice for strategy innovation will provide a stimulus for fresh thinking in the organization and, thereby, invigorate its culture.

From the very beginning of the company, the culture at Motorola reflected the commitment that the Galvin family had to innovation. It has been a result of their constant pursuit of new technologies and new markets that the company has survived nearly three-quarters of a century in the volatile electronics industry. According to Bob Galvin, "You need to have a culture of renewal. My father, Paul, knew that he would be out of business in a year, so he had to find something else to do when that happened. He would always be in motion for motion's sake. He had to renew the day he opened up. Our driving thrust has always been renewal. How can we renew what we are doing?"

Penetrating the Corporate Immune System

Formalizing strategy innovation in a corporation appears, on the surface, to be a relatively easy process. Just hire a creative person, give him or her an office and a budget, and prepare for the breakthrough that will fund all the retirement accounts. Nothing could be further from the truth. Integrating any new function to an organization is a complex process of addressing reporting relationships, accountabilities, turf battles, salary disputes, and office locations. Integrating innovation is even more complex than most functions.

Innovation, by its very nature, "breaks the rules." Pablo Picasso has been quoted as saying, "The act of creation is first an act of destruction." What he meant was that creativity seeks to look at things a different way. By doing that, the creator is willing to "destroy" the old perceptions or assumptions about something in order to give it new and different meaning.

Think about this dichotomy for a moment. Corporations are created to standardize and control. In order to survive, the company must create consistent, reliable product to customers in a way that maintains the financial integrity of the organization. Internal systems are created to control internal processes—systems that are rule-driven with reporting processes that alert management to any deviation from the norm so that corrective action can be taken. "No surprises" is the operative mantra. Nearly everyone in the management of a company is responsible for preventing actions that might affect the company's standard operating procedures.

The result of these internal processes and controls is a corporate "immune system" that develops, protecting the company from surprises and deviations.

Clayton Christensen, in his book *The Innovator's Dilemma*, observed, "One of the dilemmas of management is that, by their very nature, processes are established so that employees perform recurrent tasks in a consistent way, time after time. To ensure consistency, they are meant *not* to change—or if they must change, to change through tightly controlled procedures. *This means that the very mechanisms through which organizations create value are intrinsically inimical to change.*"[1]

Innovation, however, is all about change and surprises. It is finding new ways of doing things, new ways to create value. It leverages surprises in the marketplace, and can create very positive surprises in the corporate boardroom—"what a great idea!"

But what happens when innovation tries to navigate the corporate hallways on its way to the corporate boardroom? To meet the changing needs of customers, someone in the company creates a new product design, signaling a change to your current product line. The innovation "champion" in the company then takes this new design concept to the R&D department, where she is told that the project will have to wait due to higher priority projects. She then shares it with the people in operations, where she is told that it will require new equipment that is not covered in this year's budget. The champion then goes to the finance group, which runs some numbers that show the projected ROI for the new design is not as good in the first year as the planned line extension

Strategic Point of Tension

Successful innovation can be very beneficial to a corporation but, in the process, will require it to change. Most corporate systems are established to *prevent* corporate change in order to maintain predictability. The challenge for management is to foster innovation and change without putting the organization at risk for its predictability.

that is coming up. Three strikes, and the champion is out. The immune system wins. Innovation cannot penetrate the corporate defense system, the controls designed to maintain the status quo and eliminate surprises.

This tale has played out thousands of times within companies across all industries. While well-intentioned senior managers desire the benefits that innovation can provide, they do not realize the systemic roadblocks that internal innovation champions encounter.

The Blueprint for Formalizing Innovation

It is possible to integrate innovation into any corporation. It must, however, represent a commitment on the part of senior management to provide the support and resources necessary to overcome the corporate immune system.

The following four elements must all be addressed for an innovation system to become *integrated* into the operating systems of a corporation:

1. Management mandate
2. Corporate infrastructure
3. Innovation process
4. Corporate culture

Management mandates for innovation will never get off the ground unless resources are provided via the corporate infrastructure. Information generated in an innovation process will dissipate without a receptive infrastructure. Even when the right infrastructure and processes are in place, the wrong corporate culture will ignore the new knowledge and kill the new ideas created by them. Innovation processes that begin at the company's grassroots with the support of the culture will wither without a management mandate. All four of these elements must work together for the integration of innovation to a corporation.

In the early 1990s, Eastman Kodak had an Office of Innovation, which was located outside the main headquarters building in Rochester. Although the staff there offered valuable advice and support to Kodak employees who had come up with new ideas, its ultimate demise was most likely due to its not being integrated into the mainstream corporate business systems. Recognizing their need for innovation and the shortcomings of the previous office, Kodak redesigned this group, integrating it more fully to the ongoing organization and its systems. Today, Kodak has a very impressive organization, called Systems Concept Center (SCC), aimed at identifying and integrating innovative business opportunities. Funded by a portion of the R&D budget, the SCC identifies, develops, and screens innovative business opportunities and coordinates their smooth transition to the commercialization group. Unlike the original Office of Innovation, which was "added on" to the Kodak organization, the SCC is "built into" it and appears significantly more productive.

> **Process Tip:**
>
> *Innovation needs to be integrated into your company, not merely added on.*
>
> Trying to add innovation to a company by setting up an innovation department would be like transplanting a human heart in a recipient but not attaching the important arteries and veins. Without somehow being integrally connected to the rest of the body on a constant, ongoing basis, the transplant will lose its nourishment and vitality and will ultimately fail.

Management Mandate

The integration of strategy innovation into a corporation must begin with a management mandate. Because senior management is responsible for the corporate strategy, anything that helps feed the process of strategy creation must be initiated by them. In addition, senior management has the ultimate responsibility for the corporate infrastructure. Changes in the infrastructure that will be required for strategy innovation must have the proactive support of the senior management group.

What form should this "management mandate" take? We believe that management should *not mandate a process* for strategy innovation, but should *mandate the desired output*.

Employees in many corporations have been inundated with processes over the last several decades. In an effort to streamline operations and increase the bottom line, management has mandated quality control, reengineering, Six Sigma, and many other internal processes. The goal for strategy innovation is not to have employees implementing a new process. The goal should be focusing on an output—a portfolio of viable new business opportunities for the company.

Therefore, we recommend that the management mandate be for a specified *outcome* of a strategy innovation process. We most admire how the management mandate was carried out at 3M under the leadership of Bill Coyne. When Coyne became senior vice president of R&D for 3M in the early 1990s, he began looking for ways to improve the level of innovation in the company. As he talked with people across the business units and laboratories of 3M, he discovered that there were many exciting new technologies that were languishing in the labs because higher priorities were being placed on a large number of lower-risk line extension products. Although 3M had successfully evolved an innovation culture that was aggressively proactive and not constrained by a corporate "immune system," still it required fine-tuning to increase the emphasis on the nonincremental to breakthrough opportunities. Coyne explained, "We knew that we had to produce fewer, but better, products. Their time lines were longer, and they represented greater risk to the company, so the business units were not supporting these opportunities on their own." Knowing that the depreciation rate of technologies was increasing, Coyne searched for a way to stimulate the development and introduction of these technologies to the marketplace.

Building off a previous program already in place, Coyne created what he called Pacing Plus programs throughout 3M. Pacing Plus was an attempt to find one or two products or new business platforms in each business unit that were strong enough to make a significant impact on the market. Specifically, Pacing Plus programs were defined by the following characteristics:

- Capable of "changing the basis of competition" in a market
- Projected to generate $100+ million in revenues
- Global in scope
- Able to leverage a proprietary 3M technology

Proposals for Pacing Plus programs poured in and were given a strict review to determine if they were of Pacing Plus caliber. Not all the business units were able to identify one or two programs to meet the corporate goal and were instructed by management to go back and "try harder." Those that qualified were then provided with corporate resources to support them. Coyne designated nearly 20 percent of the total corporate R&D budget to helping business units develop and get these Pacing Plus programs to market. In addition, they would get priority allocation of resources from the corporation for engineering tech center support. With this assist, business units were able to develop their higher-volume, higher-risk programs to help break the cycle of reliance on incremental line extensions to meet yearly growth targets. Without this support, the business units were reluctant to support these programs because of the longer time lines and greater risk to the company.

One of the first Pacing Plus programs to reach the market in 1996 was Dual Brightness Enhancement film, which increases the brightness of LCD screens in laptops and other electronic displays. A year later, the 3M Pharmaceuticals Division introduced Aldara, an immune response modifier in cream form for the treatment of genital warts. In 1998, CEO and board chair L.D. DeSimone announced that "Pacing Plus programs have the potential to reach over $6 billion of annual sales at maturity."[2] Although current 3M CEO Jim McNerney is using a different approach to innovation, his corporate R&D commitment to the development of innovative new technologies at the business unit level has increased from 20 percent to 30 percent. While the form of strategy innovation initiatives will change as the market needs change, 3M's management mandate for innovation will continue.

In addition to stating the desired output of strategy innovation, the management mandate should include a tangible infrastructure change, clear accountability for results, an impassioned appeal, and the identification of a strategic frontier.

Tangible Infrastructure Changes

The management mandate for strategy innovation must include tangible infrastructure changes. Employees do not "hear" mandates; they recognize them when they "see" them. Tangible changes of some type from senior management represent a commitment to what they are proposing. The greater the tangible change that is made, the greater the perceived commitment. Examples of tangible changes to consider might include reallocation of budgets, the creation of a new group or department, or new guidelines for bonuses or yearly reviews.

When Procter & Gamble launched its Corporate New Ventures organization, a net was cast wide across the organization to identify the most capable P&Gers to staff the effort. While identification of the right individuals was easy enough, recruitment was a challenge. There was no precedent of successful career paths that went outside of a corporate sector and through an organization like Corporate New Ventures. The solution to this dilemma demonstrated a clear management mandate. Senior officers met with individual candidates and informed them that their promotion paths would likely accelerate due to this innovation assignment.

At Eastman Kodak in the early 1990s, R&D budget changes were implemented that helped stimulate the change in strategic direction of that imaging giant. Bob LaPerle explains, "There is no question that it takes a while to change the strategy and culture of a large organization. We were able to first make a dramatic change in the

R&D spending. By 1992, there was a significant shift in spending away from silver halide projects toward projects aimed at digital and hybrid approaches. QuickTake, the world's first digital camera, was an early success."

The Carl Zeiss company pioneered the science and business of optics in 1852. In 2001, the Zeiss board and management team, led by chairman and CEO Dieter Kurz, conducted a worldwide strategy innovation initiative that created a future road map and vision for the future of the company. The tangible infrastructure change that signaled this commitment to strategy innovation was the creation of a vision office, led by Vice President Marc Vogel. This office coordinates a series of global strategy initiatives, acts as a communications hub, and keeps the organization's scorecard on its metrics for success.

Clear Accountability

A successful management mandate must be clear about who is responsible for the results. Because new business opportunities involve most functional areas in the organization, it may not be clear to the functional groups that will be held accountable for the results.

At the same time, we recommend that the person or group responsible for the new business opportunities be involved in the establishment of the mandated results. Holding people accountable for unrealistic goals or providing them with inadequate resources to achieve those goals is counterproductive to the mandate and will jeopardize the formalization effort. Because people support what they help create, allow the responsible group to be part of the creation of the goals and identification of the required resources.

Impassioned Appeal

A mandate for innovation is different from a mandate for operational efficiency. Senior management can convince the company, through a myriad of charts and financial analyses, that they need to cut costs to remain competitive in their market. A rational, quantitative appeal will appeal to the rational, quantitative need for greater efficiency.

Strategy innovation is not a typical, quantitative goal, so it should not be communicated to employees in a rational, quantitative way. Strategy innovation is a bold leap into a new future. It is a rallying cry for growth, a clarion call to lead others into the future, to achieve new levels of performance and success. It is often vision- or mission-based. It speaks to what is possible to achieve. It taps into the wishes and aspirations of everyone—customers, employees, shareholders, and other stakeholders. For these reasons, we suggest that the management mandate for strategy innovation in a company include an impassioned appeal. Tap into people's aspirations, cite their need for challenge, or highlight the opportunity for everyone to make a difference (and grow in the process). Appeal to their hearts through emotions, not to their heads with numbers.

Strategic Frontier

The management mandate for strategy innovation should include reference to the company's strategic frontier. In 1961, U.S. President John F. Kennedy delivered his famous mandate for stimulating the growth of the U.S. space program by specifying a new strategic frontier, an American on the moon by the end of the decade. Highlighting the focus of strategy innovation will help people see that this is just not a random process being introduced to the organization, just in case it might help the company. Instead, identifying the strategic frontier as the goal to be achieved through strategy innovation will help employees see it as a tool to help the corporation get where it wants or needs to be in the future.

Corporate Infrastructure

There is no one-size-fits-all recommendation for corporate infrastructure to implement strategy innovation. Every corporation is different, sometimes radically different. For example, a small, highly entrepreneurial company may require only minor fine-tuning to integrate a system of innovation. On the other hand, a large, hierarchical corporation that has been successfully managing and line-extending one product over the last five decades will require dramatic changes to become an organization with the capability of strategy innovation.

The integration of strategy innovation to a company must include changes to the corporate infrastructure. Strategy innovation needs:

- A home
- Resources to operate
- Metrics to assess its performance

Home

Where should the responsibility of strategy innovation report within a corporate infrastructure? We believe it should report directly to the division or corporate president. Strategy innovation is a cross-functional effort, requiring the involvement of all major departments—R&D, product development, marketing, operations, sales, and finance. To have strategy innovation report to any of the functional silos would place more emphasis on that function, which may not be warranted.

Reporting to the division president will maintain the visibility of strategy innovation and perhaps also shield it from inappropriate budget squeezes. Whenever budget concerns force a company to make trade-offs in their spending, the budget for today's programs will always win out over the budget for future programs. The urgency of today triumphs over the importance of tomorrow. By reporting to the president, strategy innovation will be more shielded from this inclination, assuming that the president is being held primarily responsible for the future.

The location of the strategy innovation function is an issue that is handled differently by the companies we have worked with. Procter & Gamble set up their Corporate New Ventures (CNV) group on their main campus in Cincinnati, maintaining proximity to key people in the organization and reporting to the company's COO.

The story is told that Craig Wynett's CNV group originally shared office space with several corporate vice presidents, until they were asked to find a different office because of the enthusiastic noise they created.

In a different approach to location, Barclays Global Investors (BGI) sent the developers of iShares to a location down the street, away from the daily activities of BGI. The idea, according to Garrett Bouton, CEO of the Global Individual Investor Business of BGI, was a deliberate attempt to create a different, more entrepreneurial culture from the rest of the organization.

> We incubated iShares as a separate business outside the company and allowed it to grow independently. We put people in a different building and gave them a separate identity. They cooperated with BGI when necessary, acting more like a BGI client. It gained a lot of momentum, almost eclipsing the BGI in importance. After eighteen months, we brought them back to this building, where they were challenged to maintain that entrepreneurial spirit.

Regardless of where a company's permanent strategy innovation group is physically located, it is very important that they have their own space. Let the group design the space to fit their working style, which will likely include flexible, comfortable, stimulating common space in lieu of typical corporate-gray cubicles.

Resources

We include both people and funding as part of the resources for formalizing strategy innovation.

People

Because strategy innovation is a cross-functional effort, it should include representatives from the major functional groups. We have seen it work as either a matrix reporting relationship or a separate cross-functional group. If the strategy innovation group is not a full-time responsibility, it is critical to have a commitment from the people involved that it will nevertheless be a high priority in the allocation of their time and attention. If it is a full-time responsibility, you will want to carefully consider both career path and compensation issues involved, to be sure you are getting the strongest people possible in this group.

As for the type of people who should be involved in strategy innovation, it is not necessary to staff it with only "creative" people. Creativity plays an important role in the strategy innovation process but other skills are useful also. For example, you need to have people who are good at gathering insights, from customers and other information sources. You will also need employees skilled in evaluating or assessing market viability for new products and people who can help plan implementation strategies.

The people who are most effective in working in strategy innovation are those who are open-minded and comfortable dealing in ambiguity. Open-minded people are more likely to see the potential for opportunities in a situation than those who are more closed-minded and judgmental. Because the strategy innovation process is heuristic and iterative, there is no one pathway or progression of steps that will guarantee success. There will be dead ends and times of uncertainty, particularly when dealing with the future. People who appreciate structure in their work and need to follow a delineated plan will find the "fuzzy front end" of strategy innovation to be frustrating.

Funding

The other major resource component to formalized strategy innovation is funding. How much should you invest in strategy innovation? Obviously that will differ significantly by industry and by company within an industry. We have seen a spectrum ranging from tens of thousands of dollars to hundreds of millions of dollars. One way to approach this question would be to ask how much you would be willing to spend in order to identify a new business that would be capable of generating $XX million per year. What is that worth to you? Think of it in investment terms, perhaps looking at the net present value after calculating the discounted future cash flows.

Another approach to the funding dilemma is to consider how money is currently allocated to new products throughout the company. Some companies have five or six groups all pursuing, in an uncoordinated way, new products. By pooling funds and providing a focus for the work (the strategic frontier), you may find strategy innovation to be no more costly and much more efficient and prolific than the programs that are currently in place. Also consider carving out some portion of your R&D budget for this effort.

To find the right level of funding, think about experimenting with strategy innovation using a "beta" approach. Start small. Identify a few good people, give them some money to spend, and see what they come up with in terms of new opportunities for the company to consider. Then, debrief their process after a period of time and see what could have been done had additional funds been available. Decide if it would be worth the additional investment. If so, let them run a little longer and check their results again. Experiment, learn, adjust, experiment again. How ironic to think you might be able to create quantum leaps in your business through incremental steps in this beta process.

Metrics

Some people consider the "fuzzy front end" of new product development to be like a black hole in a black box. It draws vast quantities of people and resources into it but nobody is really sure what happens inside or when results can be expected. When asked, the people in charge of the process claim that it is a creative process and creativity cannot be rushed or scheduled. This only adds to the mystery.

We see it a little differently. It is true that because creative processes are heuristic and iterative, it is difficult to schedule exactly when "success" will be achieved. However, that should not imply that anything short of the final "success" does not have value. New business opportunities do not just emerge from nothingness. They evolve from earlier forms, which can be tracked and measured.

This book has outlined the strategy innovation process as a progression of outputs leading ultimately to new business opportunities (see Figure 12-1). For example, the first output is a prioritized
listing of strategic frontiers. If you are in a company that knows
its strategic frontiers, you have something valuable that remains a
mystery to the vast majority of companies we talk to. Strategic frontiers are a goal; they are defined, and they can be tracked.

After strategic frontiers come insights. Each insight gained in the
Exploring Phase has value to the company, because it represents
value in the marketplace. Once identified, insights can be put in a
database, where they will continue to have value until the marketplace changes significantly. Set a goal for the number of insights
you want to generate per year and then track that number.

The next step in the evolution of new business opportunities is
"beginning ideas." A beginning idea is an insight translated into an
initial description of a business opportunity. However, because this
initial description serves only as a stepping-stone to the creation of
a finished business concept, we do not believe that there is value in
archiving and tracking beginning ideas.

Finally, the output of the Discovery Process is finished business

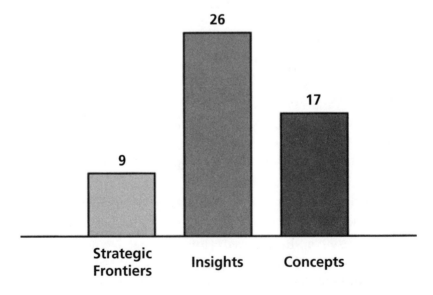

Figure 12-1. Strategy innovation metrics.

concepts. These are the beginning ideas that have been further developed and refined, perhaps several times. Concepts are what you evaluate in your new product evaluation process. They represent new business opportunities and, as part of a portfolio of options, are significant assets to your company. Concepts should also be included in the metrics of the strategy innovation process.

At some point, the Discovery Process outlined in this book becomes a quantitative game. If you want to come up with one viable new business opportunity, that means you may have to generate at least twenty to thirty new business concepts. For each business concept, you may have to create more than twenty to thirty beginning ideas. Each beginning idea may require ten to twenty new insights. Of course, these numbers will vary by the size of business desired by the company.

According to Bob LaPerle, Kodak assumes that it will take 3,000 "beginning ideas" to create one significant new successful business opportunity. The numbers will vary by team but the point here is that the process is not an unpredictable black box. The components can be identified and appropriate metrics established. This aspect of the Discovery Process is quite similar to the approach of most successful venture capital companies that monitor their prospective investments.

Innovation Process

As mentioned earlier in the chapter, the management mandate should not specify that the company will take part in a strategy innovation process. It should specify the outcome that management desires and let the organization decide the appropriate process to achieve those results.

We highly recommend that you use the five-phased process outlined in this book for your strategy innovation process. That's why we wrote the book. It is a proven, hands-on technique that works. Whether you are using an ad hoc team or a dedicated team, have them go through the Staging, Aligning, Exploring, Creating, and Mapping phases.

Keep your focus aimed externally, on customers and markets. Don't try to force their needs into your system of doing things or your areas of competence. This is a very common way that teams want to start the search for new businesses—identifying their core competencies so they can understand what they have to leverage. This approach will significantly narrow your range of vision on the frontier, allowing you to see only those opportunities that fit your abilities. Besides, the way you operate (and your competencies) may no longer be valuable in a dynamic market. Ask travel agents, or companies that make typewriters or carbon paper.

Start the process with insights about customer and market needs, not with product ideas. Procter & Gamble's Craig Wynett shared with us his story of an "electronic suggestion box" created by his Corporate New Ventures group, called myidea.com. When it first started, they asked employees to contribute suggestions for new product ideas, such as ways to improve Tide or many of P&G's other products. The number of suggestions they received for product improvements was quite limited. So they changed the suggestion criteria and asked people to answer the question, "What do you see that is interesting and provocative?" The number of suggestions increased dramatically. People are more comfortable identifying insights than translating insights into implications for new products.

And don't start the process with one or two insights, start with more than you think you can ever use. The creative process described here is one of divergence (generate a great quantity) followed by convergence (selection of the best ones to meet your criteria).

Corporate Culture

Strategy innovation will thrive in an innovative culture. When people in a company celebrate newness and uniqueness, value nonconformity, practice tolerance and flexibility, and tolerate mistakes, innovation will flourish.

Stan Gryskiewicz describes the basis of a creative corporate culture in his book *Positive Turbulence: Developing Climates for Creativity, Innovation, and Renewal.* He suggests that corporate attempts to institute a sense of order, control, and focus on their current business will unwittingly eliminate the sources for innovation and renewal. Organizations need to introduce sources of turbulence, diversity, and dissenting opinions so that employees will constantly question how the company should change to address business opportunities of the future. He writes, "Every big trend starts as a small, one-of-a-kind blip on the screen, easy to overlook and easy to dismiss. Only those paying close attention to the turbulent periphery will see it, and only those predisposed to thinking that turbulence can be positive will see its strategic potential. The task for visionary leaders is to create an environment where new information is embraced, not feared."[3]

But strategy innovation can survive in a noninnovative culture too. The key to survival in a more rigid culture is to isolate and protect the corporate pioneers. Barclays Global Investors did this by sending its iShare development team to a separate location outside company headquarters. If off-site locations are not an option, consider creating a separate space in your building for this group. They need a place to call home that is not subject to constant comparisons with the rest of the organization.

While we do not pretend to be experts on corporate culture, we believe that corporate cultures are a by-product of how a company runs its business. If rules, strict controls, and punishment for mistakes are the primary tools used by senior management in running the business, the resulting culture will probably be risk-averse, fearful, and unwilling to experiment. If people are empowered to act, encouraged to take chances, and celebrated for both successes and failures, the culture will be much more innovative.

If it is true that corporate culture is a by-product of management activities, then it does no good to try to "change the culture" if you do not also change the management activities that drive it. We have heard of many attempts to make a corporate culture more innovative, through innovative awareness campaigns in the lunchroom or "innovation fairs" highlighting new ideas throughout the company.

Without a management mandate, infrastructure changes, or process changes, these efforts, while noble, will fail in their attempts to change the corporate culture.

BGI's Garrett Bouton says about corporate culture. "An innovative culture has to start at the top. The CEO has to want it and to celebrate new ideas that result. It could take years to establish but it's a valuable thing to have in an organization."

This positive reinforcement of innovations and special recognition of those who contribute (at any level) to innovation are valuable tools in establishing the right culture for strategy innovation. Senior management must be vigilant in communicating the company's goals and future vision, highlighting the need for constant innovation and change to reach them.

Beware of other cultural norms that might run counter to the goals of strategy innovation. For example, some corporations celebrate "heroes," those people who single-handedly champion a project and, against all odds, succeed. In an environment where people are looking for opportunities to be a hero, they will be less interested in joining a Discovery "team." Or worse, they will join a team and attempt to be its hero, destroying the collaborative dynamics that are critical to its success.

Teresa Amabile, Harvard Business School professor and author of *Creativity and Context*, says this about an innovation culture:

> Dynamics within a team can determine the creativity of both the individual members and the team as a whole. Our research in organizations suggests that the most effective creative teams are those that are composed of individuals who have diverse skills and perspectives and who are open to each other's ideas, able to constructively criticize those ideas, and eager to help each other. All of this is more likely to happen when the team members communicate freely, trust and respect each other, and feel that their teammates are committed to their project's success.

We have worked with a valuable tool for assessing the corporate culture as it relates to innovation. It is called KEYS to Creativity, is authored by Amabile and Gryskiewicz, and is available from the Center for Creative Leadership (CCL). This assessment tool measures six aspects of corporate culture that support the work environment:

- Organizational encouragement
- Supervisory encouragement
- Work group supports
- Sufficient resources
- Challenging work
- Freedom

It also measures two aspects of corporate culture that can undermine it: organizational impediments and workload pressure. The survey, taken by all members of a work environment, can be compared to other corporate environments in the KEYS database as well as serve as a "pre" level for any change management initiatives in innovation.

Summary

- For many companies, the intermittent use of ad hoc strategy innovation initiatives is not enough. If your company could benefit from having strategy innovation as a core competence, consider the formalization of a strategy innovation system.
- To be successful, a formalized strategy innovation system must penetrate and co-exist with the corporate "immune system," which protects it from undesirable change.
- The four elements that must all be addressed for an innovation system to become *integrated* into the operating systems of a corporation include:
  - *Management mandate*: The senior management commitment to strategy innovation, which could include tangible infra-

structure changes, clear accountability for those involved, an impassioned appeal, and the focus on a strategic frontier.

- *Corporate infrastructure*: The establishment of an infrastructure for strategy innovation so that it has a home, resources with which to operate, and metrics to assess its performance.

- *Innovation process*: The development of a specific process for identifying and evaluating new business opportunities, such as the Discovery Process.

- *Corporate culture*: The establishment of rules, norms, and recognitions in support of strategy innovation will ultimately create a culture that is supportive of strategy innovation.

Endnotes

1. Clayton Christensen, *The Innovator's Dilemma* (Boston: Harvard Business School Press, 1997).
2. L.D. DeSimone, 3M News, www.3m.com, May 12, 1998.
3. Stan Gryskiewicz, *Positive Turbulence: Developing Climates for Creativity, Innovation, and Renewal* (San Francisco: Jossey-Bass, 1999).

EPILOGUE

I. The New World of Innovation

The Innovation Boom Continues

When Alex Osborn encouraged brainstorming in his advertising agency in the 1950s, he was the first to introduce creativity to the world of business. For many decades, creativity found a home in the areas of advertising and marketing, where new and innovative ways to promote products often resulted in greater sales revenue.

But creativity was not considered appropriate for other areas of the business, where logic and analysis drove decision making. That began to change in the 1970s and 1980s when we started working with corporations to develop innovative new products using creative techniques. Throughout the 1990s, a few of our clients began experimenting with creativity to identify whole new strategic platforms for growing their businesses.

Ten years ago, we wrote this book as a way to bring together creativity and corporate strategy in the pursuit of new growth opportunities. It was our hope that using new insights and perspectives to look at any existing business challenge can result in the creation of innovative new opportunities—anywhere in the corporation.

We couldn't be happier with the continued growth of creativity and innovation in business over the past decade. Corporations are demanding it, business publications are constantly writing about it, business schools are teaching it, and a new field of expertise is based on it.

Since 2003, Boston Consulting Group has been conducting a global annual survey on innovation with senior management members of the *BusinessWeek* Market Advisory Board. The most recent report (2010) reflects the strategic importance of innovation to corporations around the world. The authors write, "Seventy-two percent of respondents said that their company considers [innovation] a top-three priority, versus 64 percent in 2009. This percentage matches the highest reading seen in the seven years we have been conducting the survey."[1]

Setting Up Permanent Residence

There have been sightings in recent years of a new species roaming the hallways of corporations, often found nesting in the C-Suite. Its behavior is sometimes unconventional by C-Suite standards but appears to be effective in the identification of new breeding grounds. It goes by a variety of different names, most commonly called the Chief Innovation Officer (CINO).

There was a time, not that long ago, when creativity was not welcome in the C-Suite. It was considered a loose, undisciplined process that was no match for data-driven analysis in corporate decision making. It seems as though the C-Suite is now open to what creativity can do, recognizing its potential through the establishment of a senior position and a new function.

Gina Colarelli O'Connor, Director of the Radical Innovation Research Program at Rensselaer Polytechnic Institute's Lally School of Management, has been researching innovation in corporations for many years, and finds the emergence of this CINO role to be exciting. "First, it signals a recognition that innovation is distinct from other functions, including R&D, Corporate Strategy, and Marketing. . . . Secondly, it shows there is a mandate for companies to build a strong capability for breakthrough innovation."[2]

Because these early CINOs are pioneers, they are having to discover and define the role they will play in corporate life. O'Connor believes that the Chief Innovation Officer has two primary functions: To manage the innovation function, and to be the interface between it and the rest of the organization. Others highlight the importance of CINOs in establishing the language, vision/strategy, budgets, and resources for innovation. In the near term, the specifics of the role will likely be different in every corporation, depending on the location of this new function (corporate or business unit), the industry, and the role that innovation is intended to play within each corporate strategy.

While this new role is very promising for the future of corporate innovation efforts, there is research that shows that these innovation leaders will have their work cut out for them. In a recent survey of corporate innovation leaders conducted jointly by IESE Business School and Capgemini Consulting, only 42 percent of respondents said that they have an explicit strategy for innovation, 30 percent have an effective organizational structure for innovation, and 24 percent have an effective organizational alignment of innovation efforts.[3]

The Globalization of Innovation

When we wrote this book in 2003, the United States was clearly playing the lead role in innovation efforts around the world. Since that time, the U.S. leadership role has been shrinking as global companies and economies ramp up their innovation efforts.

This shift can be seen in the evolution of the Product Development and Management Association. The PDMA is a global organization dedicated to innovation. When we first met the board of PDMA in 2003, they were a large, splintered group made up of corporate product development professionals and academics in search of alignment on their future. After we led them through an exploration of their future opportunities, they selected several strategic frontiers for consideration, including a focus on innovation and desire for globalization.

Believing that innovation was to be the future in the area of product development, the PDMA adopted this as their new strategic focus in the 2003 timeframe. Their website now proudly proclaims "PDMA accelerates the contribution that innovation makes to the economic and professional growth of people, businesses, and societies around the world."

At the same time, PDMA committed to a 2020 globalization strategy. They changed their governance process to include vice presidents of four global regions. They then opened up membership opportunities globally, and the response has been impressive. PDMA went from 40 U.S.-only chapters in 2003 to add 20 international affiliates in 2013. The appetite for innovation around the world has been growing significantly.

The Boston Consulting Group survey cited earlier confirms this globalization trend for innovation. In their 2010 report they concluded, "The world's economically mature countries, led by the United States, have been the principal players on the innovation stage for decades. But there is much to suggest that this era of unquestioned dominance is fading. RDEs [rapidly developing economies] led by Brazil, India, and China (the BIC countries) are in the ascendancy and appear poised to put a major dent in the mature economies' self-image and position, if not to assume their leadership role outright."[4]

And the *Forbes* 2012 list of the top ten most innovative companies in the world includes one from China (Tencent Holdings), two from India (Hindustan Lever and Bharat Heavy Electricals) and one from Brazil (Natura Cosmeticos). These are companies to whom investors have paid an "innovation premium," based on expectations of future innovative results.[5]

Two years ago, Bob had the opportunity to visit China, delivering a speech on innovation on behalf of PDMA. He tells of a visit he took to a place called Innovation City:

> "With a population of over 10 million people—one million university students—the city of Wuhan, China, on the Yantze river, pulsates. Centrally located in the Hubeii province, it has been described as an entrepreneurial hotbed and a model of urban innovative growth.

One day we were invited to visit Innovation City on the outskirts of Wuhan, the newest symbol of the government's mandate for innovation. With two dozen gleaming structures (none reaching more than 10 stories), a park-like setting with a lake, emerald open spaces and walkways, Innovation Park draws you in.

But, the most surprising secret regarding Innovation City is captured by a black-and-white photograph in one building's lobby of rolling, empty farmland dated precisely 24 months earlier. This was the rural landscape that became Innovation City. In China, innovation can't wait."

Meanwhile, Europe is also embracing the role of innovation. In 2010, the European Commission, the executive body of the European Union, established "Innovation Union—A Europe 2020 Initiative." Its goal is to create the conditions where the European Union is able to compete globally for future economic growth and jobs. They have been actively involved in developing programs to increase the flow of venture capital funding, patent and intellectual property rights, and access to scientific data across the European Union. One of their goals is to create a European Research Area, a single market for research and innovation across Europe that will help attract science and technology talent and funding to compete with the U.S. and Asian markets.[6]

II. The Corporate Innovation Journey

The emergence of a corporate role of Chief Innovation Officer is the signal of a significant shift taking place in the role of innovation in business—movement in the Corporate Innovation Journey.

Corporate Innovative Journey

Ad Hoc Teams	Dedicated Office and Infrastructure	Enterprise Innovation

In the 1990s, the infrastructure for innovation was mostly ad hoc, cross-functional teams that would complete their innovation initiatives and then disband. This was the experimental era of innovation, when corporations were trying out this creative process to see if it would create value before committing overhead funds to it.

With many of these ad hoc innovation group initiatives producing successful results, corporations were then willing to commit their innovation efforts to a more permanent place in the organization. This is an important step along the Innovation Journey—the movement from an ad hoc structure to a dedicated office. We use the term "dedicated office" here, but it can represent forms that go beyond a literal "office" to include things such as Innovation Institute, Innovation Center, or even just a Chief Innovation Officer. The key distinction is that it is a more permanent part of the corporation than ad hoc teams, reflecting a commitment to make innovation ongoing and sustainable.

So with the movement that is currently taking place along this innovation journey, the question is: Where does it go next? Is this the end of the line for the corporate growth of innovation? We would like to argue that it is not. While there may be some who consider innovation to be a fad that will run its course, we believe that it will eventually make its way into every nook and cranny of an organization.

The reason for our optimism is in the definition of innovation: the creation of new value. That means the pursuit of ever-improving customer satisfaction, providing all customers (and other key stakeholders) with more value. And that applies not just to the external customers who purchase products and services. Every employee in every corporation is providing value for someone—their customer. It may be a vice president, the marketing department, or external investors; everyone provides value for somebody they consider a customer. If someone is not providing value, that person should not be collecting a paycheck. So if they are providing value, there must be a way for them to provide *more* value. That's where innovation comes in.

Wouldn't it be terrific if every two years the Distribution Department, for example, would use the tools of creativity to rethink how they carry out their function and spend their budgets? What if they were challenged in the work they do to create more value for their customers, their corporation, their community, or their planet?

We experienced that recently, with the Distribution department of one of our clients. Free to ask "why" and "what if" for all of the work they had been doing for years, this distribution group reconsidered and reconfigured their entire role. They knew where all of the bottlenecks, roadblocks, and inefficiencies were. For the first time, they were given the freedom and autonomy to address them. They took on their assignment with gusto, and delivered an amazing result that saved their company a significant amount of money for both the short and long term.

This is the future potential for innovation, a destination we call Enterprise Innovation. It is not only pursuing breakthrough new business opportunities aimed at external customers, it is using these same creative tools to improve the internal operations. When an entire organization is focused on creating new value, it provides a sustainable competitive advantage for any corporation in a dynamic global marketplace.

The Corporate Innovation Journey: Procter & Gamble

As of this writing, few corporations can be considered firmly entrenched in Enterprise Innovation. However, we have had the opportunity to play a role in the innovation journey of Procter & Gamble over the years. To us, they are the avant-garde corporate innovators that provide a model for how corporations can and should make this Corporate Innovation Journey.

Procter & Gamble has always been an innovative company, developing products with advanced technologies in laundry detergent (Tide), toothpaste (Crest), disposable diapers (Pampers), and fabric softeners (Bounce), to name a few. In the late 1980s, a corporate review of the innovation practices being used across the many divisions of P&G revealed more distinct practices than there were divisions. While the divisions had all produced innovative successes, there was no one innovation process that could be learned and shared across the corporation.

We were selected by P&G to help them develop a creative process for innovation that could be used across their divisions. Called Concept Lab, it was a two-day, creativity-based program for the development of new product concepts. For several years, ad hoc, cross-functional brand teams created portfolios of new product ideas that filled their new product pipelines for many years.

Then in 1994, future CEO John Pepper recognized that the innovation engine at P&G was focused on creating new products in the categories that already existed at P&G. In order to grow the business, P&G would have to find new business opportunities in the white spaces between their siloed divisions. So he appointed Craig Wynett, a brand manager in the healthcare area, to head up an office of innovation called Corporate New Ventures. We worked with Craig to help launch this CNV group, one that went on to bring the billion-dollar opportunities of Swiffer, Crest White Strips, and ThermaCare to P&G. But as important, it created a dedicated office of innovation at the corporate level of P&G to pursue growth opportunities beyond the existing business units.

In 2001, the innovation landscape at P&G changed again when A. G. Lafley took over the CEO role. Convinced that innovation was the key to P&G's long-term success, he greatly expanded the responsibility for innovation to include most everyone in the company. In his book, *Game Changer: How You Can Drive Revenue and Profit Growth with Innovation,* Lafley writes, "Innovation is all about connections, so we get everyone we can involved. . . . To succeed, companies need to see innovation not as something special that only special people can do, but as something that can become routine and methodical, taking advantage of the capabilities of ordinary people, especially those deemed by Peter Ducker as knowledge workers. . . . Every day, more P&Gers are involved in innovation."[7]

With his deft and focused leadership on innovation, P&G rose to great levels of prominence during the Lafley years. They completed their innovation journey by making innovation the responsibility of everyone in the organization, not just a select few. They reached the level of Enterprise Innovation. With systems, structures, and a culture in place to support innovation throughout the entire corporation, P&G is poised to remain a competitive global force into the future.

III. Four Pillars for Enterprise Innovation

Ten years ago, in Chapter 12 of this book, we introduced the idea that eventually every company would have a formalized system of innovation because the benefits of innovation would be critical for sustained growth. Today, we believe more strongly that a formalized system, which we now call Enterprise Innovation, will not only be important for sustained growth, it will be necessary for long-term survival.

To be sure to address the key elements that go into creating a corporate system, we proposed a framework of four key pillars of this innovation system:

1. Management Mandate

2. Corporate Infrastructure

3. Innovation Process

4. Corporate Culture

If any one of these pillars lags behind the others, the innovation system will be incomplete, and innovation efforts will suffer. For example, if mandate is strong but infrastructure is weak, the organization may not have the resources to carry out the mandate. Or if the mandate, infrastructure, and process are all in place but the culture remains stuck in the "way we have always done things around here," innovation will succumb to the weight of history and never get off the ground.

The past ten years have taught us that these four pillars remain a valid and useful framework for the development and evolution toward Enterprise Innovation. We revisit them here with some observations built on our experiences this past decade.

1. Mandate is THE critical pillar.

If the leadership of an organization does not actively commit to the support, encouragement, and recognition of innovation as a key element of the organization's future success, the organization will not likely adopt Enterprise Innovation.

Using the tools of creativity to rethink how an organization creates value requires a change in the traditional behavior of employees. More important, changes could bring about strategic and structural changes in an organization. Before employees embark on such a voyage, they will want to be sure that the mandate for innovation is real. To do this, they will look carefully at the *behaviors* of their senior leaders to assess whether this call to innovation is a commitment or merely the latest fad attempt to improve corporate performance.

No matter how impassioned or expertly staged, speeches or letters in the internal newsletter are not enough to convince skeptical employees of a mandate. Employees are looking for hard evidence of commitment in what the leaders do. Are they putting someone with credibility and respect in charge of the innovation effort? Have they articulated an innovation strategy and how it will fit into the organization's overall strategy? Are they funding a department or hiring staff? Are they demanding that presentations to them include innovative options? Are they themselves using creativity and innovation in the work they do?

We worked with two different companies that were in stark contrast in their mandates for innovation. In one, the CEO *said* all the right things in meetings with the innovation team we were working with. He spoke of the importance of innovation to the company's future and how the work of that group was critical. The problem was, he was reluctant to provide the funding necessary for the group to do its work, did not follow up on the group's progress, and would only consider the low-risk, incremental opportunities developed by the team.

On the other hand, we had a CEO lead group cheers for innovation (literally), provide whatever funding and support was necessary for the team to operate, and kept pushing for even bigger and more innovative suggestions. Mandate is all about the behavior.

According to recent research conducted by McKinsey, senior leaders agree with the importance of this C-level mandate on the impact of innovation. In their report of an online global survey conducted in May of 2012, they state, ". . . the results suggest that the most important factors for success are the extent to which innovation is integrated in corporate strategy and to which company leaders support and engage with innovation efforts."[8] They go on to say that companies where innovation is fully integrated into the overall strategy are six times more likely to meet financial objectives of innovation, compared to those without strategy integration.

The successful adoption of Enterprise Innovation begins with, and is dependent on, a strong innovation mandate from leadership. This mandate is both the expression and behavioral proof of:

- The reason innovation is key to the organization's success
- How innovation will be integrated into both the strategy and operations of the organization
- The vision or goals of innovation
- Who will be held responsible/accountable for innovative results
- How and where resources will be made available
- The processes to be used for innovation
- The anticipated cultural impact of innovation

2. Infrastructure must be dedicated.

Establishing an internal system for innovation requires the creation of an innovation infrastructure, which we defined earlier in this book as a home, resources, and metrics for innovation.

That home for innovation is now being constructed. Corporations, recognizing the need for sustainability in their innovation efforts, are committing to the practice of innovation by creating permanent positions. This dedicated infrastructure, often led by the Chief Innovation Officer, is charged with developing and maintaining an ongoing system of innovation.

Where should innovation live within an organization? There are many viable options to consider:

- A corporate office or function reporting directly to the C-Suite
- A business unit function to be closer to operations and markets
- A distant laboratory or institute, to be less market-influenced and more cutting edge
- Part of an existing functional area, such as R&D, Product Development, or Marketing

As of this writing, there is no consensus on the best place to locate the dedicated innovation function. A McKinsey global online survey report in 2012 found that ". . . companies rely on various organizational approaches to execute innovation: 62 percent of executives report the use of multiple structural models to drive innovation efforts."[9] It seems that the innovation infrastructure varies by the current corporate organization and the strategic role that has been identified by its leaders.

However, the placement of the innovation function today may affect its future evolution. As we have projected, many corporations are on an innovation journey that will ultimately lead to Enterprise Innovation, where responsibility for creating new value through innovation is an integral part of everyone's job. If a company believes that Enterprise Innovation is its ultimate destination, that may inform where and how the initial dedicated office should be established. For example, a corporate innovation function reporting to the C-level would be a better launching pad for Enterprise Innovation than the creation of a detached innovation technology institute or making innovation function-based (e.g., in R&D).

There are also other considerations in the creation of a dedicated infrastructure, beyond where the office sits on the organization chart. These questions deserve careful consideration and made part of the creation of an overall strategy for innovation:

- ◆ How will we fund the innovation infrastructure?

- ◆ What are the important stages of the innovation process and how will we make decisions about advancing innovation programs?

- ◆ Will there be organization "hand-offs" involved?

- ◆ Where will innovation products be produced and commercialized?

- ◆ Who in the organization will be responsible for what aspects of innovation?

- ◆ How will we measure progress and the success of innovation?

3. Innovation Process should include the unconventional.

We are delighted to report that the Discovery Process, outlined in this book, has stood the test of time as a reliable process for the identification of innovative new business opportunities for both large and small companies. We continue to use this five-phased approach to guide teams through the innovation process, regardless of whether the goal is a breakthrough strategic business opportunity or a tactical improvement in an internal process.

Key to the level of innovation (incremental or breakthrough) that results from this process is the selection of the strategic frontier. For more innovation that is more incremental, choose a strategic frontier that is very close to your current business model—for example, a different target audience or different geographic location. For more breakthrough innovation, select a strategic frontier that's more distant from your current business, such as a nascent technology or trend.

When it comes to the Exploring Phase of the Discovery Process, it is important that the methods used for insight generation be unconventional for your company. We have seen companies setting up the Exploring Phase turn immediately to their traditional methods of customer insight methods, such as focus groups. If you have always done focus groups, then the chances of getting new and different insights to drive innovation is limited. Instead, use a technique that is new and different for your company. For example, set up an online community, conduct co-creation sessions with customers, start a Twitter campaign, set up a mock retail store, or shadow your target customers for a day. New insights are much more likely to emerge from unconventional processes.

In the world of Enterprise Innovation, everyone in the organization is looking for ways to create new value for the organization. That means for many employees, customers (who are the arbiters of value) are other internal employees. So the Exploring Phase to identify insights for an internal customer will likely be less complex than an external customer—perhaps only an in-depth conversation. For example, someone in Finance who wants to raise the value of the services that Finance offers, might set up discussions with those internal customers who receive financial reports to understand how they can be delivered better, faster, cheaper.

4. Culture can be changed.

Corporate culture is one of those nebulous entities that is difficult to define and recognize until it appears to get in the way of what you want to do. The internal innovation champion runs into corporate culture when she requests something for her team, and is told that it can't be done because "we've never done it before."

Ten years ago, we said that culture is difficult to change directly, as it is a by-product of all of the other things you do in an organization. An email from the C-Suite telling people to be more collaborative will not make a collaborative culture. You will get a collaborative culture when you have good cross-functional communication networks, recognize and reward cross-functional group efforts, train people in interpersonal skills and techniques, create cross-silo budgets and goals, and get rid of employees who don't play nice. The net result of all of these efforts aimed at collaboration will be a collaborative culture.

However, we have learned since then that it is possible to have a very significant impact on a corporate culture through more direct means. Insigniam has built a business on changing corporate cultures in order to achieve breakthrough performance. Shideh Bina, cofounding partner of Insigniam, tells of a recent dramatic change in corporate results that occurred at Cone Health.

Cone Health is a regional community health care system located in North Carolina, consisting of five hospitals, approximately two dozen outpatient clinics, and more than 8,000 employees. In 2010, senior leaders recognized they could not survive in the changing landscape of healthcare by doing business the way they always did it. What was needed was a dramatic change in the culture of Cone Health that would allow for a dramatic improvement in operating results.

Insigniam found through its initial assessment that there were nine elements of the corporate culture that were holding back the ability of employees to achieve breakthrough results. So they established a cross-functional, cross-level team called the Guiding Leadership Coalition that would take a leadership role in changing the culture of Cone Health.

This grassroots coalition, along with Engagement Teams, worked for two years to establish and disseminate new corporate values, operating principles, and practices aimed at improving both employee engagement and healthcare delivery throughout the system.

The results were dramatic. Employee engagement levels, measured at the 51st percentile in 2010, were at the 87th percentile in 2012. Employee turnover levels fell from 14 percent to under 10 percent, and 90 percent of employees said that they had changed the way they operate to be consistent with the new corporate values. In addition, one of their hospitals, Annie Penn, received a national Distinctive Workplace Award as being one of the best hospitals to work for in the country—99 percent level of employee engagement, 96 percent doctor satisfaction, and 94 percent patient satisfaction.

So we now see that corporate culture can be changed through direct efforts.

*   *   *

We had the opportunity in the last few years to test these four pillars as a framework for Enterprise Innovation in a place on the
other side of the globe. . . .

Case Study—Year of Innovation

We journeyed to a country rich in natural resources, with valuable
deposits of many precious metals hidden underground. Specialty
Products (not its real name) is a large consumer products company
that also had hidden assets. Deep within their nearly 1,000
employees was a capability for creativity and innovation that was not
being used to its potential. While the company had been a family-
owned jewel for many generations, the family believed it was capable
of more.

So in November 2009, we received a call from the CEO of
Specialty Products, asking if we could conduct a workshop on
creativity and innovation that would unleash the potential of their
people, and create significant growth opportunities for Specialty's
future.

Our past experience told us that a workshop would create some
new insights and high energy with their employees, but unless they
had some internal structure for using these outputs, the impact of skills
training would have a negligible longer-term impact on their business.

Sensing that there was a strong mandate from the leadership team
for growth through innovation, we proposed instead that the
workshop become the first step in the creation of enterprise-wide
innovation for Specialty Products. In other words, we were suggesting
that they condense the typical Innovation Journey mentioned earlier;
skipping over ad hoc innovation, skipping over a dedicated office for
innovation, and moving directly to the end of the innovation spectrum,
and implement Enterprise Innovation.

Specialty Products' leaders bought into the idea of a Year of
Innovation, aimed at establishing the basis for Enterprise Innovation
that would make innovation a sustainable process long-term. That
meant that we would need to use the leadership mandate for
innovation to develop the other three pillars within Specialty:
infrastructure, process, and culture.

Working closely with the COO and his management team, we proposed an infrastructure that would maintain and extend the momentum created by the creativity workshop. The plan called for the creation of Innovation Teams (or I-Teams) that would use creativity tools and techniques to develop solutions to existing Specialty Products issues and opportunities. The I-Teams would consist of people who volunteered to be part of this process, as it would be work above and beyond their day jobs. Each team would not be considered a permanent part of the Specialty Products organization chart, but would fold when their charters were accomplished. However, the concept of an ongoing structure of volunteer teams that was separate from the operations of the company was established.

Thinking that we would get enough volunteers following the creativity workshop to establish three or four I-Teams, we were shocked to learn that 26 I-Teams had been chartered by senior leaders to operate over the coming year! They would address a wide range of both tactical and strategic issues, with some teams representing one functional area, and others being cross-functional in their make-up.

Providing I-Teams with a creative process to use in their work was the next step toward Enterprise Innovation. We used a version of the Discovery Process outlined earlier in this book, which continues to be a valuable way of pursuing innovative opportunities for growth. Specialty's senior leaders also created two Discovery Teams, and used this Discovery Process to explore two strategic frontiers for significant growth opportunities for their overall business.

In one of our coaching visits during this process, we asked I-Team members to describe their experience on the I-Teams compared to being on typical project teams. Nearly all of the people we asked claimed that I-Team work was a better, more enjoyable experience. As one employee said, "When you are on a project team, you are only carrying out what the leaders want done. On an I-Team, you can do what you think is best, and explore ideas that have never been considered."

To successfully establish innovation as a sustainable part of the Specialty Products business, we needed to make innovation a part of their culture. So Specialty's leaders created recognition programs, and built innovation into yearly objectives. But it was the "jam session" that probably had the biggest cultural impact on the

Specialty employees. For the session, each of the I-Teams was assigned exhibit space in a large meeting area, and was provided with a budget and professional assistance to be creative and share with the rest of the company the work they were doing. On the day of the day-long session, the atmosphere in the room can only be described as "electric." Colorful, creative exhibits of concepts, prototypes, and innovative ideas communicated to the entire company that Specialty Products was on the move, driven by innovation. At one point during the session, several employees brought their children in to see the exciting new things that were taking place in their company. (Go to www.insigniam.com/jamsession for photographs of the jam session.)

By the end of Specialty Products' Year of Innovation, many of the I-Teams had successfully completed their work, resulting in pipelines of new business opportunities as well as significant cost-saving opportunities. There were celebrations and a look back over the road traveled and progress made in one year. Enterprise Innovation was off to a great beginning.

Enterprise Innovation Infrastructure

With the successful launch of Enterprise Innovation at Specialty Products under our belts, we were delighted to read that other companies have adopted a similar infrastructure for innovation. John Kotter, the Konosuke Matsusjita Professor of Leadership Emeritus at Harvard Business School, is the world's leading authority on leading corporate change. In his recent article in *Harvard Business Review* called "Accelerate: How the Most Innovative Companies Capitalize on Today's Rapid-Fire Strategic Challenges—and Still Make Their Numbers," Kotter talks about the fact that most established companies are set up to maximize the efficiency of their current operations, not to maximize flexibility in pursuing innovation opportunities. His experience showed that attempts to change the hierarchy of the current operations to be more flexible often leads to problems, as efficiency-oriented hierarchies are built to be stable, not flexible. But in a dynamic marketplace, the ability to detect and quickly pursue innovation opportunities can be crucial for the success of the organization.

A solution to this inherent tension, according to Kotter, is to create "a second operating system, devoted to the design and implementation of strategy that uses an agile, network-like structure and a very different set of processes."[10] This separate operating system should be complementary to, and coordinated with, the hierarchy but free to chase opportunities as they arise. He describes the employees in this networked system to be a "volunteer army," recruited from the ranks of the hierarchy because of their skills of energy, commitment, and enthusiasm. "They are not a bunch of grunts carrying out orders from the brass. Rather they are change leaders."

This is exactly what we saw at Specialty Products with the infrastructure of the I-Teams and the recruiting of volunteers. There are some people working in organizations who enjoy the structure, guidelines, and stability that comes from hierarchical living. Putting them on I-Teams and asking them to be creative would make them uncomfortable and unproductive. However, there are often many people in organizations who yearn for the challenge, the freedom/autonomy, and the opportunity to contribute to the building of the organization's future. When these types of people are on I-Teams with others who feel the same way, they get things done. They also get noticed, as cutting-edge work makes its way to the boardroom pretty quickly. Doing I-Team work at Specialty Products has already proven to be a way to advance the impact of the company while advancing your career.

(Go to the Insigniam website for a fun way to test your current capabilities on these four pillars.)

IV. Six Factors for Dramatic Growth Through Innovation

While you can put structures, incentives, communications, and goals for innovation into place, this will not insure a reliable flow of innovative new opportunities. Within every organization, there are important, usually invisible forces at work that serve as barriers to the creation and pursuit of innovation.

In order to launch a rocket into space, it must achieve an escape velocity sufficient to overcome the force of the earth's gravity. We believe that the same is true for launching innovation in your organization. By leveraging the positive forces for innovation and identifying and minimizing the negative forces, you stand a much greater chance of having your innovation efforts succeed.

To achieve growth through innovation, you need the following six factors.

1. Greater Innovative Thrust

When one person in an organization does something, it is an aberration. When several people do it, it becomes a trend. When enough people do it, it becomes a standard behavior. Once something reaches a critical mass of people, it seems to take on a momentum that is difficult to stop.

This same thing holds for innovation. Once enough people look for new, out-of-the-box ways of getting things done, ask "What if we tried something else?" or generate a long list of possible solutions, innovation will be the standard way of doing business. But it must reach that tipping point first.

Senior executives can influence this innovation thrust by committing to innovation as "the way we do things around here." By demanding to hear breakthrough ideas, looking far out into the future, and daring to try new things, leaders can create a set of innovation expectations that the rest of the organization will begin to honor.

This suggests an aggressive, focused effort by senior leaders to launch innovation in an organization, similar to our Year of Innovation at Specialty Products. This will create a critical mass of people involved in innovation, and the establishment of innovation as an expectation in the operations of the organization. Begin the process with enough thrust to get it off the ground.

2. Less Corporate Gravity

Corporate gravity is "an invisible force that prevents employees from venturing too far from the current business model." It comes from years of focus on operating inside the current business model, as that is the way that the company typically does business. An employee's thoughts, reading, problem-solving are all done within the confines of the business model, so it is natural that it becomes their frame of reference. It also becomes their comfort zone, creating boundaries that define what is permissible, and therefore what is possible to achieve within acceptable corporate limits.

As a result, innovation leaders must take special steps to overcome corporate gravity to allow unconstrained exploration of what else is possible in the way of customer interactions, marketplace changes, and new business models. It is the exploration *beyond* the business model that reveals the innovative opportunities.

There are several different ways of dealing with corporate gravity. Corporate gravity often takes the form of tacit assumptions that a team makes, based on its past experiences of how corporate decisions are made. One way to deal with the constraining power of corporate gravity is to reveal these assumptions. For example, a team member might say, "I assume that we would never do online selling." Get a list of these gravity-producing assumptions, and then agree, as a group, that they are all invalid until further notice. This creates a blank slate, on which innovative ideas can be built.

Another approach is for a C-level executive to give permission to explore beyond the current business model, considering things that are not currently being done. Better yet, have that executive *demand* that this exploration beyond the business model be done—on a regular basis.

Thirdly, you can redefine the team's role to be outsiders, rather than employees. Tell them they are venture-funded entrepreneurs with significant resources that want to redefine how this marketplace operates. This removes all of the corporate issues that constrain creative exploration, eliminating corporate gravity completely.

3. Innoculation Against Corporate Immune System

The corporate immune system is "the role played by current corporate systems and processes to 'repel' anything that threatens the current stability of the overall business system." This force tends to be more tangible than corporate gravity, as it often appears as internal rules, policies, or guidelines that define actions and decisions as acceptable or not.

The immune system is most visible in the financial area (e.g., budget sign-offs, financial hurdle rates, and financial ratios). Done for control and efficiency purposes, these guidelines keep the financial system operating within limits deemed acceptable by the C-level.

However, innovations often fall outside these typical corporate guidelines, as they may require new investment in infrastructure, product development, or special promotional efforts. The corporate immune systems will flag these aberrations and, worst case, shut them down, or require lengthy internal discussions to override them.

The best way to deal with the immune system is not to ignore or defy it but to sensitize everyone involved to its existence. To define the corporate immune system before starting an innovation initiative is to alert everyone to the potential conflict. This will prompt a discussion on where the corporate immune system might appear, what exceptions/risks will be tolerated, and what hurdles will be non-negotiable. This discussion could also open the possibility of other funding options, including venture funding (internal or external), partnerships, grants, etc.

4. Elevated Capability of and Capacity for Creativity

Creativity is the force that drives innovation. Without it, corporations would operate primarily on rational thinking that comes from using past experiences and historical data to make future decisions.

In a meeting at the Dallas headquarters of 7-Eleven many years ago, an executive told us a story about how strong of an influence the past had on their decision-making process. It seems that back in the late 1930s, 7-Eleven hit on the idea of selling gasoline out in front of their stores as a way to offer customers a one-stop convenience option that is so common today. As it turned out, however, that experiment was not as successful as they desired, and was shut down. In the 1960s, 7-Eleven again considered gasoline sales at their stores. The number of cars on the road in the U.S. had more than tripled from the 1930s to the 1960s, and interstate highways had made long-distance car travel much more common. However, at least one of the 7-Eleven executives initially rejected this proposal, claiming, "We already tried that and it didn't work."

Creative thinking allows for consideration of options that are not grounded in past experience, and not even yet tangible. By using our imaginations, we can "see" things that do not yet exist, and evaluate them as if they were real. Thus, the effective use of the imagination to create new, higher-value options for corporations is the heart of the innovation process.

As for capability, everyone has the potential to be creative. We worked with a company recently that wanted to raise the creativity of their employees at their corporate headquarters. At our insistence, we convinced them to also offer creativity training to their factory employees, many of whom were illiterate or struggled with the English language. After a couple of days of hour-long workshops to train their 500+ factory workers, our client was astounded by the level of creativity they saw! The output included ways to improve the layout of the factory, many of which were adopted by the senior leaders. While everyone is capable of creativity, many are not provided with the environment, the permission, or a process for tapping into this valuable source of innovative ideas.

5. Corrected Corporate Myopia

We define corporate myopia as "a condition where the urgency of today's business supersedes the importance of future business, resulting in a near-sighted perspective."

There is no question that corporations are pressured to run with a short-term perspective. Wall Street anxiously awaits the quarterly earnings reports that drive the financial viability of many corporations. By cutting investment spending on R&D and other longer-term innovation initiatives, those cost-savings improve the short-term bottom line. That makes Wall Street happy, but cuts off the potential for the identification of future growth initiatives.

Another area of corporate myopia we see is the selection of what new business opportunities to pursue. Given a choice to develop a short-term, incremental improvement to an existing product versus a new, longer-term breakthrough product, the short-term improvement typically wins out.

While there is no easy answer for this conundrum, it is important that organizations maintain the forces that keep short-term and longer-term interests in balance. Earlier in this book we referred to bi-focal vision as an important executive skill to keep the urgent present and the important future in the right balance.

Having a Chief Innovation Officer as an advocate for the future is a good way to keep the discussions in the executive suite balanced. Without someone to champion the needs of the longer-term future of the business, corporate myopia can take over and starve the future to fund the present.

6. Effective Execution

When we first wrote this book in 2003, the focus of our consulting company was on delivering a portfolio of new business opportunities to help our clients grow.

Throughout the 1990s, much of our work was with large organizations with strong capabilities in new product development, sophisticated stage-gate processes, and histories of successful new product introductions. After delivering the portfolio of growth opportunities to most of our clients, we left the execution of them in capable hands.

However, we also had a number of clients who were not as seasoned in the execution of innovative opportunities. More times than we would like to admit, innovative growth opportunities sat in a binder somewhere, a buried treasure that would become obsolete because of our client's execution incompetence.

Our partnership with Insigniam opened our eyes to the powerful potential of a rigorous execution process. By enrolling execution team members in a commitment to the successful implementation of breakthrough results and using language and coaching to maintain accountability, incredible results can be achieved. A very recent example of the power of effective execution comes from a fast-moving consumer products company headquartered in the midwest (we'll call Acme) that had historically been the leader in a highly competitive household products category.

Faced with two aggressive competitors about to introduce strong new entries, Acme knew it had to respond quickly to this market threat. Historically, new Acme products took about two years from start of development to market entry, which would be unacceptable in this situation. At the same time, there was poor communication between two key functional areas that could cause further delays plus a culture of consensus that caused projects to drift.

Insigniam entered this challenging situation, and first assembled a cross-functional execution team made up of on-the-ground decision makers. This team then committed to an extraordinary result —the introduction of a consumer-preferred new product in *nine months*, less than half the typical timing. Acting as committed partners, the team then uncovered the beliefs, assumptions, and process hurdles that would prevent the successful launch of this new product. And they vowed to address or overcome all of them.

Their interactions with each other were direct, transparent, and highly efficient. Their results were the introduction of a new product two weeks earlier than their nine-month target! Not only that, the product was so superior that one of their competitors never launched their product. The net result was an additional $10 million of value to Acme from this one introduction.

The amazing results of this team became legendary inside Acme, which has since begun a transformation in how they do business. Effective execution of innovation is key to sustainable competitive advantage.

How Leaders Can Manage These Six Growth Factors

Create lofty goals. When the goals are set "outside" the current way of doing business, it forces a search for new ways of operating (and not just incremental improvements within the current ways of operating). Dare to stretch their thinking by asking for a five-year roadmap of breakthrough improvement options.

Remove obstacles. The future is your friend because it automatically removes the perceived obstacles of lack of resources and lack of time. Promise support, particularly for the political battles and corporate conflicts that are sure to be encountered along the way.

Manage the energy. Search for the spark of excitement or energy in others because that will lead to commitment and not just compliance. When you see it, recognize/reward it and encourage it because the energy will make it "their" initiative rather than yours.

Endnotes

1. Jim Andrew, Joe Manget, David C. Michael, Andrew Taylor, and Hadi Zablit, "Innovation 2010: A Return to Prominence—and the Emergence of a New World Order," www.bcg.com, Boston Consulting Group, April 16, 2010.
2. Gina Colarelli O'Connor, "The Real Role of a Chief Innovation Officer," *Center for Innovation Management Studies Newsletter*, Spring 2012.
3. Paddy Miller, Koen Klockgieters, Azra Brankovic, and Freek Duppen, "Managing Innovation: An Insider Perspective," Innovation Leadership Study, Capgemini Consulting, March 2012.
4. Andrew, Manget, Michael, Taylor, and Zablit, op.cit.
5. "The World's Most Innovative Companies: How Innovative Leaders Maintain Their Edge," *Forbes*, http://www.forbes.com/innovative-companies, September 5, 2012.
6. http://ec.europa.eu/research/innovation-union/index_en.cfm?pg = intro, http://europa.eu/rapid/press-release_MEMO-12–564_en.htm?local e = en.
7. A.G. Lafley and Ram Charan, *The Game Changer: How You Can Drive Revenue and Profit Growth with Innovation* (New York: Crown Business, 2008), pp. 5, 7, and 26–27.
8. Maria M. Capozzi, Ari Kellen, and Rebecca Somers, "Making Innovation Structures Work," McKinsey Global Survey results, by McKinsey & Company, May 2012.
9. Ibid.
10. John P. Kotter, "Accelerate: How the Most Innovative Companies Capitalize on Today's Rapid-Fire Strategic Challenges – and Still Make Their Numbers," *Harvard Business Review*, November 2012.

Glossary

Aligning Phase—The second phase of the Discovery Process, where the Discovery team and senior management align themselves on the focus and scope of the strategy innovation initiative, agreeing on the strategic frontier(s) to be explored.

Bifocal vision—The ability of senior management to balance the realization of both near-term and long-term opportunities.

Business model innovation vector—One of three areas to be explored by the Discovery team for the identification of insights on how innovations in business models could add value to the company.

Business opportunity—Any new product, service, or significant change in a company's current business model that results in a new or improved revenue stream for the company.

Collaboration—A style of group interaction where all team members enter the process with an open mind and a willingness to explore together, define together, and select together the opportunities that will meet the shared objectives.

Convergent Phase—The second step of any creative process, when the ideas and options generated in the first (divergent) step are prioritized, according to some evaluation criteria.

Corporate gravity—An invisible force that prevents employees from venturing too far from the current business model.

Corporate immune system—The role played by current corporate systems and processes to "repel" anything that threatens the current stability of the overall business system. While it repels things that threaten the system, it also acts to repel things that could improve the system.

Corporate myopia—A condition where the urgency of today's business supersedes the importance of the future business, resulting in a nearsighted perspective.

Creating Phase—The fourth phase of the Discovery Process, where the Discovery team uses its new insights from the strategic frontier(s) to create, refine, and develop a portfolio of new business opportunities for the future.

Creativity—The innate developable skill for generating novel ideas.

Customer value vector—One of three areas to be explored by the Discovery team for the identification of insights on what has value to customers.

Discontinuities—Events, products, or technologies that dramatically alter some aspect of the future because they cause large-scale changes in behavior.

Discovery brief—A document prepared by the members of the Discovery team that contains information that would be helpful to begin the Discovery Process initiative.

Discovery drift—The perceived gap between new strategies being considered by the Discovery team and the company's current strategy. If this gap becomes too large, senior management often rejects the new strategy as too much of a change for the company to handle.

Discovery Process—A five-phase process for the identification and mapping of new business opportunities that leads to strategy innovation. It is also referred to as a strategy innovation initiative.

Discovery team—The core group of people responsible for the implementation and results of the Discovery Process.

Divergent Phase—The first step of any creative process, when new ideas or options are generated in great quantity, without regard for feasibility, practicality, efficiency, or effectiveness.

Dreaded delta—The gap between projected future revenues and the company's growth targets, which often triggers the need for strategy innovation.

Ethnography—The growing field of observational research, a term first used to describe a research method in the field of cultural anthropology.

Evaluation criteria—The screening criteria used by the Discovery team to prioritize the new business opportunities they develop in the Creating Phase.

Exploration vectors—The areas to be explored by the Discovery team for the identification of insights with value-adding potential. The three vectors recommended are: customer value, market dynamics, and business model innovation.

Exploring Phase—The third phase of the Discovery Process, where new insights are identified on the company's strategic frontier(s), providing the raw material necessary for the development of new business opportunities.

Extended Discovery team—A group of managers who participate in the Discovery Process on a part-time basis, typically attending high-profile exploration activities and review or alignment meetings. They are normally asked to be involved in the process because of their experience, expertise, or implementation responsibilities.

Focused exploration—A streamlined alignment process between the Discovery team and senior management based on the identification by senior management of the specific strategic frontier(s) to be explored by the Discovery team.

Foresight—An understanding of what is possible in the emerging future.

Formalizing—The process of creating a permanent, internal corporate system for strategy innovation.

Future-pull—The aspirational attraction that one feels towards the identification or creation of some compelling future state.

Fuzzy front-end—As part of the new product development process, often the name given to the early part of the process where new product ideas are first identified.

Immersions—In the Exploring Phase, the involvement of the Discovery team in a new environment (of customers' lives, in the marketplace, etc.) for observing new insights.

Incrementalism—The strategy of meeting revenue growth targets through the introduction of products that are only marginally different from (better than) existing products. Frequently the products are "new, improved" versions of current products, or line extensions.

Innovation—The process for implementing creative ideas.

Insight—Any new understanding or perception about customers, market dynamics, or business models that could reflect added value in the marketplace. Insights form the basis of new, value-creating business opportunities that, in turn, form the basis of strategy innovation.

Interactions—In the Exploring Phase, events set up by the Discovery team for the exchange of information (with customers, market experts, etc.) that could lead to insight identification.

Mapping Phase—The fifth phase of the Discovery Process, where the Discovery team creates a strategic road map, outlining key events, trends, market discontinuities, and milestones to move the company into its new strategic future.

Market dynamics vector—One of three areas to be explored by the Discovery team for the identification of insights on what could represent value in the marketplace of the future.

Open exploration—The alignment process between the Discovery team and senior management, where the Discovery team explores and recommends to senior management the specific strategic frontier(s) to be explored.

Opportunity format—A tool (form) used by the Discovery team in the Creating Phase for the development of new business opportunities.

Provocateur—The role played by outside experts (or thought leaders) in a thought leader panel, where the goal is to stimulate the Discovery team with provocative thoughts and insights rather than give coaching or advice.

Safaris—An immersion technique for the Exploring Phase, often consisting of customer visits for observing their environments.

Sponsor—The senior management individual who serves as liaison, mentor, and spokesperson for the Discovery team throughout the Discovery Process.

Staging meeting—The time when the Discovery team gathers to understand the scope of the initiative, to share the Discovery Brief, and to create the team.

Staging Phase—The first phase of the Discovery Process, where the Discovery team is selected, key roles are identified, the objectives of the initiative are established, and the team is prepared for the process.

Stake-outs—An immersion technique for the Exploring Phase, consisting of observing customers outside their living environments, such as retail stores or public places.

Strategic frontier—The unexplored area of potential growth that lies between today's business and tomorrow's opportunities. It is usually a market, product, technology, or business process that represents potential new growth for your company.

Strategic Opportunity Spectrum (SOS)—The wide range of new business opportunities that can result from the Discovery Process. The spectrum runs from shorter-term, lower-risk, market-entering opportunities that are on the "visible" part of the strategic frontier to the longer-term, higher-risk, market-creation opportunities on the "visionary" part of the strategic frontier.

Strategic planning—The process of deciding on the company's tactics for competing in the marketplace.

Strategic road map—A corporate time line into the future that identifies the crucial activities, milestones, and marketplace events that must take place for the new business opportunity to succeed.

Strategy innovation—Shifting a corporation's business strategy in order to create new value for both the customer and the corporation.

Team captain—The Discovery team member who is the leader of the team and primary contact for the Sponsor.

Thought leader panel (TLP)—An insight-gathering technique for the Exploring Phase, consisting of the interaction of five to six "experts" in a variety of areas relevant to the future of a strategic frontier.

Unarticulated needs—The opportunity areas for products and services that could add value to the lives of customers but that, because of their limited experiences and perceptions, customers are not able to describe or define.

ValueProbe—A customer interaction technique for the Exploring Phase, consisting of a group discussion with customers around what has value in their lives.

Visible opportunities—New business opportunities that are currently "visible" on the strategic frontier. They tend to be shorter-term, lower-risk opportunities, where markets are established but new value can be created.

Visionary opportunities—New business opportunities in a strategic frontier that are not currently visible. Visionary opportunities tend to be longer-term, higher-risk opportunities, where markets would need to be created.

Visual illumination—The process of graphically portraying an idea or opportunity to bring it to life and aid in its communication to others.

RECOMMENDED READINGS

"Inspiring Innovation," *Harvard Business Review*, August 2002.

Amabile, Teresa, Constance N. Hadley, and Stephen J. Kramer, "Creativity Under the Gun," *Harvard Business Review*, August 2002.

Christensen, Clayton M., *The Innovator's Dilemma: When New Technologies Cause Great Firms to Fail*. Boston: Harvard Business School Press, 1997.

Christensen, Clayton M., Michael Raynor, and Matt Verlinden, "Skate to Where the Money Will Be," *Harvard Business Review*, November 2001.

Collins, James C., and Jerry I. Porras, *Built to Last: Successful Habits of Visionary Companies*. New York: HarperBusiness, 1997.

Collins, James C., *Good to Great: Why Some Companies Make the Leap . . . and Others Don't*. New York: HarperCollins, 2001.

DeBono, Edward, *Lateral Thinking for Management*. New York: AMACOM, 1972.

Dell, Michael, *Direct from Dell: Strategies that Revolutionized and Industry*. New York: HarperCollins, 1999.

Drucker, Peter F., "The Discipline of Innovation," *Harvard Business Review*, August 2002.

Florida, Richard, *The Rise of the Creative Class*. New York: Basic Books, 2002.

Foster, Richard and Sarah Kaplan, *Creative Destruction*. New York: Currency/Doubleday, 2001.

Gardner, Howard, *Creating Minds*. New York: Basic Books, 1993.

Gerstner, Louis V., Jr., *Who Says Elephants Can't Dance: Inside IBM's Historic Turnaround.* New York: HarperCollins, 2002.

Gordon, W. J. J., *Synectics.* New York: Harper, 1961.

Govindarajan, Vijay and Anil K. Gupta, "Strategic Innovation: A Conceptual Road Map," *Business Horizons,* July/August 2001.

Gryskiewicz, Stan, *Positive Turbulence: Developing Climates for Creativity, Innovation, and Renewal.* San Francisco: Jossey-Bass, 1999.

Guilford, J. P., *The Nature of Human Intelligence.* New York: McGraw-Hill, 1967.

Hamel, Gary and C. K. Prahalad, *Competing for the Future.* Boston: Harvard Business School Press, 1994.

Hamel, Gary, *Leading the Revolution.* Boston: Harvard Business School Press, 2000.

———— "Strategy Innovation and the Quest for Value," *Sloan Management Review,* Winter 1998.

Johnston, Robert E., Jr., and Soren M. Kaplan, "Harnessing the Power of Strategic Innovation," *Creativity and Innovation Management,* June 1996.

Kaplan, Soren M. and Robert E. Johnston, Jr., "Dislocations—Drivers of Industry Evolution, Innovation, and Corporate Growth," *Strategic Change,* February 1998.

Kim, W. Chan and Renee Mauborgne, "Value Innovation: The Strategic Logic of High Growth," *Harvard Business Review,* January/February 1997.

Kotter, John P., "Leading Change: Why Transformational Efforts Fail," *Harvard Business Review,* March/April 1995.

Krinsky, Robert and Anthony C. Jenkins, "When Worlds Collide: The Uneasy Fusion of Strategy and Innovation," *Strategy & Leadership,* July/August 1997.

Leifer, Richard, et al., *Radical Innovation.* Boston: Harvard Business School Press, 2000.

MacKinnon, Don W., *In Search of Human Effectiveness.* Buffalo: Creative Education Foundation, 1978.

Markides, Constantinos, *All the Right Moves.* Boston: Harvard Business School Press, 2000.

————— "Strategic Innovation," *Sloan Management Review*, Spring 1997.

————— "Strategic Innovation in Established Companies," *Sloan Management Review*, Spring 1998.

————— "To Diversify or Not to Diversify," *Harvard Business Review*, November/December 1997.

McGrath, Rita Gunther and Ian MacMillan, *The Entrepreneurial Mindset: Strategies for Continuously Creating Opportunity in an Age of Uncertainty*. Boston: Harvard Business School Press, 2000.

Mintzberg, Henry, *The Rise and Fall of Strategic Planning*. New York: Prentice-Hall, 1994.

Osborn, Alex F., *Applied Imagination*, 3rd edition. New York: Scribners, 1963.

Parnes, Sidney J., *Source Book for Creative Problem Solving*. Buffalo: The Creative Education Foundation Press, 1992.

Peters, Tom, *The Circle of Innovation*. New York: Vintage Books, 1999.

Porter, Michael E., *Competitive Advantage*. New York: Free Press, 1985.

————— "What is Strategy?," *Harvard Business Review*, November/December 1996.

Prince, George, *The Practice of Creativity*. New York: Scribners, 1970.

Schwartz, Peter, *The Art of the Long View: Planning for the Future in an Uncertain World*. New York: Doubleday, 1996.

Slywotzky, Adrian J., *Value Migration: How to Think Several Moves Ahead of the Competition*. Boston: Harvard Business School Press, 1995.

Slywotzky, Adrian J. and Richard Wise, "The Growth Crisis—and How to Escape It," *Harvard Business Review*, July 2002.

Tucker, Robert B., "Strategy Innovation Takes Imagination," *Journal of Business Strategy*, May 2001.

Tushman, Michael L. and Charles A. O'Reilly, *Winning Through Innovation: A Practical Guide to Leading Organizational Change and Renewal*. Boston: Harvard Business School Press, 2002.

Utterbach, James M., *Mastering the Dynamics of Innovation*. Boston: Harvard Business School Press, 1994.

Wynett, Craig B. and T George Harris, "Yes, You Are A Creative Genius," *Spirituality & Health*, Winter 2003.

Zook, Chris, *Profit from the Core*. Boston: Harvard Business School Press, 2001.

INDEX